Struggling to Forgive

Struggling to Forgive

*Nelson Mandela and South Africa's Search
for Reconciliation*

Brian Frost

HarperCollins*Publishers*

HarperCollins*Publishers*
77-85 Fulham Palace Road, London W6 8JB

First published in Great Britain in 1998 by HarperCollins*Publishers*
1 3 5 7 9 10 8 6 4 2

A catalogue record for this book
is available from the British Library.

ISBN 0 00 274002 8 (hardback)
ISBN 000 628095 1 (export edition)

Printed and bound in Great Britain by
Mackays of Chatham plc

To the South Africans from so many backgrounds and experiences who in the autumn of 1995 helped me in my researches for this book, which was dedicated to God in the private chapel of the Anglican Bishop of Kimberley and Kuruman in December 1995.

'My only wish before I die is to see blacks and whites living harmoniously in a united South Africa.'

Nokukhanya Luthuli[1]

'Before they can get on with their lives it is important that people ask for forgiveness.'

Professor Adam Small[2]

'We have to reconcile, accept and enjoy our differences.'

Moses Mapalakanye[3]

'Forgiveness is not an end in itself ... Forgiveness is a bridge that leads to a new land.'

Dr Mmutlanyane Stanley Mogoba[4]

'If you forget the past, you will lose the future.'

Jan Gruiters[5]

'This richly endowed, highly favoured tip of Africa could be a real vanguard for world community as the twenty-first century breaks.'

Rev. Arthur Blaxall[6]

Contents

Foreword

by Mary Robinson
United Nations High Commissioner for Human Rights
President of Ireland (1990–1997)

I still remember my thoughts as Impala jets of the South African Airforce flew over the Union Buildings in Pretoria, trailing the new national colours in salute to Nelson Mandela – inaugurated as his country's first democratically elected President.

Their roar symbolized for me the final transfer of state power, and the end of a regime of racism and oppression. But in my mind was an anxiety about what might lie ahead for South Africa. Would it be possible for the different communities to come to terms with their past? Or, as has happened so often elsewhere, would their future be lost in vengeful score-settling?

In his own description of the day, President Mandela wryly noted that the same officers saluting him would, not long ago, have been rushing to arrest him. But close to the President were prison officers invited as his guests, a sign that this man would not seek revenge on his persecutors. Instead he has built his politics on his belief that 'to make peace with an enemy one must work with that enemy, and that enemy becomes one's partner'.

Brian Frost's book looks at the history of the struggle against apartheid through the lens of religious belief, in particular the doctrines of forgiveness, reconciliation and redemption. These words are usually foreign to the world of diplomacy and politics, their absence certainly diminishing the effectiveness of international efforts to restore communities shattered by internal divisions and strife.

The story that unfolds is heart-rending in its detail of how a racist ideology would distort religious beliefs and tear apart the lives of those who fought to be true to their faiths. It is a story which weaves in the lives of Mahatma Gandhi, Jan Smuts, Chief Albert Luthuli, Archbishops Trevor Huddleston and Desmond Tutu, climaxing in the courage of F.W. de Klerk in releasing Nelson Mandela and beginning a process of freeing South Africa from its history of hatred. Sadly, it is also a story of many deaths – some such as Steve Biko have become famous; most were reduced to faceless numbers as all sides resorted, out of fear, desperation and frustration, to lethal force.

Ironically, apartheid had its birth in 1948 as the General Assembly was moving to adopt the Universal Declaration of Human Rights. South Africa abstained in that vote and was gradually ostracized by the international community. The campaign against apartheid became the entry point for people around the world to learn about human rights and their own responsibility to realize the principles elaborated in the Universal Declaration and which were so thoroughly trampled upon in apartheid South Africa.

In 1997, I was privileged to mark Human Rights Day in South Africa with President Mandela and also met again Archbishop Tutu and his colleagues on the Truth and Reconciliation Commission. I came away with views I find echoed in this book. The first is that South Africa can still offer us lessons in practical human rights through its willingness to explore the complex relationships between justice, truth, forgiveness and reconciliation. The second is more simple: that the world community must not leave South Africa alone in its immense task of constructing a society where economic and social benefits are shared equitably. These too are basic human rights.

Preface

African Rain

African lightning
You streak across the sky,
Your forks and tongues dominating
The tower-blocks
Above so many thousand neon lights and hopes.

   African rain,
   African rain,
   You pour your blessing on
      this parched city and land.

African town
You illuminate Johannesburg
As we thunder by
Soweto's highway
And see its homes
To the right
As far as the distant skyline.

   African rain,
   African rain,
   You pour your blessing on
      this parched city and land.

African driver
Your Zulu strength and poise
Calm my starry night
As I make a final journey
Through the city
For my London home,
Watered with forgiveness stories
Despite the pain and suffering of
    your beautiful land.

    African rain,
    African rain,
    You pour your blessing on
        this parched city and land.

In our dryness,
African Christ,
African Christ,
Pour your forgiveness on my parched
    city and land.

    African Christ,
    African Christ,
    Pour your forgiveness on all the people
        of this rainbow city and land.

I wrote this poem in Johannesburg Airport at the end of an eight-week visit to South Africa in the autumn of 1995, to try to express Britain's need for forgiveness for her involvement there. Like so many British people I came originally from a very ordinary background, with little knowledge of South African history and Britain's role in it. Yet, over the years, a number of incidents have led me to greater and greater involvement, which culminated in my visit during 1995 at the invitation of the (then) Presiding Bishop of the Methodist Church, the Rev. Dr Mmutlanyane Stanley Mogoba.

The first incident which aroused my interest was an impassioned sermon against apartheid from a normally undemonstrative curate at evening worship in the Anglican church in Surrey where I grew up. Then at a university meeting one night (I was secretary of the Oxford branch of the Student Christian Movement) I had to introduce Father Trevor Huddleston to 1,000 undergraduates. He enthused us then, as he did many more for decades, to struggle against racism.

I began to read about South Africa's problems and during my eight years with Christian Aid (1960–68) represented it on a committee concerned with the future of the High Commission Territories, now, of course, Botswana, Lesotho and Swaziland.

In 1969, as Director of the Notting Hill Ecumenical Centre, I played 'host' to the World Council of Churches' Consultation on Racism, one of whose focuses was Southern Africa. An invitation to visit South Africa itself came in 1973, through the Christian Fellowship Trust. It was a tense time in the country, with the rise of Black Consciousness, the SPROCAS (Study Project on Christianity in an Apartheid Society) Reports on South Africa's future and the work of the Christian Institute. Indeed, while I was there, black leaders such as Steve Biko were banned, along with white student leaders.

Once back in Britain I wrote a 'Litany for the Banned', which was used in many places in Britain and elsewhere on 16 December 1973 (16 December is the Day of the Covenant when Afrikaners remember their victory over the Zulus at Blood River in 1838). I also published a poster-poem, using some of the poetry I had written during my visit, had South Africans to stay in my home and created a multi-cultural festival in London, an idea first discussed with a friend in Cape Town. Throughout this time I also prayed nightly for Nelson Mandela, as a symbol for all those in prison in South Africa.

In London in 1991 I published *The Politics of Peace*, a book on forgiveness and politics in many continents throughout this century. Then, in 1995, I visited South Africa's main urban centres again, but this time to find material which would enable me to write about forgiveness in one country alone.

On my way by coach from Port Elizabeth to Cape Town I had an encounter with one of the returned ANC (African National Congress) exiles which I recalled often while writing *Struggling to Forgive*. He had been in Maseru, Lesotho's capital, on the night South African military forces murdered a group of ANC activists, as well as Lesotho citizens, and narrowly missed death himself. Nevertheless, he now agreed with President Mandela who was urging South Africans to let bygones be bygones, for through the 1994 free elections there had been a resolution of the conflicts which had engaged Afrikaner and African nationalism for decades.

During a stay at John Moores University, Liverpool, my friend had found healing from the trauma he had experienced and now wanted to play a constructive role and help build a different future for South Africa. But later, as I read about so many other atrocities, I asked myself: had he really forgiven? If, as I believed, forgiveness took the sting out of remembering, perhaps that was a healthier way to relate to the past; remembering also that forgiveness also freed people from the past to face a new – and hopefully different – future even though it would contain new wrongs to forgive.

As I recollect this encounter, I continually throw my mind back to the incredible beauty of so much of South Africa, including the 'Garden Route' to Cape Town and the coach ride where I met my friend. I remember, too, the many conflicts in South Africa's history and with remorse realize afresh how Britain, with its colonial attitudes and attempts to overcome Afrikaner and African aspirations, has contributed to them.

Is there a profound meaning in all the pain? I believe there is. South Africans are in a unique position in the world, straddled as they are between Africa, Europe and Asia. At the theological level, too, they are unique. The Truth and Reconciliation Commission, for example, is acting on behalf of the state to try to heal the wounds of many who were caught up in and damaged by group conflicts, the dynamics of which they seldom understood in all their complexity. The Commission can therefore be seen as an organization created by a nation, which demonstrates how the reconciliation Christ has brought through his death and resurrection can affect not only individuals but the fabric of society itself.

South Africa's search for reconciliation has a global resonance, too, because of its pivotal position from which may emerge a vital exploration of the meaning of forgiveness in relation to justice, healing, restitution and repairing, as well as to love, remembrance, reconciliation and repentance. This exploration may well be of help not only to South Africa herself as she matures and develops, but also to other parts of the world.

The Morning after Apartheid

The morning after apartheid
History was let loose from its vice
As clasped hands
Winced in their pain
And minds tried to forget
Memory's ravages.

The seasons
Were fruitful;
Autumn did not age,
Winter was pure delight,
Warm as Gulf Stream waters.

The morning after apartheid
Forgiveness danced in the townships,
The skies were rainbow hues
As scars of centuries healed
And there was ointment
For all the wounded.

Mercy cried;
Joy rampaged
In drab streets
And derelict hearts.

Saris were scattered
Weaving beauty into lives
Grown stale in a century's waiting.

The dead rose in applause
Over the Drakensberg
And Table Mountain erupted with sun.

The morning after apartheid
There were drums and singing
And loving and sweltering nights
And tender dawns.

Prologue

Forgiveness is a word human beings often use to describe an experience of handling wrongdoing in a certain way. It is not necessarily an exclusively Christian word, though there is much teaching about forgiveness in Christianity, as in the other world faith communities. It can occur both at the personal and the group level, though the two are not always so easily distinguishable. For example, in South Africa Nelson Mandela is both himself forgiving as an individual and also a leader of the ANC which has articulated a forgiveness policy that goes way beyond his own person. As his friend and colleague Walter Sisulu said to me in the ANC Headquarters in Johannesburg in December 1996, 'We are obliged to forgive. It is our policy. We may not forget.'

Walter Sisulu's comment relates forgiveness with remembering, an indication that when human beings grapple with forgiveness at whatever level, whether as a policy or a personal experience, it clearly does not stand on its own, however much people would like it to.

In *Struggling to Forgive* an attempt is made to relate seven themes to forgiveness thus:

```
Reconciliation       \
                      \      F
Remembering           \      O
                      \      R
Repentance            \      G
                      \      I
Restitution/Repairing  >     V
                      /      E
Healing               /      N
                      /      E
Justice               /      S
                      /      S
Love                  /
```

The situations – both personal and corporate – involving these issues are never neat and tidy, however. Thus in one context it may be that restitution, repairing and repentance are paramount in the dynamics. Yet there may well be overtones of other themes, too, which need attention. For example, until some measure of reparation and repairing has been made, memory will still sting those who were wronged. In order for reconciliation to occur, some measure of justice may also be required, even though impregnated with forgiveness.

Patently all the wrongs in South Africa over many centuries can never be put right, let alone the wrongs of the apartheid years. Yet as some have recognized, the 1994 election in South Africa was an attempt to put right the major wrong – the disenfranchisement of most of the black community – and that, in part at any rate, can help it come to terms with some of its suffering.

Human beings, of course, have what might be called an incurable itch to make life tidy and in the area of forgiveness often want to find a way whereby all the themes mentioned above (and others, too, like forgiveness and liberation) can clearly be spelt out and their inter-relationships made obvious and clear cut. Unfortunately the history of human communities seems to indicate that the forgiveness process does not work in this way. A certain amount of ambiguity and lack of crystal clarity is inevitable.

Nevertheless, in *Struggling to Forgive* an attempt has been made to simplify the process by marrying one great theme to forgiveness in each chapter as a way to introduce the issue. The aim is to put readers on the right road to an understanding of the dynamics of forgiveness and to draw attention to the main ingredients which are present when attempts are made to deal with history in a forgiving way.

Many extraordinary people throng the narrative, some of whom, such as Archbishop Tutu, never flinch when a call to repentance is required. Others are known only in one locality, or to a few friends for virtues just as striking and constant as Tutu's. No apology, therefore, is needed for including such a variety of people in these chapters, for apartheid traumatized and damaged everyone, to a greater or lesser extent, and all are the legatees of South Africa's conflict and costly history. By juxtaposing the great and the lowly, the small incident and the grand moments – either of rebellion or legislation – it is possible to catch something of the dramatic way in which people have tried to grapple with a political and social conflict in South Africa which has also engaged many others elsewhere.

Chapter 1

Forgiveness and Reconciliation –

The Role of Nelson Mandela and Desmond Tutu

Sometimes in the life of nations significant personalities emerge who highlight key aspects in the dynamics of society. In South Africa's case Nelson Mandela and Desmond Tutu, both of whom have focused on forgiveness and reconciliation as the paramount need, have emerged to lead that society forward into new ways. Mandela has been the politician, Tutu more the theologian in action. Yet both, cradled in the Christian Church, the one in Methodism, the other in Anglicanism, have had a personal faith which has enabled them to exhibit a strength beyond themselves. Indeed both have focused on the idea that all human beings have been made in the image of God.

There has also been a distinct difference, however. Mandela has urged people time and time again to let bygones be bygones, in order for there to be reconciliation, whereas Tutu has emphasized continually the need for repentance and confession to achieve reconciliation. Nonetheless, whatever may be their lack in preaching a systematic theory about the relation of forgiveness to reconciliation, it is more than made up for by their charisma and their courage and determination.

In Mandela's case he has had to work out the meaning of specific acts of reconciliation in the context of extremely complex political realities, which must often have tested to the uttermost his capacity to forgive. In Tutu's case he has often had to test the reality of his theological views in the hard school of day-to-day encounters and crossfire from political groups not in the least committed to his spiritual and theological interpretations.

THE ROLE OF NELSON MANDELA

'We may never forget, but we must forgive,'[1] Nelson Rolihlahla Mandela said to Miriam Makeba, rather to her surprise, when he was encouraging her to return to South Africa from exile. 'To make peace with an enemy, one must work with that enemy,' he wrote elsewhere, 'and that enemy becomes your partner.'[2]

Miriam Makeba was not the only person to be surprised by Mandela's capacity to remain free of bitterness as, from the moment of his release from prison on 11 February 1990, he exhibited an amazing self-control when talking about the past and a magnanimity towards those who had imprisoned him.

Some, however, had detected this quality in Nelson Mandela much earlier, like the British life peer, Lord Walston, who with Prime Minister Vorster's permission, had visited him on Robben Island for most of an afternoon. 'Mandela,' he wrote years later, 'showed no bitterness. He did not revile his jailors, nor rail against the government that had incarcerated him.'[3] Leaders of the Commonwealth, who visited Mandela in the 1980s, also found him unmarked by bitterness. 'His overriding concern was for the welfare of all races in South Africa in a just society; he longed to be able to contribute to the process of reconciliation,' they reported.[4]

The Commonwealth leaders found a similar spirit in Mandela's friend and colleague, Oliver Tambo, and among other leaders, too. 'Their idealism, their genuine sense of non-racialism, and their readiness not only to forget but to forgive, compel admiration,' they concluded. 'These are precious assets a new South Africa will need...'[5]

Nelson Mandela, of course, was not always like the leader who walked out of prison in 1990. Influenced when young by Tatu Joyi, a Thembu sage who maintained that the *ubuntu* (humanness) of the African kings had come to an end and a tyranny set up by white people instead, Mandela was inspired to regain that *ubuntu* for every South African.[6] Yet, as he came to know Sophiatown, Alexandra and other areas of Johannesburg in the early 1940s, with their rows of single-barrack blocks where more than forty shared a toilet and a tap, and the limited public housing in the townships, it was difficult for him not to seethe with hatred.[7]

'I was,' he has commented, 'sympathetic to the ultra revolutionary stream of African nationalism ... I was angry with the white man, not at racism. While I was not prepared to hurl the white man into the sea, I would have been perfectly happy if he had climbed aboard his steamship and left the continent of his own volition.'[8]

At that time, and throughout the 1950s, when Chief Albert Luthuli had become President of the African National Congress (ANC), its emphasis was on non-violence and passive resistance, an idea Luthuli in particular had learned from Mahatma Gandhi. Mandela, however, who became a dynamic leader in the Youth League of the ANC, began to suspect that the legal and extra-constitutional protests, such as the 1952 Defiance Campaign, would become impossible because the state would tolerate them no longer. The Gandhian model was only effective if those opposing you played by the same rules. If peaceful protest was met by violence, what good was it doing? he asked himself, even raising the question in the ANC National Executive. Here he was admonished, so continued to defend the ANC's official policy. 'But in my heart,' he decided, 'I knew that non-violence was not the answer.'[9]

The path to violence seemingly became inevitable when in the late 1950s the Treason Trial of 156 leaders was followed by the Sharpeville massacre in 1960 and the banning of the ANC, the Pan-Africanist Congress (PAC) – a breakaway from the ANC led by Robert Sobukwe – and other groups. 'Our preference, and that of every true African patriot, has always been for peaceful methods of struggle,' Julius Nyerere once observed. 'But when the door of peaceful progress is slammed, shut and bolted, then the struggle must take other forms; we cannot surrender.'[10]

By creating the Spear of the Nation (*Umkhonto we Sizwe* or MK for short) with others like Walter Sisulu and Joe Slovo, Mandela made it inevitable that a civil war would develop when on 16 December 1960 (the Day of the Covenant when Afrikaners held a special remembrance of past victories) they performed their first act of sabotage against the state.

Mandela, the Xhosa teenager who had once been a cattle herdsman in the Transkei, and who later set up a law firm in Johannesburg with Oliver Tambo, had come a long way. He always bore himself with dignity, a trait he had doubtless developed when part of the Thembu royal household, which he had been invited to join on the death of his father. Now he lived like a 'scarlet pimpernel', directing clandestine operations and never staying anywhere long enough to be detected. 'I will not leave South Africa,' he had written from the underground, 'nor will I surrender. Only through hardship, sacrifice and militant action can freedom be won. The struggle is my life. I will continue fighting for freedom until the end of my days.'[11] However, shortly after a secret meeting with Chief Luthuli, he and other leaders were arrested in Rivonia and put on trial.

The trial which opened in Pretoria on 22 October 1962 was marked not only by the solidarity African supporters gave the trialists, but by Mandela's speech from the dock. 'The violence which we chose to adopt was not terrorism,' he argued. 'We did not want an inter-racial war, and tried to avoid it to the last minute …'[12] In fact, he added, African people had been talking for a long time about winning back their country by fighting 'and we, the leaders of the ANC, had nevertheless always prevailed upon them to avoid violence and to use peaceful methods.'[13]

Yet the ANC's belief in non-racial democracy and in negotiation had got nowhere. The Freedom Charter, agreed at Kliptown in 1955, had been regarded by the Government as a seditious document and draconian legislation was introduced throughout the 1950s to prevent any change. Now apartheid policies were developed systematically, which Mandela and others opposed. 'I have cherished the ideal of a democratic and free society in which all persons live together in harmony and with equal opportunities,' he declared. 'It is the ideal which I hope to live for and achieve. But if needs be, it is an ideal for which I am prepared to die.'[14]

Nelson Mandela's years in prison – for he was sentenced to life imprisonment, along with many of the other Rivonia trialists, including Walter Sisulu – were formative. 'In his political life in the early years he gave vent to the anger he felt,' 'Mac' Maharaj has observed. 'In prison he got his anger almost totally under control. That control has come about through a deliberate effort by Mandela, for political reasons as well as personal.'[15]

Mandela regarded his role in prison not just as the leader of the ANC but as a promoter of unity, 'an honest broker, a peace-maker'. He was even reluctant to take sides in a dispute which was raging at one time between protagonists of the ANC, the PAC and the Black Consciousness Movement (BCM).[16]

The prison regime was tough. For years he and his fellow prisoners chipped stones in a quarry and for well over a decade their diet was mostly boiled corn, porridge and soup. Bread was forbidden, but after protests prisoners were permitted to buy a loaf at Christmas.[17] Yet Mandela's friendliness and capacity to negotiate was evident even in his relationships with his warders, as his lawyer George Bizos found on his first visit to Robben Island. 'Eight guards marched towards me and in the middle was Nelson, wearing sandals, shorts and tunic, at ease among them,' he has noted. '"George," he said, "I want to introduce you to my guard of honour," and he introduced all eight of them.'[18] 'Even in the grimmest times in prison,' Mandela wrote later, 'when my comrades and I were pushed to our limits, I would see a glimmer of humanity in one of the guards, perhaps just for a second, but it was enough to reassure me and keep me going.'[19]

In keeping with this outlook, Mandela made sure that when he was to be inaugurated as President on 10 May 1994 three warders were invited, for he wanted them to share 'in the joys that have emanated around this day, because in a way they also contributed'. To Mandela the prison experience was profound, both at the political and the personal levels, for his friendships with some warders had undermined attempts by prison authorities to persecute blacks and had also given him the ordinary contact with people he needed, as he demonstrated on leaving prison when he left a card for one warder saying, 'The wonderful hours we spent together during the last two decades end today. But you will always be in my thoughts.' As he was released he embraced him and said: 'We'll meet again.'[20]

Mandela's desire for reconciliation encompassed all. At a press conference in Cape Town shortly after his release he was asked about the fears white people had. 'I knew that people expected me to harbour anger towards whites,' he commented subsequently. 'But I had none. In prison, my anger towards whites decreased, but my hatred for the system grew. I wanted South Africa to see that I loved even my enemies, while I hated the system that turned us against one another.'[21]

The way Mandela handled his guards was a harbinger of how he would treat those with whom he disagreed profoundly later. Perhaps it was his awareness of his own frailty which enabled him to understand more deeply the weaknesses of others. Certainly he exhibited a marked capacity not only to negotiate and compromise, where possible, but also to appreciate others' points of view. In an interview on local radio, when his autobiography revealed his frailties and weaknesses, he explained that because the mass media especially seemed to have made him a messiah, 'it was necessary for me to tell the public who I am, that I am an ordinary person. I have made serious mistakes, I have serious weaknesses.'[22]

Something else happened to Nelson Mandela in prison, an understanding of which is needed to appreciate later actions. 'It was during those long and lonely years that my hunger for the freedom of my own people became a hunger for the freedom of all people, white and black,' he has recalled. 'I knew as I knew anything that the oppressor must be liberated just as surely as the oppressed,' for all had been robbed of humanity. 'When I walked out of prison,' he added 'that was my mission, to liberate the oppressed and the oppressor both.'[23]

This is the clue to Mandela's subsequent actions, some of which have puzzled many in the black communities within South Africa and elsewhere. But to do this he needed not only the moral authority gained from his inheritance and the prison years (which makes him virtually unchallengeable) but also a temperament which would enable him to handle difficult and explosive situations calmly and deliberately. That he has this latter quality is clear from an incident Richard Stengels, who helped him write his autobiography, has made clear. They were together on 10 April 1993, after one of Mandela's long walks in the Transkei countryside, when his housekeeper came to tell him that 30 members of the Transkei Police rugby team were in his driveway wanting to say 'Hello'. Mandela went to greet them, but was suddenly called back for an emergency phone call. The caller had bad news: Chris Hani, the former head of the ANC's military wing, had been assassinated by a white extremist. Mandela put the phone down and looked off into the distance, revealing his shock and concern. Then, standing up and apologizing to his co-writer for the interruption, he returned to shake the hands of the remaining police.[24]

Mandela handled the crisis following Hani's death with both wisdom and maturity. Effectively he was already acting as President when, on television, he called for calm and pointed out that it was a woman of Afrikaner origin who had risked her life to get the necessary information which had led to the arrest of the assassins. How South Africans handled the pain, grief and outrage would determine whether the country moved forward to an elected government of the people. It was 'a watershed moment for all of us,' he warned.[25]

As President, Mandela continued to show outstanding leadership qualities, urging South Africa 'to come to terms with its past in a spirit of openness and forgiveness and proceed to build the future on the basis of repairing and healing. The burden of the past lies heavily on all of us,' he added, 'including those responsible for inflicting injury and those who suffered.'[26]

In the years preceding his presidential inauguration he worked with his former enemies and jailers in the National Party (NP) to take South Africa into a new future in a Government of National Unity (GNU), which was the result of the negotiations prior to the 1994 General Election, though the ANC won over 60 per cent of the popular vote. He also worked hard to build bridges with Chief Mangosuthu Buthelezi, who, as head of the KwaZulu Government in apartheid days, had privately urged the Government to release Mandela from prison. President P.W. Botha had said he was willing to do this if Mandela would renounce violence, an offer Mandela rejected at the time. President Botha had, however, responded to Mandela's initiatives by setting up a secret committee of senior figures in 1985 to hold talks with him, and had in a sense crossed the Rubicon with his tea meeting with Mandela in July 1989.

Before becoming President himself, Mandela had made attempts to check the growth of violence in KwaZulu-Natal. At a meeting in Durban in February 1990, for example, he had urged some 100,000 activists, most of them Zulus, to take their guns, knives and pangas and throw them into the sea.[27] There was little response. In January

1991 he and Chief Buthelezi had their first encounter for 28 years, but the meeting of delegates from Buthelezi's Inkatha Freedom Party (IFP) and the ANC, which the media attended, was difficult because Chief Buthelezi listed ANC verbal attacks on him and criticized the ANC's negotiating demands about the framework for a new constitution and government.

Mandela, wanting to emphasize reconciliation, did not respond directly, choosing rather to thank him for trying to secure his release from prison. He cited, too, their long relationship and drew attention to the things that united the IFP and the ANC. During private talks later the two made more progress and signed an agreement which contained a code of conduct between the two movements.[28] It was never adequately implemented by either side. Another agreement signed in April 1991 and backed with strong statements from both leaders had little effect either.

By now Mandela suspected that in some way the Government was behind the violence and began to wonder about President F.W. de Klerk himself, a man he had hitherto regarded as someone with whom the ANC could do business.[29] It was perhaps a presentiment of things to come, for over the ensuing years the two leaders developed a relationship which had several striking ups and downs. 'He needs me; I need him,'[30] he said in November 1995 of his relationship with the second Deputy President (as F.W. de Klerk had become) after a difference of opinion following de Klerk's comments about the arrest of former Defence Minister Magnus Malan and whether he ought to have been indemnified.

At the beginning of the year there had been another incident after F.W. de Klerk had threatened to resign from the Cabinet because he had been verbally attacked in a vicious way during one meeting. He even indicated that the National Party itself would withdraw from the Government, to which Mandela had replied: 'That will cause hardly a ripple.' Mandela's judgement here was faulty, for shares on the Johannesburg Stock Exchange began to plummet when news slipped out of the row between the two Nobel Peace Prize winners. After a private meeting, at which Mandela apologized, he emerged to say yet again of the past: 'Let bygones be bygones.' And in a joint statement the two declared, 'We have agreed to make a fresh start.'[31]

The clash had occurred when ANC Cabinet ministers refused to accept amnesties for 3,500 policemen and the Chief of Police, which F.W. de Klerk had granted in secret shortly before the 1994 General Election, along with amnesties for two Cabinet ministers, Magnus Malan and Adriaan Vlok. Mandela was not against amnesties in principle, however. Indeed, ANC activists had been granted indemnities earlier but in a much more open manner. Also during the negotiations which led to the Government of National Unity, Mandela had been back to Robben Island to persuade 25 MK political prisoners to accept the Government's offer of an amnesty. 'Every soldier would like to defeat his enemy on the fields,' he had said then, 'but, in this case, such a victory was out of reach. The struggle was now at the negotiating table. I argued that they were not advancing the cause by remaining in jail. They could be of greater service outside than inside. In the end, they agreed to accept the Government's offer.'[32] But this blanket amnesty by de Klerk for so many was unacceptable.

Despite this friction – and at times downright hostility – the two lawyers, Mandela and de Klerk, had found themselves together at Oslo to receive jointly the Nobel Peace Prize for 1993. In the citation the judges acknowledged that both were 'politicians in a complicated reality and it is the total picture that was decisive'.[33] Looked at in close-up, of course, both men had been in situations where violence had occurred in which they were implicated, the one in Government, the other in a military wing of the ANC. Yet, as Carl Niehaus has suggested, both men 'were delivered to each other by history'.[34]

To ensure his goal of a non-racial, majority-ruled South Africa, 'Mandela had to forgive conduct toward himself and all South African blacks that his own moral code tells him is unforgivable'.[35] This he found at times difficult to do, even saying to 3,000 people gathered in a high school in Bonteheuvel: 'We want to bury de Klerk and his government for ever. They have committed crimes against humanity. We want to ensure that they never again rule this country.'[36] Yet at Oslo he was able to say he could envisage sharing power with de Klerk, 'despite all the mistakes he had made and continues to make'.[37] 'He had the courage to admit that a terrible wrong had been done to our country and people through the imposition of the system of apartheid,' he wrote on reflection. 'He had the foresight to understand and accept that all the people of South Africa must, through negotiations and as equal participants in the process, together determine what they want to make of their future.'[38]

For his part F.W. de Klerk had to ensure peace and a future for the Afrikaner people, which meant he had to stop a political process which was leading South Africa to ruin. Both had the courage to react creatively to their situations, helped of course by their aides; but it was inevitable in the new, transitional process, that there would be clashes.

In the run up to the 1994 General Election, for example, ANC members on the ground tried to disrupt township election rallies the NP was holding there. Mandela ordered them to desist, a directive de Klerk welcomed, adding that it had to be backed by firm action. He said Mandela had phoned him to express concern at recent violence, including an incident in one township when de Klerk had been hit by a stone.[39]

Mandela's attitude to the white communities – the Afro-Europeans – continued to be firm and clear. He recognized early on perhaps that there were two power bases in South Africa: the whites, who held economic power and by and large were very skilled, and the black nationalists. The two nationalisms in particular, Afrikaner and African, had to come to terms with each other. This, it is true, left out of account Zulu nationalism, which was another aspect of the equation. But to those who criticized him for his sensitivity to the whites Mandela was firm. 'Why should we not pacify them?' he asked. 'In putting aside quarrels of the past we have a country which has the opportunity to acquire education, skills and expertise in many fields. We want this. Let's forget the past. Let's put down our weapons; let's turn them into plough-shares. Let's build our country.'[40]

There was obviously a political aspect and awareness to Nelson Mandela's stress on forgiveness and reconciliation, but whether human beings can forget the past so easily may be doubted. Nevertheless Mandela continued to say and do daring things, especially as he reached out to the Afrikaner community.

Four incidents stand out above many others which show the

President's sure and steady touch in this respect. One is his meeting after 21 years with Dr Percy Yutar, his prosecutor in the Rivonia trial who, it appeared, had been urged to charge the accused with high treason. He had resisted and tried them only on a charge of sabotage. In July 1983 he claimed he had approached four Cabinet ministers and pleaded with them to set the Rivonia trialists free. 'My part was a small one,' he said to the media who had gone to his home for the lunch date with Mandela, which the President had requested. 'I wonder in what other country in the world would you find someone you prosecuted thirty years ago coming to see you.'[41]

A second incident did more to heal the wounds than many debates, arguments and political manoeuvres. During the period of the Rugby World Cup Final in Cape Town in 1995, Mandela phoned the Springbok captain every day. And in due course, when he came to give the prize to the Springboks for their win, he was seen to be wearing the captain's number 6 jersey and cap. In prison he had said he would never watch rugby, because it was the oppressor's game. Now here he was before the eyes of all South Africa – most of whom had identified with the Springboks – giving the prize to members of the very group which had caused so much sorrow and pain. In Johannesburg on the night of the Final there had never before been so many street parties. 'Thank you for what you have done for the country,' Mandela said to the captain. 'It is nothing to what you have done,' Francois Pienaar replied. A little later, on the 19th anniversary of the 16 June 1976 school children's uprising, precipitated by the forced teaching of Afrikaans in black schools, Mandela turned up to speak to 30,000 in Ezakheni, a township near Ladysmith in KwaZulu-Natal, wearing a Springbok rugby cap. 'This generation,' he declared, 'stands at the borderline between the past oppression and repression and the future of prosperity, peace and harmony.'[42]

But the event towering above all others in daring and imagination occurred in July 1995 when he held a lunch for the women, both black and white, who had stood by their husbands during the apartheid era. Mandela called them 'the heroes of both sides'. Standing behind Marga Diedrichs, widow of the former State President Nico Diedrichs, and putting his hand on her shoulders,

Mandela said 'I will tell you a secret: this lady was the first to congratulate me and wish me well after my inauguration as president.' Visibly moved, she touched his hand saying: 'We are doing well, aren't we?'

Among the eighteen women attending the luncheon were Susan Strydom, widow of the former Prime Minister, J.G. Strydom, Tini Vorster, widow of the former Prime Minister, John Vorster, and Elize Botha, wife of the former State President, P.W. Botha. Wives of former liberation movement leaders included Ntsiki Biko, Steve Biko's widow, Albertina Sisulu, wife of Walter Sisulu, former ANC president Oliver Tambo's widow Adelaide and Amina Cachalia, widow of the Indian Congress leader Yusuf Cachalia.

Mandela said he had brought the wives together as a 'practical way of forgetting the past'. 'We have fought our fights in the past. We have forgotten that and by attending this occasion, each of them is putting an important brick in that new building.' Adelaide Tambo said Mandela had set an example of the spirit of reconciliation: 'We cannot forget the past, but we can endeavour to forgive.'[43]

Mrs Betsie Verwoerd, then 94 years old, had been unable to attend the meal, so Mandela paid a special visit to meet her in the private, whites-only settlement of Oranjia, where he promised to continue talks with Afrikaners about self-determination. He also went to see the statue of Dr Verwoerd on a *koppie* (small hill) above the town but made it clear during his visit that he remained convinced South Africa had a non-racial future. He added two things: much anger and bitterness remained about the apartheid past; and the removal of Verwoerd statues in several parts of the country should have been done only after guidelines had been set up on dealing with apartheid symbols and movements. Albertina Sisulu and Amina Cachalia also accompanied Mandela, who was with the Free State Premier Patrick Lekota and his Northern Cape counterpart Manne Dipico.[44] Mandela said later his reception had been as warm as Soweto's; and Mrs Verwoerd said she was glad he was there.[45]

One further incident stands out. The Cabinet had met in Mandela's absence and decided to change the name of the Hendrik Verwoerd Hospital in Pretoria. On his return Mandela questioned F.W. de Klerk about this, who reported that the Cabinet had agreed

STRUGGLING TO FORGIVE

to the name change. 'Had I been there,' the President replied, 'I would not have agreed. Mrs Verwoerd is still alive.' Moreover, he added, one of Dr Verwoerd's relatives was a member of the ANC.[46]

'What can one wish President Mandela on his birthday this week?' the South African satirist Pieter Dirk Uys asked in July 1995. 'A long life? Yes, yes, yes. A happy life? With all our hearts. A normal life? How!' He went on: 'He doesn't have to prove anything. Now, dangerously, he can tease and challenge, jeopardizing his position as a rare and protected species, in order to get across his point of view. It is so obvious what that is. The man is committed to forgive and reconciliate. The man embodies the best in all religions. Love your neighbour, even though he locked you up for twenty-seven years!'[47]

Nelson Mandela has not always been able to forgive easily: that much is obvious from some of his statements. Despite his latter-day emphasis on forgiving and forgetting, this has not always proved possible even for him. At the funeral of Victoria Mxenge – her husband had already been brutally murdered by a hit squad as admitted subsequently by Dirk Coetzee, who was in charge of it[48] – Mandela sent a message which said the murder was 'an atrocity we shall never forget or forgive'.[49] And, of course, he did justify killing in self-defence as when MK men, approached by security forces whose policy was to shoot and kill rather than arrest, opened fire and killed a South African officer, though several of them lost their lives, too.[50]

When Magnus Malan and others were committed to trial in KwaZulu-Natal for alleged complicity in atrocities, the former State President, P.W. Botha, warned Mandela not to rouse the sleeping tiger in the Afrikaner, but Mandela, who earlier had recognized that Botha had been the first 'from the other side to try to turn the direction of the stream,'[51] was firm. 'Nobody should lecture me about reconciliation,' he said forthrightly. 'I started reconciliation in South Africa after a lot of humiliation. I am the architect of reconciliation.'[52]

Reconciliation, however, did not mean irresolution, or lack of direction. So at one point he even threatened to cut off government funds to KwaZulu-Natal, having told 20,000 militant ANC supporters in the province that Inkatha was using government funds to foment violence there, only to find that his suggestion was unconstitutional.[53] He also sent the Army into the province in an effort to control the violence there and admitted in June 1995 that he had told guards to shoot to kill opponents marching on the ANC Headquarters in 1994. He had acted, he said, on information that Inkatha planned to attack Shell House to destroy information and kill party leaders.[54] 'This is nothing more nor less than a statement of the common law right to self-defence,' he maintained during a debate in Parliament about the deaths outside the ANC's Headquarters in Johannesburg on 28 March 1994.[55]

Views were mixed about Mandela's actions. Local media commentators accepted that he was not giving guards *carte blanche* to blaze away, but also argued that the ANC had been slow to give details of the shootings. The ANC's reply, however, accused Nationalists in particular – who, unusually for them, had focused their attack directly on the President – of 'selective morality', saying that they sat 'comfortably in their mansions while South Africa burned', and that they only highlighted killings when it suited their agenda.[56]

Is Mandela a saint or a politician of great subtlety? The answer must be a mixture of both. 'Nelson Mandela has forgiven and has no desire for revenge,' considers the Rev. Theo Kotze, who visited him three times on Robben Island. 'It is an act of grace.'[57] Dr Percy Yutar, at the time the President visited him, referred to the great humility of this saintly man. Yet Mandela himself, when questioned about his religious beliefs, explained how he was 'not particularly spiritual', adding, 'I am just an ordinary person interested in trying to make sense of the mysteries of life.'[58]

Nevertheless, he has shown himself very sensitive to the faith dimension in public life, calling himself a Christian (he was brought up within a Methodist context) and making sure that at his inauguration as President all the world faith communities present in South Africa were given acknowledgement. At the time he became President, for example, he visited a mosque, a synagogue and a Christian service, and later a Hindu temple.

South Africa, of course, is an intensely religious country, where over 80 per cent of people express allegiance to some form of Christian belief, the largest group of supporters being in the

African Independent Churches. So it is not surprising to find Mandela as President acknowledging this fact. But there is more to it than this, surely. There is also an awareness that South Africa needs the resources religious faith can bring to help its leaders build a new nation out of the ashes and histories of the old. 'In a period of transition,' Mandela has said, 'in which we will experience many things for the first time, we are bound to make mistakes and experience failure. We must make sure we recognize these quickly, assess them, criticize ourselves where necessary, learn what has to be learnt, and emerge from these stronger and better, able to carry out our historic mission.'[59]

To be willing to admit mistakes implies forgiveness for our common fallibility. This is a rare gift in any politician and shows a wisdom and maturity which has few equals. 'Mandela is,' suggests George Alagiah, 'coaxing a nation to maturity.'[60] This was epitomized during the run up to the 1994 General Election when he gave guarded recognition to the former Life President of the Ciskei, Lennox Sebe, appearing on an election platform with him and asking the people of the region to forgive those who had changed their former pro-apartheid stance.[61]

Later he suggested in an interview that he could have destroyed his political opponents with ease, yet he had not retaliated when they had said damaging things because he had the responsibility of keeping the nation together. 'I have to suppress my feelings and think through my head rather than my blood,' he observed.[62]

'The vast majority of black South Africans are not racists, they are generous to a fault towards their white compatriots and oppressors,' the journalist John Carlin considers. 'The message that has struck a chord has not been the Pan-Africanist Congress's "one settler, one bullet". It has been the ANC with its bedrock principle of "non-racialism" that had captured the popular imagination.'[63] Though this attitude has a long history in the ANC it goes even deeper. 'There is something ingrained in Africans,' Mandela himself has explained, 'where people are able to express their views without bitterness, to fight for what we regard as being wrong without bitterness. The message of the African National Congress has merely consolidated that historical pattern.'[64]

'Perhaps if I was idle,' Nelson Mandela has summed it up, 'and did not have a job to do, I would be as bitter as others. But because I have been given a job to do, I have not had time to think about the cruel experiences I've had. I'm not unique – others have every reason to be more bitter than I. There are countless people who went to jail and aren't bitter at all, because they can see their sacrifices were not in vain, and the ideas for which we lived and sacrificed are about to come to fruition. And that removes the bitterness from their hearts.'[65]

Undergirding Nelson Mandela's life, but always regarded as a very private matter and therefore not at all obvious to some, is his view of religion, which he believes is about 'mutual love and respect for one another and for life itself'.[66] His God, if he understood the Bible correctly, required human beings to fight against evil and social ills, including poverty and disease. Indeed, on Robben Island, where he had frequently received Holy Communion, he never missed a service and often read the Scripture lessons. 'Come to think of it,' he told one interviewer, 'I was quite religious.'[67]

THE ROLE OF DESMOND TUTU

Whereas Nelson Mandela is a politician with an instinctive theological undertone, Desmond Mpilo Tutu is first and foremost a theologian-teacher and priest. 'I am not,' he once stated categorically, 'a politician trying to be an Archbishop.'[68]

His schoolmaster father, Zachariah Tutu, was a somewhat proud Fingo, he once explained to the Eloff Commission investigating the affairs of the South African Council of Churches (SACC), of which he was then General Secretary, who 'inexplicably married Aletha Matlhare, a Motswana woman who washed clothes for a white household. Am I a Xhosa or Motswana?' he asked.[69]

He and his sisters learned to speak Xhosa and Tswana, English and Afrikaans, so, though his roots are essentially African, he is intensely South African, too. 'In the African world view,' he once explained, 'God is understood as the source of all life and creator of heaven and earth. There is an emphasis on the continuity of life

STRUGGLING TO FORGIVE

after death … Land is … not a piece of real estate; it has a very deep significance. Land is perceived as an organism that sustains the bond between the unborn, the living and the dead.' He went on to suggest that these aspects of African culture, 'together with what I term South African culture, which embraces a mixture of African, English and Afrikaans, could deeply enrich our spirituality and our understanding of God and the world.'[70]

Two remarkable people deeply influenced the young Desmond Tutu at a time when he might have become radicalized in the way so many blacks were later in the 1970s and 1980s in the townships across South Africa. One was Florence Blaxall, who founded a home for blind people in South Africa and helped many to hope again. 'Knowing you,' Tutu once said to her, 'has made it virtually impossible, I think, for people to be embittered because of how they were treated in this country, because they would recall how you had treated them as if they were what they knew themselves to be, human beings made in the image of God.'[71]

The second person was Trevor Huddleston who, like Tutu himself, lived in Sophiatown near Johannesburg in the 1950s. One day Tutu's mother was walking along a street and Huddleston tipped his hat to her. Tutu had never seen a white person make such a gesture before and the event lodged itself in his mind for decades. So, too, did Huddleston's pastoral concern for him later, when in 1953 the 13-year-old Tutu contracted TB and Huddleston visited him in hospital every day for 20 months.[72]

Tutu's upbringing was rough. A sewage bucket system was in operation and a candle lit the home at night as his mother cooked on coal or paraffin stoves. Like many other African boys he played soccer barefoot in the street with an old tennis ball and was 'a typical street urchin'. Music, too, enthralled him, especially that of Fats Waller, Louis Armstrong and Nat King Cole.[73]

In 1955, when the family was living at Munsieville on the outskirts of Krugersdorp, nearby Sophiatown was demolished. What happened when the families were loaded on to trucks and taken to Meadowlands – a new location further from their work where they had no land tenure – one wet February morning and Sophiatown was bulldozed and reduced to rubble, etched itself in Tutu's memory. 'Houses, land that people had actually owned, were taken away from those owners without consultation, without compensation, without compassion,' he wrote later as he recalled the injustice of it all. It was the beginning of Soweto and a new white suburb called, provocatively, Triomf (Triumph). In 1996 Triomf became Sophiatown once again however.

Tutu experienced firsthand what it was like to live with inadequate housing, for even after he had been ordained and had his first curacy (in 1960 at St Alban's Church in Benoni), living conditions for his wife and three children were not good. They lived in a garage, which served as main bedroom, children's bedroom, sitting room and dining room, with a small second room used as a kitchen.[74]

Living out of South Africa for many years, Desmond Tutu and his family learned to breathe in a new atmosphere and shed apartheid restrictions. But he returned in 1975 to become Dean of St Mary's Cathedral in Johannesburg, then in quick succession Bishop of Lesotho, General Secretary of the SACC in 1978, then Bishop of Johannesburg and finally, in 1986, Archbishop of Cape Town.

He was thus in the country when many of the upheavals of the 1970s and 1980s occurred – the 1976 Soweto uprising, the murder of Steve Biko in 1977 and the banning of many organizations, including the Christian Institute and the Black Consciousness Movement – as well as the installation of the Tri-Cameral Parliament for whites, Coloureds and Indians only, instituted by President P.W. Botha in the early 1980s. He also experienced the 1984 State of Emergency and growing disaffection, as blacks in the townships responded to the ANC's call to make South Africa ungovernable, and as the United Democratic Front (UDF), an association of some four hundred anti-apartheid groups led by the Rev. Allan Boesak, among others, grew in strength.

'It is as well that our Lord expects us not to like but to love our enemies and neighbours,' Tutu had written to a friend in 1966. 'It will be extremely difficult to love the white man as it is. Awful sentiment, isn't it?'[75] Now, as violence and conflict escalated between Government and governed, Desmond Tutu was to find both his theology and practice tested to the limit. Though never banned, nor arrested for long, he and his family used to receive death threats on the telephone,[76] an experience he found 'almost unforgivable'.[77] Sometimes his passport was withheld until the last moment, too, or withdrawn to prevent him making speeches or giving lectures abroad. Yet invitations came to him thick and fast, the more so after he was awarded the Nobel Peace Prize in 1984. These even included an address to the Political Committee of the United Nations General Assembly in New York in 1985, where he called for universal sanctions against South Africa.

Again and again he was thrust into the limelight, often at points of great pain, suffering and difficulty. In 1977, for example, he was one of the speakers at Steve Biko's funeral. 'We are experiencing the birth pangs of a new South Africa,' he said, 'a free South Africa where all of us, black and white together, will walk tall …'[78] In 1982 he was preacher at yet another funeral of a prominent activist, the Durban civil rights lawyer Meungiso Mxenge who was killed by a hit squad under Dirk Coetzee, as he later admitted when recounting the details of this most terrible atrocity.[79] 'Many more will be detained,' he warned. 'Many more will be banned. Many more will be deported and killed. Yes, it will be costly. But we shall be free. Nothing will stop us becoming free – no police bullets, dogs, tear-gas, prison, death, no, nothing will stop us because God is on our side.'[80] Later, in 1993, in the most explosive situation of all, he had to speak before a crowd of 100,000 in a soccer stadium in Soweto at the funeral of Chris Hani.

Once in Soweto, when two large white policemen were beating an elderly black man, he put himself between them, holding up his bishop's cross until they ceased. He risked danger, too, at a political funeral in the Ciskei by flinging himself across the body of a black security policeman who was being stoned by a large, angry mob. Thinking the stoning was over, he returned to his rostrum, his clothes saturated in the policeman's blood. Later, however, the crowd dragged the policeman away and beat him to death.[81]

Always Desmond Tutu seems to be at the point where forgiveness or reconciliation is needed. Sometimes he exemplifies it. On one occasion he astounded an elderly man, who made it clear he disliked him greatly, by visiting him regularly as he recovered from an operation. In like manner he went to the funeral of a woman who hated him.[82] It was a working out of a conviction, from which so much of his reconciliation activity stems, that there is (as the Quakers have taught) something of God in everyone.

'We are created in the image of God,' he has written, 'who shows a marked bias in favour of the marginalized, the poor, the weak – the widow, the orphan and the alien ...' If we take our theology seriously, he went on to argue, 'we should really genuflect before one another'. God has created human beings for family, for a togetherness and interdependence, which leads to friendliness, sharing, laughter and joy, peace and prosperity. We are God's stewards over creation and like God in creativity through our relationships and work, the arts, drama and literature and even as gardeners. He affirmed that we are made in the image of the Trinity and if the laws of interdependence are broken, 'all kinds of things go horribly wrong'. Moreover, we have to exhibit a compassion like God's, for we were created by God and made to reach out to the transcendent: 'a remarkable paradox – the finite made for the infinite'.[83]

Unlike many peace workers, Desmond Tutu starts with clear theological perceptions and his actions in any given situation or context must be seen as the inevitable outworkings of his beliefs. His comment on Winnie Mandela, therefore, to whom he once administered Holy Communion in his car because the police told him he could not enter her house,[84] is illuminating: 'We must not too facilely condemn her for none of us can confidently predict how we would react under pressure and we all respond differently. The apartheid system was vicious and sought to break her.'[85] Similarly he declared 'Botha is my brother' and refused to believe that God's grace could not operate on the President.[86] In 1980, at a time when there was much popular resistance to the Government, he led senior figures in the SACC to meet him and six Cabinet ministers, for which he was severely criticized by radical black church leaders.[87] Tutu was undeterred, drawing on the biblical parallel of Moses going to see Pharaoh.[88] He was generous, too, towards President F.W. de Klerk, Botha's successor, 'for the indispensable part he has played in setting in motion the revolution happening in South Africa'.[89]

Nevertheless, before Nelson Mandela was released he was warning always of the perils of the situation. 'It is a miracle of

STRUGGLING TO FORGIVE

God's grace that blacks can still say they are committed to a ministry of justice and reconciliation and that they want to avert the blood bath which seems more and more inevitable as we see little bending on the crucial issue of power-sharing,' he said at one meeting in Durban. 'We are told that the Afrikaners have found it very difficult to forgive, certainly difficult to forget, what the British did to them in the concentration camps. I want to say that blacks are going to find it difficult, very difficult to forgive, certainly difficult to forget, what whites have done and are doing to us in this matter of population removals.'[90]

Between 3 and 5 September 1990, a reported 36 people died in violence in Sebokeng. The Anglican Synod of Bishops, gathered in Lesotho, suspended its meeting and made a pastoral visit to the area on 6 September, Tutu preaching in the Anglican church there. 'Let us not let the enemy divide us,' he urged. 'We must not allow the enemy to fill us with hatred ... Let us not be filled with a desire for revenge...'[91]

Even when there were terrible massacres, as at Boipatong, when forty or so were killed, including a nine-month-old baby who was hacked to death, Tutu reiterated his message. 'We must remember,' he said later in Memphis, Tennessee, 'that white South Africans are not demons with horns and tails. No, they are human beings, most of them very frightened human beings. Wouldn't you be if you were outnumbered five to one? And remember that quite a few have opposed apartheid and paid heavily for that stand.'[92] 'If I was white I would need a lot of grace to resist a system that provided me with such substantial privilege,' he added on another occasion.[93]

Buti Tlhagale (General Secretary of the Catholic Bishops' Conference), who considers there is a continuity between Tutu and what the silenced black leaders stood for,[94] (though Tutu, as he once told President P.W. Botha, agreed with the aims of the ANC but not its methods[95]) has explained that Tutu possesses a faith which dissipates fear and always encourages blacks to believe they will be free. 'For him, faith in God is an invisible pillar of strength,' he considers. 'And so at every event where he participates, he acknowledges God's presence by saying a prayer to the embarrassment of many disillusioned blacks who regard

Christianity and its rituals as the handmaid of the oppressive system.'[96]

Tutu's role changed with the release of Nelson Mandela in 1990. Mandela spent his first night of freedom with the Archbishop at his residence at Bishopscourt in Cape Town and the next morning Tutu bade him goodbye and wished him well on the next stage of his long walk to freedom. 'I hoped that the release would mark the normalization of the political process in South Africa,' he has commented, 'and that I could take a far lower profile in the political arena.' Prior to 1990 political rallies had been held 'under the guise of church services'.[97] But with the unbanning of political organizations Tutu believed the Church now had to render a different service to the community, leaving the overtly political work to the politicians, as it ministered to the spiritual and material needs of the people.

Tutu discovered, however, that events were not to work out quite as he hoped because of what he termed 'grandstanding and prima donna behaviour' by some politicians. So once again he found himself visiting homeland and national liberation movement leaders and meeting government representatives. 'In polite but forceful manner,' he has recounted, 'I have tried to knock their heads together ... and to get the democratic process underway...'[98]

At one moment he and Stanley Mogoba, then the Presiding Bishop of the Methodist Church, facilitated a meeting between Nelson Mandela and Chief Buthelezi. 'I had just celebrated a very beautiful Eucharist at the consecration of the Bishop of Zululand, Chief Buthelezi was present and the mood was correct,' he has commented. 'I put the question to him and he agreed. The opportunity to speak to Nelson Mandela was in an equally apt situation. We had participated in the Gandhi centenary celebration and in the unveiling of the Gandhi statue. I put the question to him and he agreed.'[99]

At other times Desmond Tutu exhibits critical solidarity with those in power, seeking always to ensure that the Church retains a perspective on them. The massive payout, reportedly totalling 17.5 million rand, made by the Nationalist Government to the police involved in 'dirty tricks' threatened to wreck the process of reconciliation in South Africa, Tutu declared in 1995. The country needed to know the degree of F.W. de Klerk's personal knowledge of the payments and the reasons for them. 'If we do not get to the bottom of this, reconciliation is impossible,' he added.[100]

The escalating violence in South Africa distressed Tutu continually. When F.W. de Klerk called a conference to deal with the issue he was not able to persuade those from the liberation movements to attend. 'It was only when some of us Church leaders ... got together with business leaders that we were able to facilitate the signing of the National Peace Accord,' he told one meeting. 'We are going to have to urge blacks to be ready to forgive all the horrendous atrocities perpetuated on them by apartheid upholders because we will say to them they are obliged to forgive,' he continued. 'And yet they will need to forgive only when those who have wronged them are penitent and contrite and ask for forgiveness ... That will pour oil on many wounded souls, three and a half million who have been wounded by the rape, for example, of District 6 and other injustices of the forced removals. We must deal effectively, penitently with our past or it will return to haunt our present and we won't have a future to speak of.'

He went on in his address to explain that wrong was wrong whoever committed it, so there was condemnation for the Government 'for its machinations' in fomenting the violence. Black leaders had been called to the Bishopscourt summit to discuss violence and the black community, an issue which was followed up by the SACC. 'I have engaged in shuttle diplomacy,' he explained, 'to facilitate an end to the bloodletting. I have not minced my words in condemning APLA (The Azanian People's Liberation Army), Inkatha, or the human rights violations in the ANC camps.'[101]

Soon after F.W. de Klerk's speech on 2 February 1990 the Anglican Church had called on the ANC to end, or at least suspend, the armed struggle because negotiations with authentic representatives were a real possibility. 'The ANC didn't like that,' Tutu commented, 'but it subsequently suspended the armed struggle.' Moreover, the Anglican Church had prohibited its licensed clergy from being card-carrying members of any political organization, a move meant to demonstrate the Church's determination to be even-handed.[102]

When it came to relations with the Afrikaans community especially, Tutu was reconciling. He once strolled down Adderley Street in Cape Town in a Springbok rugby jersey, which had been presented to him by the team after the opening match of the Rugby World Cup between Australia and South Africa,[103] and he spoke out against a proposal to drop Afrikaans from TV 1, while appealing to Afrikaners not to be 'hyper-sensitive' about their language.[104] In November 1995 he was invited to preach the sermon in the NGK (Nederduitse Gereformeerde Kerk, the largest and most 'mainline' of the three white Dutch Reformed Churches in South Africa) Suid-Oos Church in Pretoria. Talking of the need God had for human partners to make real his plan – Moses, or Mary, for example – he told the congregation: 'God has chosen you Afrikaners for a special role in this land.'[105]

He recalled how, when the only response to an SACC Consultation on Racism from the NGK had been via the press, he had persisted. He wrote a letter to them, indicating that South Africa needed them and including a request for forgiveness for the SACC and its member churches for anything they had done in the past to hurt the NGK.[106] Slowly things had changed and the NGK had been the first Church 'publicly and openly to acknowledge wrong' when its prophets Professor Ben Marais and Dominee Beyers Naudé, who had been persecuted, were rehabilitated and vindicated. 'Our land needs healing,' he concluded. 'We have all been traumatized by apartheid. We are a wounded people, all of us.'[107] The Church must therefore preach the gospel of reconciliation, which depended on forgiveness, which itself depended on confession.

Desmond Tutu believed that God was calling the Church to a ministry of healing: healing for blacks for three centuries of denial of human rights; healing for whites, who carried 'the scars from the wars of conquest and the traumas of enforced conscription', and the guilt associated with being so privileged. Originally he had wanted to be a physician and now, in large measure, he set out to perform that role. 'It was,' he maintained, ever the theologian-teacher, 'a wounded Christ whom God made the instrument of healing in our world.'[108] Christ was even tortured to death, executed for his beliefs just like a common criminal.[109] So Christians especially were in a position to be alongside those most broken by apartheid.

How could this healing come about? Since the 1994 elections, by realizing that 'we are free, all of us, black and white together. We have been transformed. We have been transfigured. The repulsive caterpillar has become a gorgeous butterfly of many colours.'[110] South Africa now needed to develop a culture of tolerance, which it had never really possessed. 'People have learned,' he explained, 'those who differ from you are enemies and the only way to deal with enemies is to liquidate them.'[111] In addition, South Africans needed to forgive. In a pre-1994 election service, which was broadcast nationally, he said, 'We must all work together for confession, forgiveness, restitution, reconciliation and peace. The interim constitution will assist in this process because we are compelled to have a Government of National Unity which will be a non-party administration that will operate on the basis of consensus and compromise.'[112]

Blacks had to turn the spotlight on themselves, too, he insisted. They could not go on blaming apartheid forever, responsible for so much evil as it was. In the struggle for justice they had shown a resilience, could laugh and forgive, refusing to be embittered in some of the worst moments of the struggle.[113] Now it seemed the black community had lost its sense of *ubuntu* – caring, hospitality, 'our sense of connectedness, our sense that my humanity is bound up with your humanity'.[114]

So Tutu continually tried to move people on, sometimes the authoritative Anglican prelate, but one who was aware of his mistakes and the hurts he had caused;[115] sometimes the humorous man of the people; at other times like one of the prophets, from Jeremiah onwards, who warned, encouraged and cajoled. 'I believe God has called South Africa to a special vocation,' he declared during one of his overseas trips. He was hopeful because God wanted South Africa to succeed for one main reason (among others) – to provide the world with a paradigm on how to solve its problems. For South Africa had most of the world's problems written small – black and white; poverty versus affluence; industrial and sophisticated versus developing and simple; large majority versus several minorities; pluralism versus diversity: 'you name it and we have got it,' he concluded.[116] 'Had there been no forgiveness and reconciliation after Mau Mau in this country, there might have been no Kenya,' he said in 1995, indicating that he regarded forgiveness and reconciliation in the lives of nations as 'the stuff of practical politics'.[117]

He was quick to praise where possible, thereby helping others to be more generous in their appreciation, too. 'Mr de Klerk must be given his due for the courage of his initiatives in 1990,' he said in an address in 1995. Nelson Mandela is 'magnanimous to a fault, regal and yet so humble, so eager to forgive,' he considered. As to the new Government ministers, people had not been 'as quick to praise as we have been to blame and pour scorn,' on them, forgetting they were not long ago in exile, or jail, or excluded from government in other ways. Equally there were magnanimous people who had been tortured or jailed who had emerged unscathed by bitterness, who were committed to the proposed Truth and Reconciliation Commission as a means of dealing with the past so that it would not return to haunt the future. These people and their attitude should be recognized.[118]

Always in his mind there was the need for watchfulness, for even the most popularly elected governments were not 'saints, but frail human beings who can succumb to the temptations of corruption and abuse of power'.[119] The Church, he said elsewhere, must speak up for the voiceless and ease, too, the fears of South Africa's white minority.[120] We must be 'watchdogs not lap dogs',[121] he said on another occasion, precisely because the community did not want its Government to fail. If he had tangled before with F.W. de Klerk, urging him to make a formal apology for the apartheid years,[122] a request he repeated during the Archbishop Stephen Memorial lecture in 1992,[123] so now he spoke up against what he judged to be too high salaries for politicians and Government servants under Mandela and the GNU.[124]

'It needs just as much courage to say "Pardon our enemies," as to say, "Let my people go,"'[125] Tutu considered, but that is what he proceeded to do, at the same time making it clear that despite the violence and troublesome crime, he saw a good future now for South Africa. As he had shown resolution over the necessity for conflict ('it did cost God the death of His son to effect reconciliation,'[126]) so now, in the context of his black theology, with its

STRUGGLING TO FORGIVE

sense of liberation, humanization, forgiveness and reconcilia-tion,[127] he pointed towards the new South Africa as 'the rainbow people of God',[128] and 'a success story waiting to happen'.[129]

Always throughout his speeches, addresses and encounters, there has been not only a toughness, both of insight and state-ment, but also a pithy humour and lightness of touch, which has enabled so many thousands to listen to what he has to say. 'Perhaps one of the chief reasons for hope that we are going to make it is that we are all learning to laugh at ourselves,'[130] he wrote in one of his pieces. And to the Cape Town Press Club in 1995 he commented: 'As a new Springbok I would say let us play the ball and not the man/woman.'[131] To members of his Soweto congregation, most of whom were not very important in the eyes of the world, he urged them to say, when they were asked who they were, 'I'm God's viceroy, I'm God's representative, God's stand in.'[132]

For years Desmond Tutu's travel documents said his nation-ality was 'not yet determined'. It would be no bad thing, he observed laughingly, if a few more were less sure of their precise identity, for 'it might help us find a new common identity in South Africa'.[133]

Chapter 2

Forgiveness and Remembering –

The Role of History

Obstacles to change are often related to unresolved events in the past, or even to ill-perceived interpretations of those events. So history suddenly becomes contemporary, influencing decisions for good or ill now and for the future. In order, therefore, to understand some of the complex forces at work in South Africa today it is necessary to sketch out a number of the conflicts which took place between (and within) the various communities earlier this century and even before that.

It is not really possible for most individuals, other than the very heroic, to blot out from their memories wrongs committed, for to be a human being is to be a creature of history. But history can be remembered in such a way that it does not obstruct the future, and that is by linking the remembering with forgiving. In this way the truth about the past is acknowledged, but forgiveness frees people from the past for a new and hopefully different future.

The South African conflict has been so diverse and protracted that it will, of course, take decades (and almost certainly longer) to create a new society. Yet it remains necessary, amidst all the striving for a different future, to learn the lessons of the past. These can then serve as a permanent reminder of what to avoid when trying to build new political patterns.

Within the story of the conflicts between Britain and Boer, black and white, white and Indian, as well as the conflict caused by the different philosophical positions taken up within the black community itself, many individuals can be seen struggling to forgive at different levels.

Such struggles have to be teased out, making assumptions from the way people are known to have acted, rather than being immediately obvious from the bare facts. Most of this chapter on forgiveness and remembering merely sets the scene and prepares the ground for the ensuing chapters, and highlights retrospectively the remarkable way in which Nelson Mandela and Desmond Tutu have transcended the past, while remaining deeply aware of its twists and turns.

Remarkable, too, within the story of the developing racial conflict in South Africa, has been the way specific individuals have stood apart from the main attitude of their community and reached out to others. Several of great distinction are mentioned in this chapter, and they are notable for the way they sometimes demonstrated forgiveness in relation both to remembering and to other themes raised in this book.

THE ANGLO-BOER WAR

'We stood alone in the world, friendless among the people,' General Smuts once wrote, 'the smallest nation ranged against the mightiest empire on earth. Then one small hand, the hand of a woman, was stretched out to us. At that darkest hour, when our race almost appeared doomed to destruction, she appeared as an angel, as a heaven-sent messenger. Strangest of all, she was an Englishwoman.'[1]

During the Anglo-Boer War, which had begun after many manoeuvres by both sides when President Kruger declared war on 11 October 1899, Emily Hobhouse had visited some of the 43 concentration camps in which thousands of Afrikaner women and children had been herded as British troops pursued a scorched earth policy. Then she returned to London and started a relief fund for them. Soon, however, disease broke out, partly because of overcrowding and an acute shortage of doctors, nurses and medicines.[2] There were many deaths, particularly among children, and by December 1901 Emily and her supporters had so aroused the conscience of the British public that the Government itself was forced to make improvements. 'Afrikaners have never forgotten her,' one Quaker writer has commented.[3] Indeed a small town near the Lesotho border was named after her.

Camps for Africans were also established. By the end of May 1902 they were settled temporarily in over 60, but Emily Hobhouse could do little for them due to 'lack of time and strength'. She hoped the London Commission would act, and when it did not she called on Fox Bourne and laid the facts about the plight of black women and children before him for action.[4]

As they sought reconciliation, Nelson Mandela and Desmond Tutu were always aware of the suffering which Africans in particular had experienced because of Afrikaner policies, but Afrikaner Nationalists themselves were more sensitive to the deep wounds of their own history, particularly the psychological effects of the Anglo-Boer War, which had left their largely rural communities traumatized. The intention of the concentration camps was 'humane', Allister Sparks has observed, 'but under the conditions of a difficult war in a hard continent, intention and outcome do not always coincide.'[5]

British–Afrikaner hostility did not begin with the Anglo-Boer War, of course, but had its roots in the eighteenth century, when the free burghers of the Cape rebelled against the autocracy of the Dutch East India Company, and in the Great Trek of the 1830s, when Afrikaners left the Cape to free themselves from British rule.[6] For them the nineteenth century was 'the century of wrong', confirmed when Britain annexed the Transvaal in 1877. Even Smuts was antagonistic, because of the way the English colonialists had behaved, writing a manifesto with that title, which he never repudiated, though later he transcended its anti-British sentiments, taking from the past only what was good, as Paul Kruger had advised.[7]

South Africa represented all that was bad about the British Empire, Thomas Pakenham has judged – feuding between white communities, as in Canada; bankruptcy among mining interests as in Australia; war with the indigenous peoples, as with the Maoris in New Zealand; and repression as in Ireland.[8] 'We have,' observed the South African writer Sarah Millin later, 'all the world's problems in one country.'[9] In particular, the Jameson raid on Johannesburg in 1895 – an abortive attempt by an aide of Cecil Rhodes to take over the gold reserves of the Boer-controlled Transvaal Republic – completely misfired. This sowed the seeds of a unique bitterness as Jameson tried to come to the rescue of the Uitlanders, backed by Cecil Rhodes and Alfred Beit. The Uitlanders were new immigrants, mainly British, swept along in the gold rush, who outnumbered the Boers but were being offered inadequate political rights by them. [10]

Before the Jameson raid, a former judge, Kowie Marais, who was an MP for the Progressive Party from 1977, remembered that his father used to write his love letters to his mother in English. It was the smart thing to do for middle-class Afrikaners. 'After the Jameson raid he never allowed English to be spoken in the house again,' he wrote.[11] His bitterness was nothing compared with the reaction when the defeated Boers signed the Treaty of Vereeniging on 31 May 1902 and British imperialism, headed by Milner and Kitchener, won the day.

There had been atrocities on both sides, of course. One eye witness, describing the murdered and unburied Africans he saw in a post captured by Smuts himself, commented: 'If this was how Jan Smuts, as high-minded as any of the commando leaders, treated the hundred or so Africans of Modderfontein, the fate of others can be imagined.'[12] The British were no better. Even Africans involved in the defence of Mafeking, allowed food by Baden-Powell, died on the veldt when they were evacuated. Most were small boys. 'Hunger had them in its grip, and many of them were black spectres and living skeletons,' wrote one reporter.[13]

One most savage incident at Mafeking involved the Baralong women, 700 of whom were persuaded during the siege to make a mass exodus. Only 10 succeeded in escaping. The others returned, many having been stripped naked and flogged by the Boers.[14] The official figure for the black dead in the camps was in the region of 14,000,[15] but it is now thought to have been much higher. Well over 25,000 Afrikaner women and children under 16 years old had died in the camps, too,[16] besides well over 5,000 British and 7,000 Boer soldiers who died in action. Many more, of course, died of wounds and disease.[17] One-fifth of the fighting Afrikaners, however, fought on the side of the British at the end of the war, 'a secret that has remained hidden till today', one scholar has added.[18]

Ramsey Macdonald visited South Africa at the time and decided it was 'the *vrouw* (woman)' who kept the war going on so long. It was in her heart that patriotism flowed into an all-consuming hate. 'She it is who returns, forgiving nothing ... The camps have alienated her from us for ever,' he remarked.[19]

Also alienated were six 'bitter-enders', who, when 54 other leaders agreed to Kitchener's peace proposals, refused to accept them, knowing they had substantial support among the 21,000 commandos who now emerged from their hiding places.[20] Smuts, who had been given an intimation by Kitchener that there might shortly be a Liberal government in London favourable to new South African political arrangements,[21] took the view that it was better 'to negotiate an orderly peace now under the best possible terms than to be crushed later and have ignominious terms thrust on us'.[22] Acting President Burger added the solemn words: 'We must be ready to forgive and forget,'[23] referring significantly not to the British themselves, or even to the Uitlanders (perhaps worried about their future if the Johannesburg gold deposits ever came under German influence via President Kruger[24]), but to those who had *sided with* the British.

Under the Peace Treaty farms were restored, prisoners repatriated and 3 million pounds allotted for division among ex-burghers who could prove war losses, whichever side they had fought for. The actual sum amounted to over 16 million pounds, however, administered by a Repatriation Department, though Africans were paid at a 17 per cent lower rate. Many received nothing because they were landless and 'bitter-enders' usually refused to take back *bywoners* (the tenant farmers) who had fought on the British side.[25] Seed and rations were provided, along with veterinary services to deal with stock disease, and though the harvest following the peace was the worst for 40 years,[26] soon the problem of food was solved.[27]

In 1903 Rudyard Kipling wrote a poem called 'The Settler', in which he envisaged a farmer indicating a will to make amends as together neighbours would atone for the waste. As God was invoked to bless the work in the fields, Kipling suggested – in an attitude similar to Nelson Mandela's – that when old fights were recalled, the sin would not be remembered, or who did what to whom.[28] Kipling's hope was not so easily made concrete, however, for, as William Plomer has indicated, unforgiveness the size of an alp arose out of the follies of the Anglo-Boer War.[29]

Mrs Smuts herself found it difficult to follow her husband's emphasis on conciliation between English and Boer when the

STRUGGLING TO FORGIVE

Union of South Africa was created in 1910, remaining so much a republican that, with the exception of the youngest, all her six surviving children were literally born under the republican flag, which was unfurled over her bed whenever a birth was expected. But as the husbands of three of her daughters turned out to be English, Jan Smuts suggested she was probably being punished for her bitterness.[30]

Lord Milner's attempt to remove the nascent Afrikaans language from schools, an Anglicanization policy going back to the Cape Governor, Charles Somerset, further alienated Afrikaners from the English as their self-consciousness grew. They did, however, still revere Emily Hobhouse, whose mortal remains were interred at the foot of the Women's Memorial in Bloemfontein on 27 October 1926. Earlier, at the memorial's opening on 16 December 1913, she had been invited to speak, but due to health problems had only reached Beaufort West. A friend read out her message instead. 'Alongside the honour we pay the Sainted Dead, forgiveness must find a place ... To harbour hate is fatal to your own self-development, it makes a flaw, for hatred like rust, eats into the soul of a nation as of an individual,' she said. 'As your tribute to the dead, bury unforgiveness and bitterness at the foot of this monument forever.'[31]

Naturally, it took decades to work through the after-effects of the Anglo-Boer War, so strong were the memories. Denys Reitz, a close companion of General Smuts who had refused to take the oath of allegiance to the Crown when his father had done so and had therefore gone into exile, was enticed back to South Africa by Mrs Smuts, and her husband taught Reitz about his approach to Boer–English reconciliation.[32] An interesting story about Reitz's father describes a reconciling encounter he had in 1943 with Lord Vivian, his earlier adversary. While sitting at his desk in South Africa House in London, a private secretary interrupted him to say, 'There is a Lord Vivian here to see you – he says he knows you.'[33] Lord Vivian entered the room and Reitz senior saw he was carrying a long parcel. In it was the Mauser rifle, with Reitz's name carved on the buff, which he had left on the battlefield by the side of Lord Vivian when he had shot and wounded him during the Anglo-Boer War.

One other incident is seldom reported. After the War, with the cooperation of the War Office, Quakers in London successfully appealed (through Lord Roberts, the initiator of the first farm burnings) for the return of stolen Bibles, some saved from the days before the Great Trek, which had been looted from some of the 30,000 homes destroyed. By 1927, 130 Bibles had been returned to their owners and in 1933, 20 more were sent to the South African High Commission for despatch to Pretoria.[34]

The memory of the War, however, continued to provide political conflict in many households. 'The Boer War was fought again in our family,' remarked Nellis du Preez, who came from an English-Afrikaner background.[35] Patrick van Rensburg, too, has described an argument from his childhood which was only stopped by his grandmother's anger when she turned on two young Afrikaner nationalist visitors who were fuelling the controversy. 'She, who had been an inmate of a concentration camp, had been able to forgive and forget, while these people, born a full generation later, were summoning up the ghosts of the past to sustain their present hatreds,' he has recalled.[36]

One legacy of the War lasted nearly a century. During the negotiations which led to the peace treaty, Chamberlain had said, but only for the ears of some, 'We cannot consent to purchase a shameful peace by leaving the coloured population in the position in which they stood before the war, with not even the ordinary civil rights which the Government of the Cape Colony has long conceded to them.' His view did not prevail, of course, for the British government had no intention of extending the franchise to the Transvaal and the Orange Free State before representative government was given to the colonies.[37] And when the Union of South Africa was established in 1910 by uniting the former Boer republics with Natal and the Cape Colony, though Africans and Coloureds in the Cape had voting rights by the early 1900s and formed in fact 16 per cent of all voters, such an arrangement was not allowed to prevail elsewhere. Moreover, Britain even refused to veto a colour bar clause in the draft constitution which prohibited Africans from sitting in the new Union Parliament.[38]

ENGLISH AND AFRIKANER SOUTH AFRICANS

In 1914, of course, a world war overtook the nascent country and after running the East Africa campaign, Smuts was invited to join Britain's War Cabinet. Prime Minister Louis Botha was invited to join Smuts, too, after his South West Africa campaign and his victory over fellow Afrikaners, who had taken up arms in the Free State in October 1914 against involvement in the war and in rebellion to restore the Boer republics. 'It was,' says W.A. de Klerk, 'unique in history', for here were two leaders of a conquered enemy being asked to advise in the inner councils of the victor.[39]

Some, of course, could never forget that Smuts had hunted down fellow Afrikaners to death to oblige the British. Jopie Fourie, in particular, became a martyr to some when, after a court martial for treason, he was executed by firing squad in Pretoria in December 1914, a death sentence confirmed by Smuts himself as Minister of Defence.[40]

When victory in World War I was achieved, both ex-Boer War Generals were unhappy about the harsh terms discussed. On 28 June 1919 Botha jotted down: 'Today I remember the 31st day of May, 1902,' as he recalled the Afrikaner defeat and the necessity of taking up arms against former comrades. On 30 May 1919 Smuts wrote to Woodrow Wilson: 'There will be a terrible disillusion if the people come to think that we are not concluding a Wilson Peace.'[41] In the end he signed, despite his misgivings about the price being exacted from Germany.[42]

While leader of the South African National Party, Louis Botha, who since 1910 had presided over a Cabinet of ex-republican Boers, British and Cape Afrikaners, suddenly died only a few months after the Versailles Treaty was signed. After three years away, Smuts was back in South Africa not only to bury his friend, but also to succeed him as Prime Minister. He had a rude awakening, however, for Afrikaner nationalism had been growing at the expense of conciliation.

In the Afrikaner Nationalist newspaper, *Die Burger*, the movement had found an intelligent new medium to support it and in the 1915 election the Nationalists polled only 16,000 votes less than Botha's South African National Party itself. Just six months after Botha's death, they had won more seats in the new Parliament than anyone else, though the English-speaking Labourites under Colonel Cresswell also gained ground. Smuts, who saw and loved the *veldt* (terrain), had lost touch with the *volk* (people), whose exclusive nationalism was obviously on the increase.[43]

For the next 30 years – Smuts finally lost office in 1948 (and died in 1950) – Afrikanerdom was split between Afrikaner Nationalists, led first by Barry Hertzog, who claimed Smuts' career was drenched in blood,[44] and Smuts himself, who dominated the political scene whether in or out of office. In the 1930s, however, the two leaders came together in government, partly because of the Great Depression of 1931–2, but also because under the constitution Hertzog needed a two-thirds majority in Parliament to push through some of the legislation concerning Africans that most whites favoured. This was effected in 1936, when Africans in the Cape were removed from the Common Voter's Roll and a Land Act was passed, adding to and strengthening the 1913 Land Act.

Later, of course, Hertzog had to experience the trauma of uncompromising opposition from fellow Nationalists, on the grounds that he, who had done so much in the preceding decade to lift Afrikaners from poverty and encourage a feeling of national consciousness, had capitulated for the sake of a doubtful coalition with traditional enemies. 'But,' W.A. de Klerk alleges, 'time favoured the Great Experiment.'[45] By 1934 Hertzog and Smuts were leading the new United Party. For the former, however, he soon found an opponent in a Cape Afrikaner whose background was different from every other Afrikaner leader since 1910. He was D.F. Malan, a minister of the Dutch Reformed Church (NGK), who represented a deep shift in the cause and nature of Afrikaner Nationalism. With him were colleagues like Eric Louw, C.R. Swart, J.G. Strydom and H.F. Verwoerd, the last destined to alter South African history drastically. All were members of the secret Afrikaner brotherhood (the Broederbond) which became a powerhouse for fresh thinking as it plotted South Africa's future behind the scenes. But despite Malan's growing influence, Hertzog broke with him in 1935, denouncing his movement as a serious threat to the peace and order of the Union.[46]

'A phenomenon which has puzzled visitors to South Africa who are astute enough to observe it,' Leo Marquard once observed, 'is that the bitterest enmity exists not between Afrikaner and English, but between Afrikaner and Afrikaner.' He went on to maintain that probably one-third of the Afrikaner population, 'following the Botha-Smuts-Hertzog tradition,' desired cooperation with English-speaking South Africans, but the rest regarded this as 'a kind of treason to Afrikanerdom,'[47] for they were being untrue both to their language and their national traditions. Already it had become apparent that the multi-cultural, multi-lingual nature of South Africa was causing problems difficult to overcome.

Here, then, is the crux of the matter when it comes to the question of forgiveness and remembering in relation to culture, history and identity. Some Afrikaners could only consider South Africa viable as a white person's country if English and Afrikaner cooperated, yet how could they after the atrocities of the Anglo-Boer War and other disputes? Others identified with a single people, rather than a multi-culture, and this was of paramount importance.

There were few like the Afrikaner academic at the University of Pretoria in the 1950s, who had inherited his father's bloodied shirt from the Anglo-Boer War, and was intent on avenging the past by driving out all English-speaking South Africans from the campus, but who then had a dramatic change of heart. Wrestling with his conscience in his bedroom at midnight after listening to a speaker on forgiveness, he changed tack and arranged a public reconciliation with Dr Edgar Brookes (an English-speaking South African academic), where he deliberately spoke English, though he had vowed he would never speak it in public.[48]

Yet inevitably there was interaction, not only between English and Afrikaner, but between black, white, brown and Indian. An event of major significance in 1938 was the hundredth anniversary of the Great Trek, when three women, descendants of the Trek leaders Retief, Pretorius and Potgieter, laid the foundation stone for the Voortrekker Monument. The black majority were only depicted on the monument's walls outside and on the frescoes inside as the forces of barbarism, in the role of servants. But though 100,000 Afrikaners had sung the Afrikaner anthem that centenary December, not all were in tune with Malan's exclusive brand of nationalism, for in the 1938 election his party won only 27 seats, whereas the United Party won 111.

Alan Paton, not yet the famous writer and reformer, let alone President of the Liberal Party, was one of those affected by Afrikaner–English interaction and had been present at the Voortrekker Memorial stone-laying. He met a bearded Afrikaner patriot there who said, with great affability, they were now going to knock hell out of the English. A descendent of the British 1820 settlers, who had given Jacob Uys a Bible when he set out on the Great Trek, 'was shouted down because he gave his greetings in English, as his forbear had done,' Paton noted. 'It was,' he added, 'a lovely and terrible occasion for any English-speaking South African who had gone there to rejoice in an Afrikaner festival.'[49]

Many could not forget that Hertzog, the very founder of Afrikaner Nationalism, had stayed behind, proud and rejected, on his farm. Yet Smuts, a traitor in the eyes of true Nationalists, was there. At a similar ceremony in Bloemfontein, 'Vader' Kestell, the revered 'father' of the Afrikaner people who was also descended from the 1820 settlers, had married a Voortrekker wife and had been a chaplain in the Anglo-Boer war, fared better, appealing for support for the local festival and speaking at it.[50] Indeed, when 'Vader' Kestell – probably the only one ever given this title as a spiritual leader of the Afrikaner people – died in 1941, he was buried at the foot of the women's monument along with President Steyn, General de Wet and Emily Hobhouse.

Alan Paton went home after the stone-laying and said to his wife that he would shave off his beard and never grow another, seeing Afrikaner Nationalism for what it was: 'self-centred, intolerant, exclusive'. He repeated this to Jan Hofmeyr, whose biography he was later to write, who replied, 'It took you a long time to find that out.'[51] 'Since 1938,' Paton explained, 'I have lived in a love-hate relationship with the Afrikaners. I have no wish to see them destroyed, but I also have no wish that they should continue to live at the expense of others.'[52]

STRUGGLING TO FORGIVE

The obverse of the coin was seen in North Africa during World War II. Here, among strange surroundings, customs and languages, the troops turned to familiar things. 'They discovered,' wrote E.G. Malherbe, 'that Afrikaans songs, speech and literature, for instance, interpreted better than anything else the sights, sounds and backgrounds which for them spelled home, South Africa. Soon it was found that English-speaking soldiers were singing, speaking and even reading Afrikaans with natural enthusiasm and confidence ... In fact in many cases it was regarded as "good form" to speak Afrikaans in the messes...'[53]

During the war Smuts, of course, became ever more prominent. In 1941 he had become a Field Marshal and Churchill himself sought his approval on many questions.[54] After World War I he had drafted part of a speech by King George V at the opening of Stormont, urging Irish people to be forbearing, to conciliate, to forgive and forget in order to achieve 'peace, contentment and goodwill'.[55] Now, after World War II, he tried to live out this advice himself – though he still had the firm hand he had shown during the war when he had interned a future Prime Minister, J.B. Vorster, for his involvement in the Ossewa-brandwag, a paramilitary organization having much in common with National Socialism. Discovering his former World War I adversary General von Lettow Vorbeck and his family half starved, Smuts gave them help, telling the General and his wife two weeks before his fatal illness: 'Both of you are favourites in my family.'[56]

'Never did he speak any words of criticism or bitterness of his political foes,' Smuts' physician recorded when he died, though he had been disappointed in Afrikaners who regarded him as unpatriotic because he 'thought wider than the South African scene'.[57] Reconciliation was a word he had used in his letter of farewell to Milner, a policy he had tried to exemplify as far as white South Africa was concerned across the decades.

Others were more muted in their estimation of General Smuts, despite his international status, which had included helping to draft the Charter of the United Nations. One commentator noted that Smuts had died 'without having reconciled the philosophies that he accepted in his library with those which he followed in practice'.[58] For while he had been dealing with world problems, the

Nationalists had been feeding on bitter memories and other South African communities had grown restive at the way they were being treated, sometimes by Smuts himself.

According to his lights he had desired to be just, voting against the abolition of the African franchise for the Cape and showing indignation when in his absence his colleagues agreed to a colour bar in the United Party constitution for the Cape. Yet his outlook was always that of a Boer.[59] 'Unless the white race closes its ranks,' he had said at his first big political meeting in Kimberley in 1895, 'its position will soon become untenable,'[60] adding that democracy as practised in Europe and America was not applicable to Africans in South Africa. Significantly, when he acted differently and gave his opponents the opportunity to make race the main focus of the elections of 1929 and 1948, he lost them.

SMUTS AND THE INDIAN COMMUNITY

Smuts' first big conflict occurred with the Indian community and with Gandhi. Indians had come to Natal to work in its sugar plantations in the middle of the nineteenth century, and in 1893 a Moslem firm in India offered to send Gandhi to South Africa for a year as their lawyer. Shortly after his arrival, an incident occurred which focused his life from then on. A lawsuit required his presence in Pretoria, so Gandhi boarded a train and sat reading in the appropriate compartment ready for the overnight journey.

At Pietermaritzburg a white official came up to him, withdrew, then returned with two railway officials who ordered Gandhi to go to the baggage car, despite his first-class ticket. When he refused, they fetched a policeman, who threw Gandhi and his suitcases onto the platform. He spent the night 'sitting in a waiting room, shivering in the bitter cold' reflecting on the experience, not knowing where his luggage was.[61] Within a week Gandhi had convened a meeting of Indians in Pretoria and spoken to Moslem merchants and a few Hindus about white discrimination. It was his first big public speech.

In 1894, disturbed by the growing number of Indian residents and their affluence, the white community changed the regulations

STRUGGLING TO FORGIVE

relating to Indians residing in South Africa. Thenceforth an indentured Indian worker must return to India after the first five year term, or become a serf in South Africa. There was an escape clause whereby a man could pay an annual tax of three pounds for himself and each dependent and remain free, but this was prohibitively high.

Indians were discriminated against in many ways. In Natal province, for example, they were required to carry passes if they appeared on the streets after 9.00 p.m. In the Free State they were not allowed to own property, trade or farm. There were equally difficult restrictions in Zululand and in the Transvaal, which made Gandhi determined to alter the situation, if not by ending prejudice then at least by making the laws just.

Returning to South Africa from a visit to India in 1896, he was nearly lynched because of talks he had given in India on the plight of Indians, and also because two boats arrived concurrently, each carrying 800 people, and a rumour went round that he was responsible for their coming, which was not the case. Joseph Chamberlain, then Secretary of State for the colonies, wanted to put on trial those who had attacked Gandhi with stones and bricks, beating and humiliating him (some even attempted to set his house alight), but though Gandhi knew some of the assailants, he refused to move against them. It was not their fault, he considered, but the fault of the Government and the community. 'This is a religious question with me,' he declared, saying he would exercise 'self-restraint'.[62]

Two years later Gandhi offered to raise a corps of Indian stretcher bearers and medical orderlies for the British in the Anglo-Boer War, but the Natal Government declined. Nonetheless, at their own expense, he and friends trained and eventually ministered as an Indian Ambulance Corps.

It was inevitable with this outlook that Gandhi would clash in due course with Jan Smuts, and also that he would handle those clashes in ways which came to be known as *satyagraha* (soul force). It received its first test when the Transvaal Government Gazette of 22 August 1906 published the draft of an Act requiring all Indians above the age of eight to submit to official registration and finger-printing on pain of fines, imprisonment or deportation from the province. On 11 September 1906, at a meeting in Johannesburg, a passive resistance campaign began, led by Hajee Habib, whom Gandhi called 'a very old experienced resident of South Africa'.[63]

Gandhi spoke at the meeting, arguing that the Government had taken leave of its sense of decency and calling on the 3,000 present to defy the ordinance or go to jail and if need be die. The struggle, he warned, would be long.[64] Inevitably the Asiatic Registration Act was passed on 31 July 1907. Gandhi led his colleagues in refusing to register and was sentenced to two months in prison. Soon, however, an emissary from Smuts came to the jail with an offer to repeal the Act if the Indians registered voluntarily. Gandhi was conducted to Smuts' office where, in prison uniform, he discussed, then accepted, the proposal and all the Indians were released.

At a meeting where Gandhi explained the meaning of *satyagraha*, a large Pathan from the mountains near the Khyber Pass, who disagreed with the result of Gandhi's negotiations, swore by Allah that he would kill anyone taking the lead in applying for registration. As Gandhi proceeded, ignoring the warning, Mir Alam advanced and struck him on the head. He was arrested with other Pathans, but Gandhi obtained their release, saying he had no desire to prosecute them because they thought they were doing the right thing.

When, in due course, Smuts refused to honour his promise to repeal the compulsory Act, more than 2,000 Indians gathered in the Kamidia Mosque in Johannesburg in August 1908 and threw their registration certificates into a cauldron filled with burning paraffin. Gandhi's law offices in the city now became the headquarters for the *satyagraha* movement, though in Natal he solicited support from his house at Phoenix Farm near Durban.

Further conflicts occurred in the ensuing years which led to a commission to enquire into Indian grievances. Some of the commission members were not as impartial as Gandhi considered appropriate. When Smuts refused to change or expand the commission, Gandhi announced that he and colleagues would march in protest from Durban on New Year's Day 1914 and invite arrest. However, he called off the mass march when white employees across South Africa went on strike. Smuts, busy with the strike, called Gandhi for a meeting, and the Indians warned him against deception as they recalled Smuts' broken pledge in 1908. In reply Gandhi quoted a Sanskrit proverb: 'Forgiveness is the ornament of the brave.'[65]

The talk became negotiations which resulted in the Indian Relief Bill after the two had exchanged letters in June 1914. By the terms of the settlement the three-pound tax on former indentured labourers was annulled and arrears cancelled; Hindu, Moslem and Parsee marriages were declared valid (a Justice in the Cape Colony Supreme Court had earlier ruled that only Christian marriages were legal); Indians born in South Africa could enter the Cape Colony, but free movement between Union provinces was otherwise prohibited; contract labour arriving from India would cease in 1920. Free Indians, however, could continue to enter and wives could come from India to join them.[66]

Gandhi considered the compromise a victory for racial equality and soul force. That July, accompanied by his wife and a friend, he sailed for England. Before leaving, he sent Smuts a pair of leather sandals he had made in prison, which Smuts wore on his farm near Pretoria. In 1939 he sent a photo of the sandals to Gandhi saying, 'I have worn these sandals for many a summer since then, even though I may feel that I am not worthy to stand in the shoes of so great a man.'[67] When Mrs Pandit left India in 1946 for the United Nations to put before it allegations of continuing discrimination against Indians in South Africa, Gandhi said to her, 'I don't mind whether you come back having won your case or having suffered defeat. But you must come back a friend of Field-Marshal Smuts.'[68] (She won her case and India and South Africa were requested to report to the next session the outcome of their negotiations.)

When it came to relationships with the African community, Gandhi was hardly involved at all. Founder of the Natal Indian Congress in 1894 – 'the first organized and disciplined political organization in this country' according to Nelson Mandela[69] – he concentrated on those to whom he felt bonded. Indeed, in *Indian Opinion*, a paper he himself published, he showed himself less than enlightened on some matters, when he wrote in 1904 suggesting that the Johannesburg Town Council withdraw Africans from the location. About the mixing of Indians and Africans he confessed he felt 'most strongly',[70] considering it very unfair to the Indian population and an undue tax on its patience. Gandhi did, however, tend numbers of Africans wounded in the Anglo-Boer War through his Indian volunteer ambulance corps. Later, of course, when the Natal Indian Congress joined with those in the Cape and the Transvaal in May 1923, there was cooperation with nascent African political groupings, which even included the Indian word 'Congress' in their title, but by then Gandhi was back in India for good.

THE RISE OF AFRICAN
POLITICAL CONSCIOUSNESS

The South African Native Congress, one of the predecessors of the ANC, had passed a resolution in 1906 affirming its belief in Ethiopianism (the African Independent Church Movement).[71] Indeed, an earlier group, Imbumba yama Afrika, formed in 1862, had been clear that divisions among Christians, inherited from the West, were to be abhorred. 'In fighting for national rights we must fight together,' said one of the founders, S.W. Mvambo.[72] Not surprisingly some of the first presidents of the ANC were church leaders, particularly from the Congregational and Methodist Churches.

Thirty-eight delegates attended the first National Convention, which in due course set itself up as a permanent body. By January 1912 its members had transformed it into the South African Native National Congress, which was the original form of the ANC.

In 1913 the Government passed the Land Act, which reserved only 7.3 per cent of the land for the African population, and followed this up with the Native Administration Bill of 1917. African politicians opposed the segregationist features in the Bill. Smuts, who was Minister of Native Affairs, was clear: in a speech in London on 22 May 1917, he spelt out what later became institutionalized as apartheid. 'Thus in South Africa you will have in the long run areas cultivated by blacks and governed by blacks, where they will look after themselves in all their forms of living and development, while in suitable parts you will have your white communities, which will govern themselves separately according

STRUGGLING TO FORGIVE

to the accepted European principles. The blacks will, of course, be free to go to work in the white areas, but as far as possible the administration of white and black areas will be separate, and such that each community will be satisfied and develop according to its own proper lines.'[73] (He made no reference to the mixed-race inhabitants of the Cape.)

Africans supported the Allied cause in World War I, though there was no provision for arming them. They served in considerable numbers in South West and East Africa, and in the Western Front campaigns, in noncombatant roles, and when the troopship *Mendi* sank on its way to Europe in 1917, some 615 Africans died.[74] Blacks accordingly had a different struggle to forgive as they remembered the way they were treated, the more so when like Sol Plaatjie – who had witnessed how Baden-Powell and others had treated the Baralong during the siege of Mafeking – they pleaded in vain in Europe for African rights. Plaatjie (1876–1932), the first Secretary of the ANC, met Lloyd George and, in America, black leaders such as Marcus Garvey and W.E. du Bois, but though Lloyd George expressed himself willing to write a letter about the distressing situation of the black community, he would not intervene directly because of the 1910 Act of Union which had given white South Africa dominion status.

Slowly African resistance was growing, with anti-pass law demonstrations in 1913 in the Free State and in Johannesburg in 1919, where some 700 arrests were made. In 1920, 40,000 miners went on strike and in 1923 police brutality resulted in 163 dying at Bulhoek.[75]

There were, of course, whites more open to African aspirations (although such people were rare), like the communist Eddie Roux who wrote a political history of blacks in South Africa, telling the story among others of Makana, the prophet and leader of the Xhosa people in the early nineteenth century, sentenced to life imprisonment on Robben Island, who died when the boat in which he and others were escaping overturned.[76] It was Roux who wrote the words of *Mayibuy'i Africa* ('Let Africa return to us')[77] which J.N. Tantsi of the ANC helped him to compose, and it became the ANC slogan. He also wrote of the early Cape liberals and others, including Dr van der Kemp, who shocked even his fellow missionaries by marrying a slave girl. He told, too, of the later Cape liberals and the tragic betrayal of their case in the 1910 Act of Union to which they consented – except W.P. Schreiner, who fought against the colour bar to the bitter end.[78]

There were also liberals such as Olive Schreiner, Sarah Millin and others, who were conscious of South Africa's racism but who often saw their roles as representing the African community to fellow whites. In April 1936, for example, both Houses of Parliament passed the Native Representation Act, and the Cape Native Franchise was replaced by a separate register of African voters, who would vote independently for three white MPs to be known as Native Representatives. People such as Margaret Ballinger, who became a Representative, liaised well with the Native Representative Council, elected by the black community itself. But such representatives were not allowed to vote on financial or constitutional matters, and often, with the four senators also appointed to represent African affairs, though open to African needs, worked in a paternalistic way.

During the second half of 1930 the Communist Party in particular was working up support for an anti-pass law campaign, to culminate in a grand pass-burning on 16 December. It was not a new idea, the ANC having had an abortive attempt in 1919, but the idea had remained dormant. A big response seemed likely this time, fuelled by the 500 people from many organizations who had attended an anti-pass conference in Johannesburg that October. In the event, however, only Durban responded magnificently.

Thousands of passes were collected and burnt at a mass meeting on Cartwright's Flats. But the Durban police arrived, the whites armed with revolvers, the Africans with assegais and clubs, and attacked the gathering. The leader Johannes Nkosi, a Zulu, was struck down and died and others were wounded. Hundreds were arrested. Many in Durban and nearby areas did destroy their passes, but the important leaders were now in prison, a pattern which continued for decades. And though thousands saw the attack on Nkosi, the first African Communist martyr, no one was ever charged.[79]

Time and again African hopes were dashed by internal legislation, by the Versailles Treaty powers and, in the 1920s and '30s, by

Government Acts, which enabled the newly urbanized Afrikaners to overcome their poverty at the expense of others. Between 1924 and 1933, for example, the proportion of unskilled white workers on the railways rose from 9.5 per cent to 39.3 per cent, while the proportion of blacks fell from 75 per cent to 48.9 per cent. In human terms this meant jobs for about 13,000 whites and the sack for over 15,000 blacks.[80]

In the year Albert Luthuli became a Government-recognized Zulu Chief, the 1936 Land Act consolidated white power, leaving Africans only 13 per cent of the land. The decades of dashed expectations, as they have been termed, here reached an inevitable and terrible climax.

There were, of course, some countervailing forces like the Garment Workers' Union, led for 24 years by Solly Sachs, who had not only a strong Communist background (though he had been expelled from the party in 1931), but also consolidated power in a non-racial trade union. Indeed, such was his group's strength that not only did it organize successful strikes to improve pay and work conditions, but it also withstood Afrikaner Nationalist attacks on it until 1952, when the Suppression of Communism Act enabled them to silence powerful leaders like Sachs.[81]

Re-elected in 1951 by the unanimous vote of 300 shop stewards from English, Afrikaans and Coloured backgrounds, Sachs was later tried for defying his May 1952 banning order, after address-ing 10,000 workers – black, white and Coloured – protesting at the ban. A month later 18,000 garment workers went on strike in Johannesburg in his support. Released on bail, Sachs tried to address another crowd but was re-arrested in July, found guilty on two counts and sentenced to six months hard labour for each. The case made headlines for many weeks, but his career was destroyed and in January 1953 Solly Sachs went into voluntary exile like so many others in the ensuing decades.[82]

'The ANC encouraged its members to go to the war overseas,' Nokukhamya Luthuli has observed. 'They hoped that if Africans fought for democracy, in a foreign land together with white South Africans, they would also gain their freedom when they returned home.'[83] During the 1943 General Election, Smuts had sharply increased his majority in the House of Assembly, despite some opposition to South Africa's war involvement. When he wrote to congratulate Smuts, and sent him a draft document of 'African Claims to South Africa', Dr A.B. Xuma, President General of the ANC from 1940 to 1949, suggested he had been given a 'last and God-given opportunity' to bring about freedom and prosperity for the non-European sections who had made such sacrifices.[84] In 1941 Smuts had already rejected African claims, however, and now he declined even the interview Dr Xuma had suggested, ignoring his document. This had been drafted as the result of a committee inspired by the Atlantic Charter's endorsement of national self-determination, which called for a bill of rights and the application of its principles to all the British Empire. As before, Africans found all doors closed to negotiations.

When, therefore, Smuts' Government was defeated and the Afrikaner Nationalists came to power in 1948 and Dr Hendrik Verwoerd made his first major speech in the Senate, he was able to claim, correctly, 'There is nothing new in what we are proposing,' adding that the Nationalists were 'propagating the traditional policy of Afrikanerdom, the traditional policy of South Africa and of all those who have made South Africa their home'.[85] Indeed, over the next decades, whether the idea was white leadership, 'Christian trusteeship', separate development, or latterly plural relations, the policy remained the same: the control of the majority by a minority of South Africa's citizens – though clearly there was continued ambivalence between the whites, the Indians and the Coloureds about their interrelationships.

AFRICAN–INDIAN RELATIONS

The Indian community did, of course, sometimes express fierce opposition against oppressive laws, and in 1946 started a passive resistance campaign which lasted two years and involved several thousand arrests. It has been called by Nelson Mandela a 'very important landmark in the struggle of the Indian community'.[86] Their protests were triggered off by the Government's 'Ghetto Bill', which limited where Indians could live and trade and prevented land transfers between Indians and others. Three months later black miners went on strike, but were soon crushed by Smuts, who thereby created yet more African disillusionment.[87]

Despite a shared experience of oppression, tragically trouble broke out in 1949 between Indians and Africans, partly from fear of African numbers, and there were riots in the Durban area in which 53 Indians, 87 Africans and one white person were killed. Leaders of both the ANC and the South African Indian Congress (SAIC) hurried to the areas of conflict to calm residents and discover the underlying grievances. For Nelson Mandela and others this coming together remained an indelible experience, though he and colleagues in the ANC Youth League remained opposed to uniting with the Indian Congress because they believed the African community needed to gain more self-consciousness. Indeed, when African and Indian leaders proposed working together for franchise rights, young African nationalists like Mandela argued that the greater need was to build up African self confidence.[88]

THE RISE OF CHIEF ALBERT LUTHULI
AND OPPOSITION TO APARTHEID

The Durban riots left a legacy of Indo-African suspicion which leaders in the two communities worked hard to break down. Looking back, Chief Albert Luthuli, then head of the ANC in Natal, was able to say: 'Who could have predicted ... that within three years Africans and Indians in Durban itself would be acting together to demonstrate their repudiation of injustice and cruelty,'[89] as in February 1951 the SAIC, the ANC and the Coloured People's Organization met in Cape Town and pledged to resist by constitutional means all racially oppressive policies. The ANC itself wrote to Prime Minister Malan that December, asking for Africans to be represented directly, for the repeal of the Group Areas Act and for an end to cattle culling in the reserves. When they received no satisfaction, they staged various mass protest meetings against unjust laws on 6 April 1952. This was followed from June 26 onwards by a passive resistance Defiance Campaign, which brought Chief Luthuli, who had become President of the

ANC that year, to national prominence – though, like his friend Z.K. Matthews, he was already widely known through his work on the Native Representative Council.

The Defiance Campaign marked a further development in the ANC's passive resistance techniques. Thousands of well-trained volunteers were chosen from all communities to break the unjust laws, though many were arrested: 8,000 by the end of 1952. Towards the end of the Campaign riots broke out and the police responded severely.[90] The Government, worried by the revolt, summoned Chief Luthuli to Pretoria and said he must choose either his Chieftainship (a Government-funded post) or the ANC. When he refused he was summarily dismissed from his role as adviser and arbitrator in disputes by Dr Verwoerd, then Minister of Native Affairs, and in 1953 he was banned, which meant he was virtually under house arrest thereafter. When the order expired he went to Johannesburg to address his first mass meeting since his election as ANC President, but before the event a second banning order was served on him. The thousands waiting for him in Freedom Square, Sophiatown, marched past his house to show their solidarity.

One major ANC campaign in the 1950s was against the Bantu Education Act, which was designed to educate Africans for a permanently subservient role in South Africa. Pupils boycotted classes and set up alternative schools, but the police soon closed them down. Thus the lines of a protracted battle emerged, with increasing cooperation between Indian, Coloured and white democrats, which set the basis for united action in the years to come.

Though Chief Luthuli was now effectively confined to one area of Natal, his influence was still strong. He brought to his work not only his deep Christian convictions – he had begun as a Methodist lay preacher and then gravitated to the Congregational Church – but also patience, fortitude and a freedom from inner turbulence.[91] He was, Fatimer Meer has observed, 'very ethical, very upright and very honest. He was always in charge of his actions. In this sense there was a Gandhian dimension to him.'[92] 'My husband and the ANC,' his wife has written, 'were deeply influenced by the non-violent philosophy of Mahatma Gandhi,'[93] an influence no doubt deepened during a visit to India earlier in his life.

STRUGGLING TO FORGIVE

Yet even Chief Luthuli had admitted, when deposed from his Chieftainship, that few results had been gained by his moderation. Indeed, the past 30 years had seen 'the greatest number of laws restricting our rights and progress until today we have reached a stage where we have no rights at all'.[94] He refused, however, to hate, even though he recognized the vast majority of whites, 'like Pharoah',[95] had hardened their hearts, and he accepted that Africans could only win their freedom through great suffering, which they must accept, as they had often done before.[96]

Sometimes at home, after a painful incident, he would say to his wife, 'Oh forgive him, Charlotte,' and even when police arrested him and people cried, he would say, 'No, Charlotte, don't cry. They have come to do their work.'[97] One incident in particular reflects the depth of his philosophy. Restricted under his banning order to Stanger, where he lived, Helen Joseph, who visited him there, found him reluctant to talk about his own restriction but eager for her to give news of the banished people she had just visited. Describing their conditions, her anger rose until she exploded, saying that when freedom came:

> ...there would be a few people whom I should like to see banished.
> 'No, Helen,' the Chief said quietly. 'Anything but banishment. We cannot do such things.'
> 'Just one or two,' I pleaded.
> 'Not even one,' he replied. And I knew he meant it. And as I have done so often before, I could only marvel at the freedom from bitterness which marks the African people. I had seen it in the banished people; here it was again.
> I asked myself, 'Could I endure so much and not be bitter?' [98]

In 1955 a key development occurred in the life of the ANC. 'I wonder,' wrote Z.K. Matthews, 'whether the time has not come for the African National Congress to consider the question of convening a national convention, a congress of the people ... to draw up a Freedom Charter for the democratic South Africa of the future.'[99] Chief Luthuli was positive and asked him to prepare a Memorandum, which he did.

In Kliptown, Johannesburg, a Congress of the People was held, from 25 to 26 June 1955, which issued a Freedom Charter. Its aims were for a non-racial and democratic South Africa where wealth and land was shared. Human rights, work, education and culture would be available to everyone, and housing and health would be the prerogatives of all in a country which wished to reach out to other sovereign, independent nations in peace and friendship.[100] 'Perhaps,' Luthuli wrote later, 'it was the first really representative gathering in the Union's history ... Nothing in the history of the liberation movement in South Africa quite caught the popular imagination as this did, not even the Defiance Campaign.'[101] He added that 'it attempted to give a flesh and blood meaning, in the South African setting, to such words as democracy, freedom, liberty.'[102]

The Charter was taken back to groups by their delegates and the ANC ratified it in March 1956, though the Africanists in the ANC, led by Robert Sobukwe, dismissed it in toto.[103]

Chief Luthuli's two-year-old banning order had recently come to an end, but by 6 December that year he had been arrested on a charge of high treason. Z.K. Matthews and over 150 others were also arrested, accused of countrywide conspiracy to use violence to overthrow the Government and replace it with a Communist state. The period of the indictment covered 1 October 1952 to 13 December 1956, which included the Defiance Campaign, the protests when Sophiatown was destroyed and the Congress itself. High treason was defined as a hostile intention to disturb, impair or endanger the independence and safety of the state. 'The punishment,' Nelson Mandela has remarked succinctly, 'was death.'[104]

Those charged were divided into three groups and the trial of the key figures began on 3 August 1959, followed by another year of legal manoeuvring, which meant it began in earnest in the Old Synagogue in Pretoria only in 1960. The verdict was reached in 1963: the accused were found not guilty and discharged. 'After more than four years in court and dozens of prosecutors, thousands of documents and thousands of pages of testimony, the state had failed in its mission,' Nelson Mandela recalled later.[105]

By and large the accused acted with circumspection despite the provocation. In April 1962, for example, Z.K. Matthews, while himself still in detention, travelled, handcuffed to a white police-man, to Pretoria from East London to give evidence on behalf of the 30 men on trial at the time. A black warder on the train, recognizing Matthews, offered to bring him food. Matthews, looking towards his guard, replied, 'I will only eat if my friend here can.'[106]

Robert Sobukwe, a founder member of the Fort Hare branch of the ANC's Youth League in 1948 and a Methodist lay preacher, while working as a language assistant (the only title allowed him) at the University of Witswatersrand, had begun to question the ANC's direction, especially white influences from the far left and its participation in the liberation struggle. He felt especially that the ANC's leadership was slipping away from Africans and that they were abandoning African nationalism, on the basis of which he had originally joined the Youth League. Accordingly, he and others broke away in 1958 and formed the Pan-Africanist Congress (PAC), which was almost exclusively black African, though even Sobukwe could not refuse Patrick Duncan, the son of a former Governor-General, from joining because Duncan was just as much an African as he was.[107]

In December 1959 the ANC held its annual conference in Durban during a dynamic anti-pass law demonstration there. It was decided to make such a campaign national, starting on 31 March and ending on 26 June 1960 with a bonfire of passes. Much preliminary work was done, but the PAC, which had been invited to join in, announced it was launching its own anti-pass law campaign on 21 March 1960, inviting the ANC to cooperate only four days before the demonstration, but it declined.

On 21 March Robert Sobukwe and the PAC executive walked into Orlando police station to surrender their passes and be arrested. Hardly anyone noticed their action and there were few other demonstrations across South Africa. But in Evaton, Transvaal, the whole township of several hundred presented themselves for arrest and in Langa township in Cape Town a young student, Philip Kgosana, held back some 30,000 who had been spurred to riot by a police baton charge, where two were killed.

Ironically it was at Sharpeville, a small black township in an industrial complex around Vereeniging, where the Anglo-Boer Peace Treaty had been presented, that an explosion occurred which changed everything. Here, stimulated by PAC activists, some several thousand people surrounded the police station, unarmed and controlled. The police numbered 75. No one heard warning shots, or an order to shoot, but suddenly the police opened fire, continuing to shoot demonstrators as they turned and ran away in fear. Sixty-nine Africans were killed, mostly shot in the back. Seven hundred shots were fired into the crowd and over 400 people were wounded, including women and children.

News of the massacre was flashed round the world and the United Nations Security Council intervened in South African matters for the first time, blaming the Government and urging policies to bring about racial equality. Now, as the PAC leader Robert Sobukwe was being hailed as a 'liberator', a small group of ANC leaders, including Walter Sisulu, Joe Slovo and Nelson Mandela, met and proposed to Chief Luthuli that now was the time to burn their own passes as an act of defiance against the unjust pass law system. The Chief called for a national day of mourning for the Sharpeville victims in two days' time and burned his pass publicly in Pretoria on 26 March, inviting others to follow him. Mandela did so in Orlando and on 28 March several hundred thousand (50,000 alone in Langa) observed a national day of mourning.

The Government declared a State of Emergency and assumed sweeping powers to act against all subversion. Over 20,000 activists and leaders were detained, and Nelson Mandela's close friend and colleague, Oliver Tambo, responded to the ANC's request and left South Africa to set up an external organization abroad. Though the State of Emergency ended that same year (1960), the Government now pushed ahead steadily with its scheme for Bantustans, whereby each black African tribe was to be confined to its own 'homeland'.

Chief Luthuli remained steadfast, notably non-violent, and in Oslo in 1961 was awarded the Nobel Peace Prize. Other counsel was gaining ground in the ANC, however, as Nelson Mandela and his colleagues argued that the Government now left them no other option but violence. Indeed, they maintained, violence would begin whether the ANC initiated it or not. Chief Luthuli resisted his colleagues' arguments, but according to Mandela he agreed in the end that a military campaign was inevitable.[108] Joe Slovo has confirmed, however, that Luthuli 'was not a party to the decision, nor was he ever to endorse it', adding: 'It was a measure of his greatness that despite his deep Christian commitment to non-violence, he never forbade or condemned the new path, blaming it on the regime's intransigence rather than on those who created MK.'[109]

A meeting including the Indian Congress, the Coloured People's Congress, the South African Congress of Trade Unions and the Congress of Democrats, turned out to be difficult, nevertheless. As it began, Chief Luthuli, who was presiding, said that even though the ANC had agreed on a decision about the use of violence, because it was such a grave matter he would like his colleagues to 'consider the issues afresh'. Indian leaders were negative, arguing that the state would slaughter the liberation movement. 'J.N. Singh,' Nelson Mandela has recalled, 'uttered words that night which still echo in my head. "Non-violence has not failed us," he said. "We have failed non-violence. "'[110]

Mandela disagreed: non-violence had failed, for it had done nothing to stop state violence, or to change the hearts of the oppressors. By dawn the Congresses had authorized Mandela to go ahead and create a new military grouping, separate from the ANC. For 50 years the ANC had treated non-violence as a core principle: now it had changed course irrevocably. The day after Luthuli returned from Oslo in December 1961, MK ('the Spear of the Nation') dramatically announced its emergence. On the orders of the MK High Command, home-made bombs were exploded on 16 December at electric power stations and government offices in Johannesburg, Port Elizabeth and Durban.[111]

FORGIVE AND FORGET?

The Afrikaans poet Totius once wrote a poem called 'Forgive and Forget' in which he described how a tree was cut down by the big wheels of a wagon as it went on its way. The thorn tree, its loveliness shattered, slowly came upright again, by its own will, healing its wounds by the balm of its gum. Eventually the wagon marks were erased, except one which would not go away. So there remained a scar which never ceased to grow.[112] At the start of the poem was a caption reminding readers not to forget what they had seen.

The poem was a stark reminder to Afrikaners about the after-effects of the Anglo-Boer War. Now the black communities were to be put through an even bigger trauma, affecting many more people, as their suffering reached a climax. How could black people ever forget the injustices they experienced as the state did all in its power to deprive them? Could the Afrikaners ever see what they had done as the once oppressed group now became the oppressors? For, as one journalist has commented, the black struggle for independence, and sense of grievance and injustice, was to become a re-run of Afrikaner struggles against the British 'through the century of wrong'.[113]

Chapter 3

Forgiveness and Repentance –

The Role of the Afrikaner Community

When most people think about the role forgiveness can (or ought to) play in society, they usually regard it as being the result of a confession of repentance by wrongdoers. There are, of course, incidents where forgiveness evokes repentance (rather than *vice versa*), but these times are rare. The demand is commonly for wrongdoing to be admitted first, with a genuine desire to make amends.

It is true that throughout South Africa's long history of struggles, many wrongs have been committed by many different groups. It is also true that the Afrikaner community – perhaps because of its theological awareness and exceptional honesty – has explored very deeply the relation of repentance to forgiveness. This is not to maintain that the entire Afrikaner community has felt this way, but rather to draw attention to certain individuals and groups who have been pioneers, both in terms of the courage they have shown and in the depths of meaning they have explored. Because of this they probably have more to contribute to the future of South Africa than many others and will always give that part of Africa an edge, philosophically and politically.

Repentance is not a fashionable idea in the life of communities: they prefer to strive for justice, or espouse the power of love. Nevertheless, the practise of repentance, although tough, can provide openings when other avenues are blocked. For genuine repentance clearly implies that a change has already occurred and a new way is desired, different from the old and sweetened maybe by the humility which genuine repentance can bring.

AFRIKANER AWAKENINGS

On 13 July 1987 Dr F. van Zyl Slabbert, the former leader of the Progressive Federal Party and one of the founders of the Institute for a Democratic Alternative in South Africa (IDASA), went with some 60 reforming Afrikaners and others to Dakar in Senegal to meet 18 ANC leaders. While there they visited Goree, an island off the coast which had once been a staging post for the shipment of millions of African slaves to the Americas.

'I found myself in the slave houses,' Allister Sparks, one of the delegation, has written, 'on an upper-level balcony where the slave traders lived in spacious quarters.' Below were the dungeons and punishment cells where the slaves themselves were kept, and the portcullis through which they went on their journey either to death or bondage.

Standing watching the shimmering Atlantic with him was a theological student, 'seemingly transfixed'. Like others in his group, he was making the connection between Goree and the prison island off Cape Town and its spectacular views. 'They'll build a museum like this on Robben Island one day,' the student said, 'and people will come and look at it and wonder how we could have lived with such evil.' Then he added that the slave owners who enjoyed such richness were Christians, yet they had not seen the degradation below them. 'How, how can we be so blind?' he queried.

The two then joined the rest of the party. Going down the stairs, they passed Thabo Mbeki, the leader of the ANC delegation, going up. 'His father is at that moment in his twenty-fourth year of imprisonment on Robben Island,' Allister Sparks later reflected. 'Thabo, who is forty-three, has not seen him since he was a teenager. He smiles at us. Warm, friendly, unrecriminating.'[1]

Even if he was unaware of it, the young theological student had joined a historic succession of those within Afrikaans society who had opposed Dr Verwoerd's visions since the 1950s, even after Sharpeville when he seemed to be triumphant, with the arrest and trial of leading ANC members, and their life imprisonment on Robben Island – though the whites were held elsewhere. Indeed, so confident were the rulers that when the British Prime Minister,

Harold Macmillan, addressed the Cape Town Parliament in 1960 and referred to the 'wind of change' sweeping across Africa, the Afrikaners were unmoved and merely angered.

With Malan and his successors in power from 26 May 1948, 'at last Afrikanerdom had come into its own, forty-six years since its defeat in the Anglo-Boer War,' wrote Alan Paton in 1979. 'All the injustice of the "century of wrong" would be righted.'[2] Now, as South Africa left the Commonwealth, there were no informal links left which could enable politicians to question the wisdom of Government policies. These were developed apace as Government attempted to establish Bantustans for all but urban blacks, controlled as before by the discriminatory legislation which had ensured that from 1916 to 1986, when the Urban Areas Act was repealed, over 17 million Africans were imprisoned for pass law offences.[3]

'The more one examines the case for complete, permanent apartheid, the less one can avoid the conclusion that its supporters are living under a delusion that belongs to a world of make-believe,' the distinguished scholar Professor Dr B. Keet of Stellenbosch had warned in the 1950s. 'And because this dream is so alluring for our peace of mind, we substitute it for the challenge that comes to us here and now: it becomes a plausible idea without content, a salve for our conscience.'[4] There were few like him, however, but two ministers (*dominees*) – Professor Albert Geyser, a teacher of theology in the University of Pretoria, and Beyers Naudé – were as troubled as the young theological student on Goree. In the late 1950s Geyser rejected the moral basis for apartheid and opposed the Broederbond's influence. As a result of this he was charged with 'heresy' by his church because of 'complaints' by three theological students, though when he took legal action the church withdrew and he was reinstated. He left for another job early in the 1960s.[5]

THE CONTRIBUTION OF BEYERS NAUDÉ

Oliver Tambo's son Dali described Beyers Naudé as an 'icon of reconciliation'[6] in 1995, but it was not always like that for the son of one of the founders of the Broederbond, of which he was also a member. Symbolizing the absolute commitment to the Boer cause among a section of the DRC (Dutch Reformed Church) was the vote of a minister, one of the six who opposed the unconditional surrender at Vereeniging in 1902. He was Dr J.F. Naudé, chaplain with the commando troops and Beyer's father, who had him baptized Beyers because it was the name of another Afrikaner hero from that time.[7]

Originally Beyers Naudé was a believer in apartheid as the best way to keep peace in South Africa and in the 1930s, as a student, he had attended Dr Verwoerd's classes. 'There was,' he has explained, 'no sudden Damascus Road conversion.' At the intellectual level he discovered the DRC's justification for apartheid was false and could not be based on biblical truths.[8] Ministers of one of the DRC's so-called 'daughter-churches' took the pastor to the 'compounds' at Crown Mines. Beyers had never seen human beings cramped together in such inhuman ways. Then came the Sharpeville massacre, after which he felt he could remain silent no longer.

A consultation of the World Council of Churches at Cottesloe introduced Naudé to the world-wide ecumenical movement, but the DRC did not accept its conclusions about South Africa. Nor did it allow him to remain Moderator of the prestigious Transvaal area of the Church and soon, when he founded the magazine *Pro Veritate* and then the Christian Institute, stripped him of his ministerial role – though he continued a DRC member until 1980. Then, when his Church rejected by an overwhelming majority a call to unite with the black, Coloured and Indian 'daughter-churches', Naudé resigned and joined the black DRC daughter-church.

Until its banning in 1977 the Christian Institute was a group of people, some 2,000 strong, who tried to prick the conscience of the white population about the effects of apartheid and persuade them to support black movements and causes. Inevitably Naudé and his colleagues were on a collision course with the Government and with some in the churches, but Naudé, who knew many Government ministers personally, continued on his way.

After he was banned in 1977, along with many others, he could meet with only one other person at a time, so began a counselling and listening ministry. 'Having been more or less silenced myself,' he has observed, 'I learned to listen to others. What a powerful blessing that proved to be especially in later years when I became the General Secretary of the South African Council of Churches.'[9] When Naudé was tried in the autumn of 1973 for refusing to give evidence in secret to a Government Commission set up to investigate certain groups whose work did not gain its approval, he argued that no reconciliation was possible without justice and that whoever worked for reconciliation had to determine the causes of injustice in the lives of those who felt themselves aggrieved.[10]

Now he was to admit that without his banning experience he would have found it very difficult 'to understand the anger of the victims of oppression'. He had learnt so many things and had indeed to struggle against bitterness. 'I asked Ilse [his wife] to tell me if there were any bitterness in my heart to anyone,' he has reflected, as above all he came to appreciate Jesus's prayer from the Cross: 'Father, forgive them for they know not what they do.'[11]

In 1994 the Dutch Reformed Church finally apologized to Beyers Naudé and to others – including Ben Marais, an earlier dissident, now frail and in a wheelchair – who had also been victimized for their outspokenness, for it now acknowledged their witness. 'There were times when you were wronged by the Church,' the Moderator declared, 'and we have to express our regret.'

'We are sorry,' said Professor Piet Meiring, who came to regard Naudé as the prophet who saw the light, for which he suffered and was ostracized, 'we should have listened to your warnings.'

'This brings a long struggle to full circle,' Naudé said in reply, as he received a standing ovation. 'I have been waiting for this day for thirty years,'[12] Ilse Naudé added.

Subsequently Naudé and his wife were invited back to his former congregation at Northcliffe, Johannesburg, an act of reconciliation on their part. And as a recognition of his stature he was invited to be a member of the ANC team for its first meeting with the Government because its leaders felt he could help each side understand and appreciate the other.

Hlophe Bam tells a story which epitomizes all Dr Naudé stands for. In 1988 he was asked to give the benediction at the funeral of

Johnny Makhatini, for many years head of the ANC's department of international affairs. Naudé said he wanted to pray for the day when Afrikaans would be seen by black South Africans as a language of blessing and not cursing and spoke therefore in his own language. 'I cannot think of any other white Afrikaner who could have got away with praying in Afrikaans in such a gathering,' Elinor Sisulu, who was present, told Hlophe subsequently.[13]

THE ROLE OF OTHER LEADING MINISTERS

Others, too, were moved by Beyers Naudé, like the elderly lady who had tears in her eyes when during the 1994 election she told Horst Kleinschmidt, Naudé's one-time assistant, how she and her husband had not supported him enough at the Christian Institute.[14] Dr Carel Antonissen, chaplain to Afrikaner students at Stellenbosch University, who went to see Dr Naudé for help and advice about apartheid, was also deeply influenced by his encounter,[15] and it was in his church that a memorial service for the assassinated Chris Hani was later held, attended by many thousands, although inevitably there were objections.

Some were less high profile than Naudé in what they did, of course. 'In my heart I have penitence continuously,' Professor Pippin Oosthuizen has remarked, 'but I don't want to advertise it, just have it.'[16] He is one of the DRC ministers who broke many years ago with the official position of their Church, in his case studying with great diligence the role of the Independent African Churches in South Africa with their 12 million members.

A more prominent minister has been Professor Johan Heyns, once a leading critic of Naudé who later welcomed him back. 'It is a terrible mess in which we are,' he would say privately, but when urged by Professor Klaus Nürnberger to make his views known would say, 'If I simply stand up and say what I know the same will happen to me as to Beyers Naudé.'[17]

He could be more influential, he considered, within the structures in which he was set, which inevitably meant there were constraints and pressures on him at any given time. He was, as he once put it, 'an incremental reformer'.[18] Indeed, he developed late, despite his doctorate in Holland in the 1950s and his job as Professor of Dogmatics and Ethics at Pretoria University. In due course, however, he became adviser behind the scenes to Cabinet ministers and at one point acted as an intermediary between the Government and the ANC, going to Lusaka in 1990 at the invitation of President Kaunda and meeting with various ANC leaders, though he said he had not intended to.

Professor Heyns believed that as the DRC had led South Africa to apartheid – he admitted that as far back as 1857 the DRC had decided to set up separate churches for different races after white protests – it now had to lead the country away from it. 'We've had white domination for three centuries,' he observed, 'and now we are entering a completely new phase in our history where that white domination is coming to an end ... We must change and learn to enter into a partnership ... There is a necessity of liberation for blacks,' he concluded, 'but also for whites. We are all prisoners of our history and we must all rid ourselves of perceived ideas about blacks and whites because only a liberated people can create a new society.'[19]

Something of a mentor to F.W. de Klerk in the months leading up to his speech to Parliament on 2 February 1990, and for four years (1990–94) meeting Nelson Mandela often to give guidance on how to reconcile the fears of the rebellious Afrikaner right wing,[20] Heyns was shot in the back of his head one Saturday night late in 1994 while playing cards in his living room with his wife and two grandsons. Thus the former Moderator of the DRC (1986–90) died by one of the most common methods used by frustrated groups in the twentieth century. 'In numerous meetings I had with him,' Nelson Mandela said in a tribute, 'he impressed me with his insight, honesty and integrity.'[21]

In December 1981 Nico Smith, a theological professor at Stellenbosch University, resigned his post and became a working minister of the black DRC daughter-church in Mamelodi, near Pretoria. His decision came only a few months after he had been confronted by the Broederbond, which controlled the theological authorities in Stellenbosch, and from which he had resigned in the early 1970s. The Broederbond objected to his involvement with 2,000 Nyanga squatters, mostly Christians, near Cape Town, whom the authorities harassed and later arrested, deporting them to the Transkei.[22]

Professor Smith had issued a statement critical of the Government's actions and of the main white DRC itself for its non-involvement – an action which brought out their anger, a new experience for him for only recently had he become such a high-profile protestor. Indeed, when he had gone to work on a mission station in a rural area as a young minister, he had refused a lunch offered him communally with other ministers because he had a psychological block about eating with Africans. A separate meal was laid for him and he sat there eating it by himself.[23]

In 1962 he had been told by the Sierre Leone president of a youth conference he attended in Nairobi that Afrikaners had to decide whether to leave Africa, or become white Africans, who were needed to help the continent, but not as rulers. Shortly afterwards he joined the Broederbond, and here he discovered 'the evil of what people can do'. It took him another ten years, however, to find the courage to leave, after which they had blocked him for a further ten years 'at every turn'.

The final drama which led to the opening of Professor Smith's eyes had started in July and August 1981, when 2,000 men, women and children were evicted from the accommodation they were 'illegally' occupying in Nyanga, in terms of pass law and influx control regulations. Although most had been working or (in the case of the women) living there with their husbands for some time, they were summarily ordered back to their 'home-lands', which some had not visited for a decade. After eviction, however, hundreds stayed on in the winter cold and rain in the Port Jackson bush and sand dunes outside Nyanga.[24]

During a massive police raid nearly 1,000 were arrested, detained and eventually charged. Some paid their fines, but those without money went to jail, including women and children. Meanwhile police dogs raided the No-Name Camp every few nights, destroying the inhabitants' makeshift shelters. This was the last straw for Professor Smith. 'Human life was just like mosquitos,' he has commented. 'You can wipe them out.'[25]

Convinced he was about to be sacked from Stellenbosch anyway, when the call came to be pastor of the church in Mamelodi two or three days after his confrontation, he accepted, with his wife's keen support. Once there he set up Koinonia, first at a local and then at a national level. The scheme aimed to bring black and white Christians together by breaking down barriers, with whites encouraged to take blacks out for meals and to theatres in Pretoria.

Nico Smith was in Mamelodi when the funeral was held of 13 blacks killed in troubles there, a funeral at which Winnie Mandela, as she then was, spoke her famous words: 'With our matches and our tyres we will liberate this country.'[26] He was also present at the funeral of his godson, Nico Smith Olivier, killed in the border war in Angola, in which South Africa had been involved. 'The pain of standing at Nico's graveside with his father,' he wrote, 'brought home to me the urgency of our work in Koinonia … No war can last for ever. Much has to be done to prepare both blacks and whites for a new future.'[27]

Nico Smith retired when he was 65, but not before he also founded a multi-racial church in the centre of Pretoria, in a church building associated with Afrikaner history in the northern Transvaal and in which many former Presidents had sat. The much depleted DRC congregation had agreed to share it with Nico Smith's group, but he found the arrangement was disputed because the building was a national monument and people involved with its preservation could not accept the developments, so the matter went to arbitration.

When Nico Smith had first come to Mamelodi, he had bought a plot of land half an hour's drive outside Pretoria and built a house there, using some of the stones from the former African settlements which had existed on the site. Here he started a farm which would make him self-sufficient and where he and his wife now live. So for one Afrikaner at least, his trek has ended as he contemplates nature and roots himself in Africa, teaching part-time in a Pretoria University (UNISA). Jean Paul Sartre, he explains, has shown how important ideology is. In South Africa the white community has been part of Western colonialism, which thought it was responsible for civilizing the world, as well as being highly self-interested. This group lived in a world of its own and 'colonized the mind of the colonized people', he has argued. People must now be helped to see what they have done and why they have done it, for 'whites now have to be servants, not rulers'.[28]

Nico Smith has not been alone in serving a black congregation, of course. Frikkie Conradie, who died in a car crash – the details of which have never been pieced together – is another. 'If we want to sum up his life,' Archbishop Tutu said at his funeral in Johannesburg in 1992, 'we should say that he was an ambassador for Christ, who lived out a costly form of reconciliation.'[29] He had left his own community and identified himself with the down-trodden, the poor and the suffering in Alexandra, working for jus-tice under a black minister to such an extent that the people came in their thousands to the funeral and the subsequent burial (at his widow's request) in the local cemetery, the first white person to be buried there.

THE CONTRIBUTION OF AFRIKANER THINKERS AND WRITERS

'I believe in a way we should repent for what we have done to the bushman,' Laurens van de Post once said as he reflected on the role all races had played in South Africa. 'Part of what I have done is to atone for that.'[30] In like manner the dissident ministers (*dominees*) have in their respective ways tried to respond in peni-tence to African suffering. There are other Afrikaners, perhaps detribalized ones, who have left the safety of their white tribe and identified themselves with the oppressed Africans.

Originally convinced that God had willed the separation of white and black in South Africa in both Church and state, even refusing to shake hands with a black person, Professor Hendrik van der Merwe came to see that all were people of one world and himself an Afrikaner in Africa. Once an elder in a congregation in Stellenbosch which had state Presidents among its membership, he objected to the politics and dogma of the DRC, so in the 1970s became a Quaker when the DRC black church would not accept him because it felt that to admit a white member could have politi-cal repercussions. Founder of the Centre for Inter-Group Studies in Cape Town (now the Centre for Conflict Resolution) which he directed for 25 years, he presided over much of the work done during that time on peace and conflict research.[31]

As a pioneer of mediation work, Professor van der Merwe had the conceptual framework which enabled him to handle the different histories of group and intergroup conflicts which surrounded negotiations as they developed. After a particularly violent interaction between the Government and the ANC in 1982–3, involving the latter's bomb attacks inside South Africa and Government army raids on ANC cadres in Lesotho and Mozambique, Professor van der Merwe issued a statement expressing disapproval of violence and stating that he had decided to make a personal contribution to all victims. Both sides attacked his comments, but nevertheless they played an important role in the development of trust between himself and the ANC, and between himself and the Government, which enabled his role as a facilitator to grow.[32]

Three other Afrikaner thinkers and writers have played a significant role in changing attitudes at the political level, though all have been derided by their community for their actions. One is the poet Breyten Breytenbach, whose brother was a senior figure in the South African military at one point, and the others are Bram Fischer and Carl Niehaus.

In the case of Breyten Breytenbach, his personal statement included marrying across the colour line and living in exile in Paris with his Vietnamese wife until he returned to South Africa, in a clandestine operation. 'Like a burning arrow from the eye of the sun you landed here,' wrote the poet Lionel Murcott.[33] Breytenbach was arrested and jailed for 10 years, serving over two-thirds of his sentence. At the end of the book which he wrote about his experience, he argued that all South Africans must realize they are brothers and sisters. There was no utopia anywhere, so they must accept the humanity and fallibility of each other.[34]

Once released, he returned for a while to Paris, and when President F.W. de Klerk made his watershed speech in 1990, he observed: 'Our historical compromise – for whites jettisoning "group conceptions" and admitting they were criminally wrong for generations; for blacks accepting pluralism and the separation of powers and the protection of the individual, and knowing also that there can be no "total victory" – our reconciliation, seasoned by black bitterness and white fears, cannot only be a *modus vivendi*. We must make it a growth point, a shared ground for the nation, the seed bed for a civil society taking care of the values and mechanisms of reconciliation.'[35]

Bram Fischer, from a very distinguished Afrikaner background – his father was Judge President of the Orange Free State; his grandfather was Prime Minister there when the British ceded power in 1910 and Minister of Land in 1913 when he pushed through the Native Land Act – did not live to see 1990 as Breytenbach did. A member of the South African Communist Party, he was defence counsel in a number of important trials, including Rivonia. In 1966 he himself was charged under the Sabotage Act and at the age of 58 was given life imprisonment. So hated was he by many Afrikaners who regarded him as a traitor, that when he died of cancer on 8 May 1975 the prison authorities would not even let his family retain his ashes. 'Sometimes they (the Boere) derive malicious pleasure from tormenting him,' wrote Hugh Lewin, who was in Pretoria Prison with him, 'rather as if tormenting him gives them social status.'[36]

At his trial Bram Fischer spoke of an ever-growing movement for freedom among blacks. 'In the end it must triumph,' he declared. 'Above all those of us who are Afrikaners and who have experienced our own successful struggle for full equality should know this.'[37]

'It struck me,' wrote one of his friends, 'that Bram's sacrifice of family, career and freedom had essentially been inspired by his Afrikaner heritage. He had implied as much in his letter to the magistrate: as an Afrikaner, he sought to make some reparation for the misdeeds of his people.'[38]

Carl Niehaus, an Afrikaner who also joined the ANC, encouraged to do so by Frikkie Conradie whom he had first met in Beyers Naudé's garden, was also arrested and imprisoned, along with his wife. While at university he experienced great tensions with his parents over his approach to race relations and in his emotional crisis was even sent by them to a psychological clinic for observation. For years he felt bitter towards them and it was only near the end of his prison sentence that he admitted, 'I could forgive them completely.'[39] While in prison he met Denis Goldberg, one of the Rivonia trialists, who like so many had a struggle to forgive. 'Carl,' he once said, 'I try not to hate, and during my years in prison I have known many good warders, but I can never forgive them for what they did to Bram.'[40]

During his imprisonment Denis Goldberg hastened his release by renouncing violence, a decision Carl Niehaus deplored, writing him an angry letter. Once out of prison Goldberg left for London, but on a visit home he called to see Carl and they shared a meal. 'Without ever referring to the letter,' Niehaus recalled, 'we made peace.' As they were parting, Denis Goldberg said simply, 'Thank you, Carl.' Niehaus said of his response: 'I felt ashamed – muttered that the years in prison were over.'[41]

Laurens van der Post once wrote: 'We should call a national convention of all races and colours, and we should sit down and say, "Look, we have all made terrible mistakes, we have hurt one another ... We have called this conference to wipe out the mistakes of the past ..."' White people, he concluded, had to accept responsibility for inflicting the greatest injury, apologize for it, and be grateful for black and Coloured patience, 'and in consultation with them move forward.'[42]

THE CHANGING AFRIKANER POLITICAL SCENE

F.W. de Klerk, the brother of the writer and newspaper editor, W.A. de Klerk, startled the world by making it possible to change Afrikaner attitudes, as his brother had often argued. Unknown to most (including F.W. de Klerk himself, until he became leader of the National Party in the Transvaal in 1988), secret talks with Nelson Mandela had been undertaken by senior Government figures for some years – though it was public knowledge that in 1989 President P.W. Botha had taken tea with Mandela, who had asked him to release all political prisoners unconditionally.

Until then, changes in apartheid structures had been incremental, with Prime Minister Vorster easing petty apartheid, allowing mixed sport, undertaking to scrutinize discriminatory policy, giving more recognition to self-determination for blacks outside the homelands, and appointing the Theron Commission to investigate the situation of the Coloured community. He also made the first moves towards parliaments for whites, Coloureds and Indians with joint decision-making on matters of mutual interest.[43] President P.W. Botha had been bolder, setting up the Tri-Cameral Parliament in 1982, and recognizing black trade unions in 1984. In 1986 the National Party itself had changed tack and agreed to some measures of power-sharing with the black community, a policy which F.W. de Klerk took an active part in formulating.[44]

At the international level major shifts were also occurring, with the *glasnost* and *perestroika* policies of Mikhail Gorbachev, the Namibia Accord, which led to Namibian independence in March 1990, and pressures from Western powers on the South African Government to negotiate with its opponents. By the time F.W. de Klerk succeeded P.W. Botha as President (Botha resigned through ill health in the autumn of 1989), the world situation was even more propitious as Communism changed beyond recognition, with the Soviets in Moscow stating that they would prefer a political rather than military solution to South Africa's conflicts. 'South Africa should be spoken to not only through threats or pounding our fists on the tables,' said the head of the Soviet Foreign Ministry's Southern African Department, Yuri Yukalov. 'There should be dialogue.'[45]

Moreover, F.W. de Klerk, a pragmatic politician with a legal background – though deeply rooted in Afrikaner history – had won the leadership vote against Barend du Plessis from the reformist wing of the National Party, albeit only by a small majority. Soon, therefore, he was meeting Nelson Mandela, who had written him a letter similar in vein to the one he had sent much earlier to P.W. Botha, urging the need for talks and negotiations to end the conflict in South Africa.[46]

In Los Angeles in 1994 F.W. de Klerk argued that apartheid had been broken down, not primarily by external pressure (military or political), but by the changes which economic growth had generated, 'by millions of ordinary people moving to the cities, participating in the economy, gaining better education and ultimately placing irresistible pressure on an outmoded constitutional system'.[47]

Though there is undoubtedly some truth in these remarks, it was also a fact that in the 1970s and 1980s South Africa had become ungovernable, or at least could only be governed by the most repressive use of the army and the police, and by destabilizing the countries surrounding it (the countries from which the ANC operated and had its bases). With the fall of the Communist empire a major threat was removed from the Afrikaner mind, however fearful its right wing (which was strong) might be of an accommodation with the majority community. Moreover, several leaders of the party F.W. de Klerk was now leading – Pik Botha, the Foreign Minister, Gerrit Viljoen, a political philosopher completely informed about black aspirations and frustrations, du Plessis and Dawie de Villiers, often seen as a champion of justice – all helped to create an atmosphere favourable to change.[48]

It was, however, Leon Wessels, later Deputy Chair of the Constitutional Assembly, who first apologized in South Africa itself for apartheid when he said in June 1990 that it was a terrible mistake which had blighted the country. We know the Government has hurt its fellow citizens, he added, echoing a statement to the same effect made in Oslo that May with full Cabinet approval, which had concluded that apartheid was the cause of much violence. 'It failed,' the statement indicated, 'because it did not address the realities of our situation, nor did it appreciate the human factors involved...'[49]

In 1991 Wessels, then the Deputy Foreign Secretary, went further, admitting that the Government had 'failed to listen to the laughing and crying of our people. That must never happen again. I am sorry for having been so hard of hearing for so long, so indifferent.'[50] Pik Botha admitted the same, putting it in more theological language in a BBC interview: 'To allocate rights and privileges on the basis of physical characteristics was really tantamount to sin ... of sinning against God because He created us all.'[51] There was need for forgiveness, he continued, but this could not be forced.

F.W. DE KLERK AND THE DEMAND FOR
AN APOLOGY FOR APARTHEID

Strangely, in all this apologizing F.W. de Klerk remained silent. His brother regretted at one point that there had been no public or forthright confession that apartheid had been a fallacy, stating plainly: 'I think F.W. owes South Africa that confession.' Indeed, even on a television programme, despite his deeply held religious views as a member of the smallest and strictly Calvinist Dutch Reformed Church, F.W. de Klerk insisted on seeing apartheid as a mistake, not as a sin. In response to a question about an apology in the manner of Pik Botha, he maintained that even when apartheid was a dominant policy, the National Party had always striven for justice for all.[52] Nevertheless, though de Klerk has never himself offered a formal apology, as some like Desmond Tutu urged him to do,[53] he had indicated in some interviews, like one in Japan, 'We are very, very sorry for the pain which was caused by that period in our history and we are glad that the period has passed.'[54]

He did not, of course, change tack overnight. 'No, I have not had a Damascus Road experience,' he told a BBC interviewer in 1991.[55] But hard work and study with many colleagues over a number of years led him to alter his position, 1986 being the watershed when the National Party decided to exchange apartheid for power-sharing without domination. 'I thank God for this new vision,' he commented.

Also significant for him was the sermon preached by the Rev. Pieter Bingle on 20 September 1989 at his inauguration service. The Doppers, as members of his church are called, believe they may receive a special call from God to perform a specific task at a particular time. This was Bingle's theme, taking Jeremiah 23 verses 16 and 22 as his text. He told the new President that he was standing 'in the council chamber of God' to learn the will of the Lord, and that he should act upon it rather than heed the words of the false prophets. As God's instrument de Klerk should have the courage to break new ground, and 'be aggressive enough to take problems and challenges fearlessly'.

The service affected the new President deeply. 'He was literally in tears after the sermon,' says his brother, who was at a

STRUGGLING TO FORGIVE

post-inaugural gathering of friends and family. 'In the tears he told us we should pray for him – that God was calling him to save all the people of South Africa, that he knew he was going to be rejected by his own people but that he had to walk this road and that we must all help him.'[56]

'One asks for pardon and forgiveness,'[57] Piet Koornhof, former minister and ambassador, is recorded as saying, yet nowhere does F.W. de Klerk use such language. Clearly, though, his thinking has developed since the time he defended apartheid policies. Thus, addressing the Transvaal National Party Congress in 1993, he said: 'I feel proud of what we are achieving in South Africa and thankful for the recognition and the courage to break with that which was wrong in the past.'[58] Already by 1991 he had abolished the Land Act, the Group Areas Act and the Population Registration Act, unbanned organizations and released political prisoners. And now as he spoke in 1993, South Africa's first ever democratic election was but a year away.

In Oslo that year, as he and Nelson Mandela received the Nobel Peace Prize, he explained that he was deeply aware of his own shortcomings and indicated that 'the single most important factor which became the driving force towards a totally new dispensation in South Africa was a fundamental change of heart. This change occurred in both sides which had been involved in conflict over decades. It was not a sudden change but a process – a process of introspection, of soul searching, of repentance; of realization of the futility of ongoing conflict, of acknowledgement of failed policies and the injustice brought with it.' This process brought the National Party to the point of making a clean break with apartheid and separate development. 'A clean break with all forms of discrimination – for ever,' he concluded.[59]

Earlier that year he indicated at a news conference in Cape Town that it had not been the intention 'to deprive people of their rights and to cause misery, but eventually separate development and apartheid led to just that. In so far as that occurred, we deeply regret it.' Asked if the words 'deep regret' were an apology, he replied: 'Deep regret goes much further than just saying you are sorry. Deep regret says that if I could turn the clock back and if I could do anything about it, I would have liked to have avoided it.'[60]

It is comments like this from de Klerk which puzzle analysts, for when Dr Hendrik Verwoerd first spelt out his vision of separate development, many political commentators pointed out that the racial statistics were loaded against apartheid; and, even if the policy could be sustained beyond even the wildest dreams, by the year 2000 there would still be a ratio of 5–1 in so-called white South Africa. 'The whole elaborate exercise would be for nothing,' Allister Sparks has concluded.[61] Surely, these analysts observe, de Klerk must have understood this basic fact about the theory of separate development.

How then could apartheid strategists have been so naive, arguing as F.W. de Klerk has that 'separate development was morally justifiable if you look at it as a constitutional option'? Though he did concede that it was not 'a good idea to tell people where to live and kick people out of particular townships. It became forced removals. That is where apartheid became morally unjustifiable … I have said time and again "We are sorry that happened."'[62]

Three other comments perhaps help illuminate F.W. de Klerk's situation. There are those who say he has no intention of inflicting economic pain on his white constituency and to admit guilt is not only a sign of weakness but would also 'acknowledge the need for restitution'.[63] Professor Colin Gardner has made a similar point: for F.W. de Klerk to make a straightforward confession of guilt would probably mean death for him as a politician, for he might well alienate the white community to such an extent that it would desert him.[64] He does also have in his ancestry a grandfather who was both a politically active clergyman and a Cape rebel during the Anglo-Boer War, and an aunt who is the widow of Prime Minister J.G. Strydom, which means he is steeped in Afrikaner politics and traditions, another factor militating against too drastic a repudiation of the past.[65]

Nelson Mandela himself takes an analogous view, albeit from a different perspective. 'I don't think it is necessary for de Klerk to apologize,' he has commented. What mattered, he said, was what people did to ensure that a 'most brutal system of racial oppression was eliminated from our society'.[66] It was a view shared by Renier Schoeman, one-time chief spokesman for the National Party, when he said in 1991: 'Personally, I do not regard myself as belonging to the *mea culpa* brigade. We should be judged by our deeds.'[67]

F.W. de Klerk's deeds certainly changed South Africa and its world role, though he was always careful through electoral procedures in the white community to obtain a mandate for power-sharing. 'It was his destiny,' his wife commented. 'I cried when he was inaugurated,' she added, 'because he loves his country so much and at last he was going to have a chance to put things right.'[68] By being non-ideological, though to begin with, as Nelson Mandela has indicated, he hoped to entrench group rights, he helped South Africa move forward in a unique way. 'President de Klerk peacefully relinquished the monopoly on power in a way which few, if any other, precedents exist in human experience,' remarked Stephen Solarz, the former chairman of the American House of Representatives sub-committee on Africa.[69] 'For one who knew only too well the hatred that the security forces felt for the ANC, it took remarkable self-possession to release Mandela from jail and unban black liberation movements,' another commentator has indicated.[70]

Yet what was the alternative? Suppose Nelson Mandela had died in prison and become a martyr? Moreover, sanctions from the Western powers, especially economic pressures from America, as well as Europe, were beginning to bite and time was clearly running out. Unlike Mikhail Gorbachev, however, F.W. de Klerk ran with the process he started, building an alliance with the ANC once his hoped-for relationship with Chief Buthelezi and the IFP proved too unstable. And though the relations between Nelson Mandela and F.W. de Klerk obviously had highs and lows, they needed one another, too.

One revealing incident gives a glimpse of the complexity of the relationship. Some journalists were having a drink with F.W. de Klerk when the subject of Mandela came up. Both had been involved in a bitter controversy over township violence, Mandela accusing de Klerk of having blood on his hands. Admitting their relationship had deteriorated, he commented, 'What I do find astonishing is Mr Mandela's extraordinary lack of bitterness.' It was, says one journalist present, as close as he ever heard F.W. de Klerk come to admitting the 'scale of the crime' he and other NP politicians had committed in imprisoning Mandela for so long.[71]

Despite F.W. de Klerk's judicious phrases, and his politician's antennae, he is, of course, aware of the need for forgiveness. Indeed, he responded to a press question on why people oppressed for over 40 years should vote for his party by suggesting that peace would not come if people clung to past bitterness. He maintained that Afrikaners had forgiven the British for the deaths of women and children in the concentration camps during the Anglo-Boer War, adding, 'Forgiveness is the very essence of Christianity, of what all peace-loving people should seek in any society. Unforgiveness is a new form of racism.'[72]

How real were the requests for forgiveness and expressions of regret by Afrikaner politicians, when every 'sorry' has the political hope of minimizing any backlash when power changes hands?[73] Firstly, of course, South Africa is a country where religion, and Christianity in particular, plays an important role. Moreover, Calvinism has always been politically alert, wanting to change both individuals and society. Secondly, F.W. de Klerk is a politician who is a Christian to his fingertips, as was clear when he once explained his belief 'that God demands of us that we do all in the light of His Word'. In addition, though forgiveness is always contextual, it does imply a changed situation in the future as well as acknowledging that people were wronged in the past.[74]

WILHELM VERWOERD AND PIERRE JEANNE GERBER

Two younger Afrikaners have been bolder in their explorations into penitence, though they have not been shouldering heavy responsibilities like F.W. de Klerk. One, Wilhelm Verwoerd, is a grandson of Dr Hendrik Verwoerd, while the other, Pierre Jeanne Gerber, is the one-time chairman of the National Party's Youth section.

Wilhelm Verwoerd is the third child of Dr Verwoerd's eldest son and was only three when his grandfather was assassinated in 1966. The picture he had of him was always positive, reinforced by his grandmother, Betsie. Years later, of course, he was presented with a different assessment when he read Chief Albert Luthuli's description of Dr Verwoerd as 'the author of our calamity'.[75] Moreover, as Wilhelm Verwoerd has put it, 'With my mother's milk I was taught that black and white people are different.'[76]

After an idyllic childhood in Stellenbosch, Wilhelm developed a deep religious conviction but never became politically active, 'partly because of the burden of the name,' as he has explained, 'but mostly because we saw it as "a dirty business".'[77] His change-round came slowly, too. In school debates he often had to argue unpopular positions and in 1982, in his first year at university, he argued the case against the Israeli occupation of Lebanon. 'Without realising it,' he has reflected, 'we were putting ourselves in the shoes of the Palestinians; that was quite significant, because many Afrikaner people took it for granted that, like them, the Israelis were the chosen people.'

In 1985 a fellow student, who had noticed his intellectual skill in questioning his own conventional wisdom, invited Wilhelm Verwoerd to tour South Africa to meet black political groups. Here he was faced with a different picture of his grandfather as he heard about Bantu education and bannings. By then his politics had shifted to the left of many in his family and his courtship and then marriage to Melanie Fourie, a first-year theological student at Stellenbosch, cemented his growing convictions.

In 1986 he won a Rhodes Scholarship – something which alarmed his father, for 'Rhodes is not an endearing concept to an Afrikaner'.[78] Before going to Oxford he lived in Utrecht in Holland on a three-month scholarship in a house with other South Africans, some in exile. Here he had many confrontations, read Donald Woods' book on Steve Biko and saw Amnesty International's figures on torture and detention in his country. Despite this growing awareness, however, Wilhelm Verwoerd could not yet break with traditional Afrikaner attitudes, partly because he was worried about Communism, but in due course his perceptions and goals changed. Deciding to study politics and economics at Oxford University, he gave up his ideas of the ordained ministry, but retained his deep religious awareness – though he has what he calls a 'problematic relation with the Dutch Reformed Church' of which he is a member.[79]

Returning to South Africa to marry before continuing his degree, he had his first contact with the ANC, meeting Steve Tshwete, Thabo Mbeki and Joe Slovo in Lusaka with other Stellenbosch academics – though he was still ambivalent about it, partly because his older brother, Dirk, had been a paratrooper in Angola. He also met other Africans in Zimbabwe, Zambia and Malawi, which made him more alert to his African identity. This matter was brought into sharper focus when a group of militant Afro-Americans threatened to disrupt a course organized by the Oxford Centre on African Studies if Wilhelm was present. He could only attend after Blade Nzimande cleared his participation by consulting with the ANC in London.

Six months later Nelson Mandela was released and from Oxford Wilhelm Verwoerd sent him a letter in Afrikaans, expressing his deep regret for what he and others had experienced. 'Naturally the history – your twenty-seven-year-long, unjust jail sentence and my grandfather's part in that – cannot be altered in a few words,' he wrote. 'But, as an Afrikaner, who at the cost of other South Africans benefitted from apartheid, and as the grandson of the Architect of "separate development" … I want to say this to you: I am very, very sorry for what happened.' He could not ask forgiveness for his grandfather, he continued, 'but what I can do is to assure you that my wife and I will dedicate our lives to putting our words of remorse into deeds…'

Nelson Mandela never received the letter, as Wilhelm discovered when he met him in 1991 and told him of its contents. Mandela replied: 'Let's not talk about the past, let's focus on the future,' adding that Wilhelm had a 'great advantage being a Verwoerd because when you speak, people will listen'.[80]

Wilhelm, therefore, began talking at meetings across South Africa, saying he did not want to forget the past. At Oxford he had written an assessment of his grandfather, partly a personal attempt to understand him as an ideologue who was neither a hero nor a villain. 'Making sense of the past, without justifying sins,' he wrote, 'is one of the more difficult tasks confronting someone with an Afrikaner Nationalist upbringing, who is participating in the formation of a truly democratic, future South Africa.'[81] He was, he said elsewhere, particularly aware of the burden of his name, a 'personal cross' he had to bear which he could not escape, adding: 'I have to confront the ghosts.'[82]

Wilhelm Verwoerd's thesis became what he now terms his own 'little Great Trek' from being a Voortrekker Afrikaner to becoming an ANC comrade. In 1992 he had joined the ANC, following his wife who had joined earlier, distressing the Verwoerd family who read about the news in the press. There was anger and tears and his father disinherited him. 'To me it is totally unacceptable for an Afrikaner to join forces with an organization that I believe is a "black power" movement intent on taking over the country that my forefathers have earned through blood and sweat,' his father stated categorically. 'Any Afrikaner, whether my own son or anyone else, who actively promotes the ANC's election campaign is a traitor to his own people.' Now Wilhelm Verwoerd had to choose between following the more limited love for family and living out the commitments he had made as a citizen.

Wilhelm Verwoerd's grandmother, Betsie Verwoerd, said she could understand his actions as long as they stemmed from conviction, not opportunism. And his first cousin, Carel Boshoff senior, has said Wilhelm remains a member of the family. Wilhelm Verwoerd himself hopes that one day his father, whom he still sees when his children visit their grandfather, will re-establish a relationship.[83]

'Joining the ANC is my understanding of what reconciliation is all about,' Wilhelm Verwoerd has explained. 'Unlike F.W. de Klerk I think grand apartheid was wrong in practise and in theory, not morally justifiable, being wrong only because it did not work out.' It was a crime against humanity more than a policy that failed as the state became involved in structural violence against its citizens through its laws. Accordingly, on Sharpeville Day 1995, Wilhelm spoke on a platform with Dr Beyers Naudé. 'I was quite confessional,' he has recalled. Indeed, in response to the comment of Archbishop Trevor Huddleston that Nelson Mandela is too forgiving, he says tersely: 'Yes; it prevents our having to face up to what we have done.'[84]

The pilgrimage of Pierre Jeanne Gerber has been very different. As a young boy he grew up in a mixed area in the Cape, one of the last to be separated in fact. Here his father was a minister of the Dutch Reformed Church. One day Pierre Jeanne came home from school to find three nearby houses empty and no-one able to explain what had happened or where his friends were. He never saw them again until in 1995 he came across one of them working as a chief official in the Western Cape Education Department.

When Pierre Jeanne Gerber was 11, he started buying property and in 1977, when he was in standard seven, bought a plot of land in Calvinia in the Northern Cape for 12 pounds. He did not go there, however, until 1990, when he discovered to his alarm that he owned land where a chapel once stood, demolished as late as the 1970s under the Group Areas Act, when the Coloured community was forcibly removed. Though churches in areas such as Porterville were also demolished, this apartheid action was most unusual and even in District 6 in Cape Town, churches were left standing. As he probed further, Pierre Jeanne Gerber found that the demolished chapel was no ordinary one, for it was dedicated to a Calvinia citizen martyred in the Anglo-Boer War. The Anglican chapel to Abraham Esau had been officially deconsecrated before being demolished, of course, and compensation had been paid, but Esau's memory lingered on, kept alive by an annual memorial Mass which drew everyone to the Anglican church in the town.

Calvinia, set on an escarpment where a high plateau starts, was a gateway to the semi-desert, the *karoo*. Established 150 years ago, it had been named after John Calvin. Jewish traders arrived there in the 1850s and the British in the 1880s. In 1899 a Dutch Reformed Church had been built and by the time of the Anglo-Boer War the town had some 300 white and 600 Coloured inhabitants. Abraham Esau, Pierre Jeanne Gerber discovered, had supported the British in the War partly because he was concerned that the Coloured citizens would lose their vote if Afrikaners came to power.

He seems to have made his first public appearance in May 1900, heading a victory parade and rally to celebrate Mafeking's relief. Within four months he was involved in the Anglo-Boer conflict to such an extent that a local sheep farmer sent a message to his brother, who was with the nearby Free State commandos, saying: 'the English Coloured Esau' was 'being the biggest trouble-maker here'.[85]

STRUGGLING TO FORGIVE

On the evening of 7 January 1901 Calvinia had fallen suddenly to some 50 Free State commandos and by 13 January about 600 were billeted in the village. The Coloured inhabitants clung to Esau, who remained firm and loyal to the British. Arrested at dawn on 15 January, he was dragged before the authorities and sentenced to 25 lashes for speaking against the Boers and having 'attempted to arm the Natives'.[86] He was roped to a tree, and flogged until he fainted, after which further brutalities were administered.

On 5 February he was dumped about five miles out of Calvinia. Here, after another beating, he was shot dead. News of the killing spread rapidly, causing such an uproar among both the Coloured and the English in the Cape that it reached Milner and even Chamberlain. Abraham Esau thus became a symbolic figure of a revivified British patriotism in Calvinia, and an annex to the Anglican Mission Church was created called the Abraham Esau Memorial Chapel.

In 1948 another twist in the story occurred when a fiery Dutch Reformed Mission pastor, working for a Nationalist election victory, pulled down the Union Jack which always flew over the Memorial Chapel and tore it in half. In his view Esau had committed treason against the Afrikaner people and 'respectable Coloured people would not honour murderers'.[87] A politically combative young schoolteacher who clashed with the pastor was first maltreated and then whipped to within an inch of his life. He later had a mental breakdown and died. According to a local doctor, the schoolteacher had been whipped near the spot where Abraham Esau was said to have been murdered.[88]

Pierre Jeanne Gerber had, albeit unwittingly, become involved in one of the most dramatic incidents of the Anglo-Boer War, one with many subtle undertones. As Gerber gradually discovered the history of his property, the Rev. Austen Jackson, who had been appointed to the Anglican church in Calvinia in 1990, also unearthed Esau's story and determined to find the land's owner. It took two years to trace Pierre Jeanne, whom he phoned up and asked if the church could buy back the land. 'I'll give it to you,' Pierre Jeanne said, believing that land belonged to God with human beings acting as God's stewards.

On 21 June 1992 St George's Cathedral in Cape Town was quite full for a ceremony during which the Trust Deed of the land was handed over to the Diocese. People from Calvinia were there, having risen at 6.00 a.m. to reach Cape Town, some of them for the first time ever. Thirty per cent of the 500-strong congregation were white, including Pierre Jeanne Gerber, his wife and mother. Bill Nasson, the author of a book about Abraham Esau, spoke about his life. Hoosain Adams, a Moslem from Calvinia, also spoke and Austen Jackson told the story of how he had become involved. When Pierre Jeanne turned to face the congregation to talk, everyone stood up. 'I couldn't get my words out,' he remembers, but was able to say clearly: 'This is the greatest day of my life,' as tears rolled down his cheek.[89] Archbishop Desmond Tutu then spoke about forgiveness and restitution, thus setting the seal on a day which became part of a process leading to the creation of the Abraham Esau Memorial Chapel Trust, chaired by Pierre Jeanne himself. Its aim is to rebuild the chapel and pursue educational and ecclesiastical purposes.

On 19 August 1995 there was a further development when 200 people walked from the former Coloured area in Calvinia to lay a wreath on Esau's grave and thence to the site of the chapel, whose ground the Archbishop rededicated. In February 1996 a community meeting was held in Calvinia to elicit grass-roots ideas about the rebuilding of the chapel and the work of the Trust. It remains to be seen how profound its work will have been by the time the centenary of Esau's martyrdom comes round, and whether Calvinia is blazing a trail for other local communities in South Africa with equally complex and difficult histories in need of similar acts of repentance and forgiveness.

Pierre Jeanne Gerber, by now a member of the Western Cape Provincial Parliament for the National Party, performed one further symbolical act. For a long time he had been distraught about the demolition of the mixed-race area of Cape Town called District 6. Stumbling on the site of a former house in the area, he removed a granite step and made it part of his house in Wellington, outside Cape Town, as a memorial. The stone now links the kitchen to the living room.[90]

One other incident reflects changes occurring in the Afrikaner community. It concerns Archbishop Trevor Huddleston, one of the most hated figures in Afrikaner history. When he was staying in a hotel in Pretoria the day after Nelson Mandela's inauguration, he walked along a corridor flanked by armed guards, at the end of which was a young white soldier. As he approached him, the soldier took off his cap and said: 'I'm an Afrikaner serving in the Army ... I am deeply ashamed at what my people have done to the black people of this country and I apologize. We have done terrible things and we knew what we were doing. I want to thank you because you are the person who opened our eyes to what we were doing.'

'I protested,' Trevor Huddleston has written, 'but he bowed his head and asked for a blessing,' which was given. 'The soldier's whole face lit up,' Archbishop Huddleston continued. 'It was a sacrament of the whole meaning of what we have been fighting for.'[91]

Chapter 4

Forgiveness and Love –

The Role of Majorities and Minorities

There are several ways to envisage love in community terms. One is to see it as 'goodwill on fire'. In this way communities can express a concern for *all* citizens through their policies. Yet in most societies there are those who find themselves marginalized or uncared for.

The task of this chapter is to explore the inter-relationships of some of the communities in South Africa and, where possible, to give an indication of where there has, or has not, been concern for others. If this has been absent, then the older paradigm of being concerned only for one's own tribe or class is operative. Now and again, however, a greater consciousness has arisen and allowed the expression of a more universal awareness of others' needs, beyond the self-interest of one's own group.

Love in community terms can, therefore, be seen as goodwill, as indicated above. But it can also surely express itself in group terms as magnanimity, compassion and caring exemplified by the kind of legislation passed. Even an attitude of toleration can be useful as a pointer to a more concerned approach to others and their right to live alongside those with different views without feeling threatened. But where South African society has remained polarized, it has to be acknowledged that love has been shown only incidentally.

This chapter illustrates the great effort needed to cross boundaries in a society as diverse and culturally rich as South Africa. It also demonstrates clearly that forgiveness has to be seen as a process and always in a context which is never free from ambiguity.

For the purposes of the chapter only certain inter-relationships have been selected. They illustrate vividly the impact different communities have had and how difficult it is to transcend regional, tribal or racial loyalties, even when some attempt to do so. It also highlights courageous individuals who have risked ostracism to reach out to others in concern and colleagueship.

There is no reason why a dominant group – whether political or cultural – should concern itself with minorities unless love in political terms guides their outlook. Hopefully, it is in this arena that the African sense of *ubuntu* (humanness) will in the long run have an increasing influence on all aspects of South African society, and beyond it, too.

THE BLACK STRUGGLE

Dissident Afrikaners were not the only ones to confront apartheid's rulers. The black political protest movement also continued, despite the ruthless elimination of its leaders, and by 1980 it was powerfully 'striving towards national freedom and national sovereignty'.[1] Yet it was not like other African liberation struggles, as Oliver Tambo, then President of the ANC in exile, explained: 'The difference between South Africa and other systems of colonization is that in South Africa colonizer and colonized live side by side within the same country,'[2] with colour and race dividing a resident white occupying group from the subject Africans, whose function was to provide them with a cheap labour pool.

Two South African poets have succinctly described part of this experience, James Matthews writing of the pain and rage he felt under apartheid[3] and Oswald Mtshali describing how a black person could never do right in white eyes, however submissive his or her attitude.[4]

From the 1960s onwards, of course, there was a growing black consciousness as the ANC and other liberation groups chose either exile, prison or revolt. Though in theory Chief Luthuli and the ANC continued their policy of non-violence, by allowing Nelson Mandela and others to create a military organization not under the ANC's direct control (which, unlike the Executive of the ANC at the time, could have white members), it was, as Mandela has confirmed, inevitable that MK 'would be a different kind of organization'.[5]

So the seeds were sown for 30 years of conflict, with the ANC in exile seeking, initially by acts of sabotage only, to continue its protest at the lack of a constitutional settlement between the majority and minority communities. The state, meanwhile, grew ever more fearful and paranoid as the black presence in both the expanding cities and the rural areas grew.

The situation was more complex than that, however, for the ANC had an alliance with the South African Communist Party, so at the international level it became caught up in the global struggle between capitalism and communism as the Cold War went through various stages. Meanwhile, inside South Africa the English, Indian and Coloured communities had to decide whom to support, either overtly or covertly.

South Africa's population estimates for 1994 give an indication of the composition of its 40 million or so inhabitants. Besides the majority black community, many living in the rural areas, but also in, or near, the main cities, there were 5 million whites, nearly half of whom lived in and around greater Johannesburg. Sixty per cent of the 3.25 million Coloured population lived in the Cape Town area and three-quarters of the million or so Indian citizens lived in KwaZulu-Natal.[6] The population in the 1960s was substantially less than these 1994 statistics, but the proportions are roughly the same.

Within the complex developments of the 1960s and 1970s, initially during Dr Verwoerd's premiership, the black presence in the cities was tolerated only for work. In addition housing was segregated, on a colour basis, so that between 1960 and 1983 300,000 Coloureds, 100,000 Indians and 3.2 million Africans were forcibly removed, often to impoverished areas in the 'homelands' set up for them.[7]

Dr Verwoerd's policies presented the African, Indian and Coloured groups, the white liberals in the Progressive Party in Parliament (a breakaway of 57 MPs from the United Party in 1959[8]) and, outside Parliament, the Liberal Party under Alan Paton and others, with an immense challenge. This was particularly so when the state used the Army, a spying system and modern methods of surveillance to quell dissent. Few then opposed apartheid, a fact which became clear when in the 1961 General

Election the United Party made a comeback, leaving the Progressive Party with one solitary MP – Mrs Helen Suzman – in Houghton, Johannesburg.[9] One of over 100,000 people with a Jewish background in South Africa,[10] Helen Suzman became a focus of parliamentary opposition for several decades. 'You are,' Chief Luthuli told her after the Parliamentary debate on the 90-day detention bill, 'the bright star in a dark chamber, where the lights of liberty … are going out one by one'.[11]

Over the next three decades four movements of protest emerged: through the Liberal Party, which had been created in the mid-1950s; through the Black Consciousness Movement (BCM), focused on Steve Biko and other colleagues; in part through the KwaZulu Legislative Assembly when Chief Buthelezi, unlike the Xhosa Bantustan leaders, refused to accept 'independence' for the Zulu homeland; and finally, in the 1980s, through the United Democratic Front (UDF), a loose federation of some 600 anti-apartheid groups under the leadership of the Rev. Allan Boesak, Albertina Sisulu and others.

THE ENGLISH-SPEAKING COMMUNITY

It would be a mistake to assume that many English-speaking South Africans took part in opposing Government policies through the Liberal Party, for their attitudes in racial matters had been shaped by their position in the social structure – 'a minority-within-a-minority'.[12] Moreover, the ambivalence between the white groups remained as difficult as ever. There was much tension between the English and the Afrikaners in Cape Town – boys used to re-fight the Boer War regularly, as the Rev. Michael Crommelin has admitted. A one-time Chair of the Young Progressives, as a child Crommelin had hated Afrikaners, but when he was converted at 21 he changed his outlook. Then, being a Methodist minister in the Free State, he had first to learn to speak Afrikaans, which he had earlier refused to do, and then to preach in it.[13] For him, there-fore, forgiveness had to begin personally.

Another cleric, Gonville ffrench-Beytagh, also came up against inherited group attitudes when, as Dean of Johannesburg, he was arrested and tried for his involvement in giving secret financial assistance to apartheid's victims. During the many hours of his interrogation he came to understand more fully the reason for Afrikaner hatred not only for Africans but for the English, too. 'For the first time,' he has written, 'I realized that we English have the same unconscious arrogance towards the Afrikaner as we and they have towards the African and indeed we may be partly responsible for the Afrikaner's taking out on the Africans the treatment which they have received from the English.' In particular his interrogators brought up British treatment of Afrikaner women and children during the Anglo-Boer War. 'What the rights and wrongs of all this were,' he reflected subsequently, 'I do not know … But I do know that the memory of this suffering, in all its horror, lies burning and deeply bitter in the Afrikaner heart.'[14]

It is within the context of such tensions that English-speaking South Africans had to live and oppose Dr Verwoerd's policies. However, the situation was even more complex for some of the origins of South Africa's 'native policy' lay in tentative experiments in segregation in nineteenth-century colonial Natal.[15]

The poet Guy Butler encapsulated one type of English contribution to the situation when he described how through all the corruption, some people remained unstained, gaining insight and learning to endure.[16] One of these was the Anglican priest the Rev. Michael Scott, with his turbulent ministry in South Africa and his fight to help South West Africa, then under its hegemony, gain independence as Namibia. He greatly influenced Trevor Huddleston, recently arrived in Johannesburg and not yet a South African citizen. 'Father Michael Scott came and lived amongst the people, and ministered to them as best he could,' Archbishop Huddleston has recalled. 'To my shame I did very little to help him. Somehow it took me a long time to wake up, and it is good to be able to apologize publicly for an apathy I cannot excuse.'[17] Once awake, of course, first in Sophiatown in the 1950s and then globally, Huddleston fought apartheid with vigour, love, fearlessness, righteous anger, and deep conviction that ultimately good would triumph.[18]

'Do you think that I can give up fighting or rest contentedly in my priestly life,' he wrote in *Naught for Your Comfort*, 'when this

STRUGGLING TO FORGIVE

is what I am trying to protect from plunder; this most precious human treasure, the opportunity of love itself?' Finding God both at Calvary and through the resurrection, he could not understand why white South Africans could not discover what he had: a personhood for God through the African experience. Yet he also knew Christ had said from the cross, 'Father forgive them, for they know not what they do.'[19]

By the time Alan Paton became President of the Liberal Party, which had been formed in 1953, he had already written *Cry the Beloved Country*, with its haunting sentence about love and hate: 'It was Msimangu who had said, Msimangu who had not hate for any man, I have one great fear in my heart, that one day when they turn to loving they will find we have turned to hating.'[20] It was Paton especially, with his biblical prose, who tried to warn South Africans of the danger they were in through fear, maintaining: 'The only power that can resist the power of fear is the power of love. It is a weak thing and a tender thing; men despise and deride it.'[21]

Nevertheless, he looked for the day when South Africa would turn to understanding and compassion rather than power to solve its grave problems, often relating his understanding of love to forgiveness. So when he came to write *Too Late the Phalarope*, based on a true story of love between an Afrikaner policeman and a Coloured woman, which was illegal at the time, he was inspired by the fact that 'the policeman's wife sat in the court throughout the trial and by her demeanour showed that she had forgiven him'.[22]

Alan Paton's political life in the Liberal Party was never going to be as successful as his writing. Indeed, the party, with its strong Indian membership in Natal, including Gandhi's son, never won a seat in the all-white Parliament. Chief Luthuli, however, did not think the party's effectiveness ought to be measured in votes, but in the appraisal it forced on whites. It spoke with a more moral authority than other parties with white members because it had leaders like Alan Paton, Senator Rubin, Margaret Ballinger, Peter Brown, Patrick Duncan and others, Chief Luthuli considered. 'Moreover, it has tried to take its stand on principles and not on expediency – a new thing in South African politics,' he added.[23]

In the 1960s, however, when state repression escalated, the Liberal Party was torn apart by conflicting approaches. Sixteen members of the party, one of whom, Randolph Vigne, was National Deputy Chairman, formed the African Resistance Movement (ARM), formerly the National Committee of Liberation, designed to commit acts of sabotage. Adrian Leftwich, who recruited several members, headed up the new group's planning committee.

Their period of activity was soon cut short, however, for in mid-1964 members of ARM were arrested in a nationwide swoop. John Harris, another member but acting alone, left a bomb in a crowded area of Johannesburg station which exploded, seriously injuring a 77-year-old lady who later died, her 12-year-old granddaughter and others. Harris, who had telephoned the police to tell them what he had done, pleaded for mercy at his trial but was hung on 1 April 1965. Adrian Leftwich, along with others, turned state witness, as a result of which Hugh Lewin, another member of ARM, was jailed for seven years. Others received shorter sentences, parts of them suspended. It was a betrayal which lodged itself in Alan Paton's mind for the next 20 years.[24]

Adrian Leftwich, now a free man, left South Africa for good. 'Nothing I can say or do, now or in the future,' he wrote later to Paton, 'can ever reduce the immorality of my decision … I judge myself harshly.'[25] Paton did not reply to the letter, but years later wrote to Adrian Leftwich that those against whom he had sinned had now forgiven him so he ought to forgive himself. In fact, some had not forgiven him, but one who did so ungrudgingly was Eddie Daniels, who spent 15 years on Robben Island.[26] Paton, who thought those advocating sabotage should leave the Liberal Party, later came to forgive Vigne, too.[27] Indeed, it was Vigne who organized the memorial service for Alan Paton in St Paul's Cathedral, London, in 1988.

Was the Liberal Party, disbanded in 1968 because of a bill making it illegal to belong to a multi-racial organization for propagating political views, of any significance? A Liberal Party Senator from a large Jewish family in Cape Town, who became Paton's closest friend, considered it an important factor in the process which has culminated in the new, non-racial, democratic South Africa.[28] Alan Paton himself, of course, continued his work by other means, occasionally losing his passport and being intimidated.

After the Soweto uprising in 1976, he called on white South Africans to repent of their 'wickedness, arrogance, complacency, blindness'.[29] The only hope lay in a rapid change of government and serious talks with black community leaders. But his calls fell on deaf ears. The Minister of Justice, James T. Kruger, said that Paton represented only one person's views.[30] Paton replied as tersely as ever, pointing out that the Government spent 500 rand per year educating a white child and only 28 rand on a black one.

THE RISE OF BLACK CONSCIOUSNESS

During this period the ANC itself had two focal points: those imprisoned on Robben Island and its leaders in exile, led by Oliver Tambo, President of the ANC from 1967 to 1991, who had taken over its leadership on the death of Chief Luthuli. The PAC, too, had an office in exile, and was supported by the Government of China, among others, but it never gained the widespread support the ANC could muster, despite the esteem felt for Robert Sobukwe who was released from Robben Island as his health faded and then banned to Kimberley.

Among the black communities in South Africa a new figure emerged to mobilize opposition and by the 1970s Steve Biko and the BCM had grown both in significance and influence, helping black South Africans rid themselves of their inferiority and dependency. If Afrikaners knew where they were with the ANC, even though they intensely disliked the aims spelled out in the Freedom Charter, they were on less sure ground with the PAC and its Africanism, and even more uncertain with Steve Biko and Black Consciousness. Biko himself had a clear perception of the situation. 'No matter what a white person does,' he wrote, 'the colour of his skin – his passport to privilege – will always put him miles ahead of the black man. Thus in the ultimate analysis no white person can escape being part of the oppressor camp.'[31]

Liberals often wasted time proving to blacks that they were liberated, when their real task should have been to deal with white racism in their own community. 'For the 20-year-old white liberal to expect to be accepted with open arms is surely to overestimate the power of forgiveness of the black people,' judged Biko.[32] Liberals must fight for their own freedom, for they themselves were oppressed. And blacks must realize they had to stand on their own. Accordingly he and others split from NUSAS, the multiracial students' organization in the universities, and formed their own body, the South African Students' Organization (SASO). 'The decision to avoid alliances with whites was based on the assumption that their participation would undermine the prospects for black unity,' C.R.D. Halsi has explained.[33] It was a necessary step towards liberation after three centuries of oppression.

Compassion gave Steve Biko and colleagues their courage, Aelred Stubbs said at a Memorial Mass for him in 1977. 'And how Steve gave it vigour and warmth and life again! He was not christened "Bantu", meaning "people", for nothing.'[34] Originally Biko had wanted to be a doctor, but another calling had claimed him. Others had preceded him but he, with Barney Pityana, Strini Moodley and others such as Rubin Phillip and Sabelo Ntwasa, had founded and developed the Black Consciousness Movement. He had a great enjoyment of life, whether involved in a rugby game, a party or a political debate, though like all people he had a darker side too. 'And then there was his greatness of soul,' Aelred Stubbs added, recalling his magnanimity.[35]

Steve Biko's impact was too threatening and in 1973 the Government banned eight SASO leaders (along with eight NUSAS ones, too, for good measure). Worse was to come in 1977 when many movements working for change were banned and Biko himself detained. Four years earlier Father Stubbs had reminded Steve Biko of his name and suggested that he might have to suffer like the biblical Stephen. Biko laughingly replied that he thought he was not the stuff of which martyrs were made. 'I do not know what stuff he thought that was; but I do know that he had the love, which gave him the courage and the steadfastness,' Aelred Stubbs has suggested.[36]

Like many others arrested, Biko was taken into detention in Port Elizabeth, where he was not only questioned but tortured and degraded. Then, naked and chained, he was driven 700 miles to Pretoria where, in September 1977, he met his death at the hands of the security police. 'It was not just the end of a vibrant life of a gifted person, with a sense of destiny,' wrote his friend Mamphele Ramphele, 'but it was the death of a dream. The dream which was killed had both personal and national dimensions.'[37]

By June 1976, however, the effect of Black Consciousness ideas was already evident in the Soweto students' uprising, ostensibly against the imposition of Afrikaans teaching in black schools. But the revolt had deeper roots. What was new was the willingness of young people to take drastic action, even if it meant 600 were to die. 'The Black Consciousness Movement has always embraced realms beyond the purely political and organizational,' wrote one commentator in 1977. 'Detaining leaders and banning organizations does not detain aspiration or ban consciousness.' Bishop Manas Buthelezi, chair of the then banned Black Parents' Association, said at the time, 'Nobody anticipated that the children's revolution of 16 June would create such an impact never before witnessed in South Africa. It just blew up. And it is going to happen again.'[38]

Biko's death brought anger and disbelief but also universal condemnation, so significant a figure had Biko become. Consistently free himself from bitterness or resentment, according to Aelred Stubbs he laughed once when questioned about this, saying that too much time and energy would be consumed by such attitudes. However, 'to suggest that words of forgiveness were at any time during his passion on Steve's lips would be in my view unjustifiable,' Father Stubbs has considered. 'But that does not make him an unforgiving person ... There is no reason to suppose that Steve did not meet expressions of repentance with demonstrations of forgiveness. The whole aim of the "selfless revolutionary" ... presupposes that the oppressor can be brought to a state of repentance for what he has done, but also at that moment he is embraced, and so liberated by the forgiveness extended to him by the oppressed. 'For himself, Father Stubbs was unable to pray for the forgiveness of Biko's murderers. 'I can and do pray for their repentance, which will then make possible and efficacious their forgiveness,' he has written.[39]

In 1991 some repentance was evident, not from Biko's killers, but from one of the doctors struck off South Africa's medical register for unprofessional conduct. 'For a long time following the events of September 1977,' Dr Benjamim Tucker wrote in an affidavit submitted to the South African Medical and Dental Council to support his application for reinstatement, 'I had attempted to deny to myself the truth of my role in what has become known as the "Biko affair". After many years of dedicated and loyal service as a medical practitioner, I found it difficult to admit to myself that my conduct subsequent to his death fell far short of the standards required of a medical practitioner…'[40]

Both Dr Tucker, chief district surgeon in Port Elizabeth, and Dr Ivan Lang, district surgeon, had treated Biko shortly before his death in Pretoria from head injuries and brain damage. Dr Tucker had been brought before the Medical Council in 1985 after six doctors had taken Supreme Court action to make it conduct an enquiry into Dr Tucker's actions. He was found guilty of disgraceful conduct for failing to prevent Biko from being sent 1,200 km from Port Elizabeth to Pretoria on the floor of an open Land-Rover without medical attention, and for other medical negligence.[41]

Dr Tucker explained that he was a changed man. 'Genuine, complete and permanent reformation was, however, the recognition and appreciation by me of my wrongful conduct,' he said, 'and the entrenchment of deep, sincere and permanent contrition, both of which had, in turn, been born from many years of psychological trauma and stress, humiliation, despair and suffering. A medical practitioner,' he concluded, 'cannot subordinate his patient's interest to extraneous considerations.'[42]

The decision to reinstate Dr Tucker in 1991 was controversial. One of the six doctors who had taken the Supreme Court action, Professor Frances Ames, thought it lacked sensitivity when South Africans were trying to promote a new image of themselves; and Advocate George Bizos, who had represented the Biko family at the inquest, said that although 'one must try to forgive and forget', he found it 'difficult to accept that Dr Tucker has paid fully for his dereliction of duty after such a comparatively short period'. Another of the six doctors, Professor Trevor Jenkins, said he did not 'feel too aggrieved', commenting that doctors can make mistakes and learn from them. A third doctor, Dr Nchaupe Mokoape, who was also deputy President of AZAPO (the Azanian People's Organization), said Dr Tucker had paid 'for his dereliction

STRUGGLING TO FORGIVE

and I would not want to be more vindictive than that. One has to understand that Dr Tucker was operating in a political milieu in which black life was cheap. 'Ntsiki Biko (Biko's widow) told the press, however, that nothing Dr Tucker did would atone for not looking after her husband properly.[43]

Farouk Asvet wrote a poem later for 'Nelson, Robert and Steve in a quest for unity in our struggle', in which he spoke of Steve Biko's hovering face still haunting 'our waking memories', an indication of his profound legacy.[44] Others have argued that Black Consciousness and Biko's 'legacy of defiance in action' infused the liberation movement as a whole 'with a new energy'.[45] Indeed, contemporary South African leaders like Cyril Ramaphosa and Patrick Lekota were influenced earlier by Black Consciousness training programmes in which they participated.[46] 'Dying, as he lived, he expressed to many young blacks a fearlessness that helped change the face of the country,' Barney Pityana has indicated. 'It is that youth … whom Biko's legacy now challenges and addresses. What is the new consciousness of the 1990s, now that one particular aspect of the struggle has begun to be overcome?'[47]

CHIEF BUTHELEZI AND INKATHA

As the movement for black consciousness emerged, another group was mobilizing in KwaZulu, led by Chief Buthelezi. Expelled from Fort Hare University in the 1950s for involvement in a demonstration organized by the ANC Youth League, he took little part as a young man in anti-apartheid activities, between 1953 and 1960 mainly ensuring his succession to the Chieftainship of the Buthelezi clan. With some encouragement from Chief Luthuli, he tried to manipulate the Bantu Authorities system from within. This tactic seemed sensible after the Rivonia Trial in 1964, when the exiled political organizations seemed to be getting nowhere. From the late 1960s, therefore, Buthelezi, who was himself deprived of his passport from 1966 to 1971, was fairly defiant, but within certain boundaries.

He first avoided recognizing the legitimacy of a new Tribal Authority in his district, then, when a Territorial Authority was created for Zululand in 1972, he ensured that it was based on the historically dubious fact that the making of decisions should reside with the Chief of the Buthelezi clan, who he claimed had traditionally been first minister. Once in power, he worked continually through the KwaZulu Legislative Assembly to prevent Government attempts to use the Zulu King as a puppet. Later, of course, King Goodwill steered a more independent line and co-operated with the ANC. Later still, Chief Buthelezi was to become not only Home Affairs Minister in the GNU, but also acting President for the day when Nelson Mandela had to be in Europe, one of six times he performed this role. It even seemed possible, as Black Consciousness was developing under Steve Biko, that Buthelezi and he might work together, the more so after 1975 when Inkatha, the Zulu cultural movement whose origins went back to the 1920s, began to develop as a broad black nationalist movement rather than as an exclusively Zulu one. But this proved wishful thinking, despite the creation of the South Africa Black Alliance in January 1978, for the effects of the Transkei decision to opt for 'independence' in 1976, and the Soweto disturbances in June that year proved ultimately more successful politically.

Earlier in 1976 Chief Buthelezi spoke in the Jabulani Amphitheatre at his annual rally. The previous year, he reminded the crowd, he had issued a friendly warning to Prime Minister Vorster that if blacks did not reach fulfilment through his policies of *detente*, 'we would have no option but to resort to unrest and possible civil disobedience'.[48] History demanded now that South Africa's rightful role in Africa should be determined by the majority of her people.

For blacks, he went on, there was hope in the future, for liberation and the realization of human dignity. Though now suffering, they must 'throw off the yoke of oppression' and tell the world how they despised 'separate development'. 'Nowhere in the world have minorities prevailed against the majority indefinitely,' Chief Buthelezi continued. Since 1910 successive governments had 'planted seeds of destruction' so that South Africa could not be defended 'morally, theologically or militarily'. Of course many whites would interpret these words as 'advocating a revolution', but this was inevitable, as Robert Kennedy had said, claiming such a revolution could be 'compassionate if we care enough'.[49] Instead of a strong unitary state, Buthelezi maintained, he had offered 'a federal formula as a compromise proposal', even though that would be difficult. He therefore urged whites to turn away from the current Government's policy and pleaded for the release of black political leaders.[50]

Aware of the Luthuli tradition of non-violence in the ANC, Chief Buthelezi seized any opportunity to reach out to the Afrikaners. In 1972 he addressed a meeting in Stellenbosch University and made it clear that both Zulus and Afrikaners had been 'forged in this African wilderness'.[51] In Natal itself, impoverished because the Government withheld funds from the Zulus for not taking 'independence',[52] Chief Buthelezi sought multiracial arrangements, first through proposals for a multiracial province (outlined in the Buthelezi Commission), and later through the Natal Indaba of leaders from all the communities, convened in April 1986 by the Natal Provincial Council and the KwaZulu Government.

In New York in 1979 he had explained to the National Council of Churches the loneliness he felt, participating in the so-called 'homeland' political institutions. He defended himself, too, for those who were writing him off as a sell-out, maintaining that KwaZulu's refusal to take 'independence' had blocked Pretoria's objectives for a white state.[53]

The situation was complex of course, with the Government skilfully employing a divide and rule policy as Chief Buthelezi tried to steer his own course. 'Those of us who were not caught up in the emotional regionalism of Soweto were appalled at the narrow focus of interest displayed by the black consciousness movement,' he observed, adding that in 1976 talk about the South African Government falling was a stupid assessment of white power.[54]

In 1977 Chief Buthelezi was chased away from Steve Biko's funeral[55] and in 1978 he and others were forced to leave the funeral of Robert Sobukwe by militant black youths also attending it. Many of these went into exile and linked up with the ANC, and by the end of the decade a clear conflict had emerged between Inkatha, now a political party claiming 250,000 members,[56] and the ANC and other movements, though roughly 50 per cent of Inkatha supporters also supported the ANC.

Buthelezi, who opposed the armed struggle and the imposition of sanctions, and favoured capitalism rather than socialism, was clearly on a collision course with these other forces. 'I cannot bring myself to the poor and suffering of this country and say that I am working for the cessation of foreign investment in South Africa,' he told an American business group in 1976. 'Investment means increased prosperity and it means jobs for the unemployed, clothes for the naked and food for the hungry.'[57] He admitted, however, that Zulus would fight if Pretoria forced independence on them.

In 1979, a key year in the dispute with the ANC, Chief Buthelezi was maintaining that political vendettas between Inkatha and the ANC were destructive of unity within a multi-strategy approach. Reconciliation did not mean that everybody must do what he was doing. Reconciliation meant the ANC had to find room in its scheme of things to give him and Inkatha credibility and likewise he had to find room to give the ANC credibility.[58]

The ANC itself had sought to encourage mass movements in the 'independent' homelands, and so had maintained contact with the Transkei, the Ciskei, Venda and Bophutatswana. They also kept in touch with Chief Buthelezi who, according to Oliver Tambo, had 'taken up his position in the KwaZulu Bantustan after consultations with our leadership'. But soon disagreements emerged, with Chief Buthelezi perceived as building Inkatha as a personal power base for himself. First he dressed Inkatha in the clothes of the ANC and later, when the base was larger, he employed 'coercive methods to force people to support Inkatha', claimed Oliver Tambo.[59] In June 1979, for example, the KwaZulu Minister of Education announced in the KwaZulu Legislative Assembly that Inkatha was to become a compulsory subject in KwaZulu schools.[60]

Chief Buthelezi saw the conflict which emerged after 1979 rather differently. 'My only sin,' he commented, 'was that I could not agree that Inkatha be the internal wing of the ANC. I was prepared to co-operate with the ANC on those strategies we could synchronize. This was clearly not sufficient as far as ANC plans were concerned.'[61] Now, as he became more critical of the ANC,

South African television went from showing unflattering pictures of the Zulu Chief Minister to using more positive ones.[62] Chief Buthelezi, of course, always insisted he was not a collaborator whenever the radicals accused him of this, pointing out that the last armed rebellion against white rule had been a Zulu one – though they had been defeated by Britain in 1879 while defending the old Zulu order.

When hundreds lay dead in 1990 from fighting between Inkatha and ANC supporters, the result of a conflict begun in the 1980s between Inkatha and the newly formed UDF and its trade union ally, COSATU, Buthelezi addressed Zulu chiefs and said, 'We will not tolerate attacks on the Zulu nation ... I call on every one of you ... to stand up now and be counted in this hour of the people's need...'[63] To the ANC, of course, with its hopes of a democratic, unitary and non-racial South Africa, talk of the Zulu nation was extremely unhelpful, reluctant as it was to consider that South Africa (like Russia) is a multinational state,[64] just as it could not, because of its claims to be a non-racial party, overemphasize Black Consciousness. Yet inevitably, the Zulu nationalist movement remains a force which is still affecting the course of South African history.[65]

As the 1980s proceeded, Chief Buthelezi's popularity (which was put on a par with that of Mandela and the ANC in a 1977 Soweto survey[66]) waned as the ANC escalated its struggle. Oliver Tambo declared that apartheid officials, many of whom (like the police) were already targets, would come under attack. By 1983, with even less restraint, the ANC had begun to cause civilian casualties and that May a car bomb exploded outside the Air Force HQ in Pretoria, killing 19 and injuring 200.[67] The ANC's ability to cause disruption soon, however, came more through the promotion of mass action via the UDF, which had announced its birth at a Cape Town rally in August 1983. When COSATU, the biggest trade union alliance in South African history, was formed in Durban in 1985, it joined with the UDF and together they became a new force working for change. Soon it claimed 2 million affiliated members from all backgrounds.[68]

Chief Buthelezi did not support the UDF and COSATU, nor did the UDF accept him. Indeed, he vilified the UDF, suggesting that it was allied with the ANC,[69] and gave his support instead to a new Trade Union, UWUSA, the United Workers Union of South Africa, whose office bearers came from the management side of industry. This was launched in Durban on May Day 1986, before 50,000 people, many bussed in from afar,[70] and in his speech at the rally Buthelezi again stressed his opposition to the disinvestment in South Africa which many were urging.[71]

Clearly there were now several distinct approaches to black politics which would inevitably lead to tragedies. Just such a tragedy occurred at Mpophomeni, an African resettlement township near Howick, which fell under the KwaZulu Legislative Assembly. Here violence escalated over a long period and resulted in many deaths. At one point, as the conflict raged between the UDF-COSATU and Inkatha, the South African police moved in to quell the violent struggle, in the process of which a five-year-old girl was killed by a police vehicle which ran over her.[72]

The escalating violence threatened to engulf Chief Buthelezi himself. 'In the early 1980s there were two cases of people who were MK guerrillas claiming they had been sent to kill Buthelezi, who were arrested and tried,' one researcher has commented, 'which Buthelezi refers to as ANC attempts.' Though neither were even remotely successful, they made Buthelezi so fearful for his life that he asked for state protection. 'The ANC did declare war on Buthelezi,' Craig McEwan considers, in words if not in deeds, showing an intolerance of the views of others.[73]

There is no evidence available to suggest that Chief Buthelezi was involved in organizing Inkatha's violent actions. Indeed, in 1987 he cried out after a particularly devastating conflict: 'What future have we if our dignity and our decency is destroyed in ongoing orgies of hatred and revenge?'[74] But the attacks on UDF and COSATU supporters did not stop, and the police were perceived as being unsympathetic and only likely to associate with the UDF when arresting its members.[75]

Indeed, sometimes Chief Buthelezi defended Inkatha's actions on the grounds of provocation.[76] He was caught in a trap: if he publicly condoned Inkatha vigilante attacks, he would compromise the organization's 'non-violence' policy. But if he publicly censured senior colleagues in the central committee involved in

STRUGGLING TO FORGIVE

vigilante actions (Dr Sibusiso Bhengu, Inkatha's one-time secretary, admitted that 'Inkatha's warriors were terrorizing people'[77]), then he risked losing support.

Certainly there is an aggressive streak in Chief Buthelezi, as he showed in September 1977 when he threatened the Indian community with Zulu revenge for calling him 'a puppet on a string', invoking the memory of the Zulu-Indian riots in Durban in 1949.[78]

But there were ANC attitudes that were wrong as well, as the ANC MP Willie Hofmeyr conceded in 1995 when he told a Moslem meeting in Cape Town, 'I don't want to say the ANC's hands are clean.' But he also suggested that revenge was a motive and some of the violence was orchestrated by criminals. 'The rotten carcas of apartheid is still lying there and smelling,' he added. The ANC, he went on, welcomed the arrest of ANC people involved in violence, who should be tried and imprisoned if convicted. There was, though, another troubling factor: suddenly, when peace talks (especially between the warring parties in KwaZulu-Natal) were near a constructive outcome, 'there is another massacre'.[79]

Faren Kassim, the representative of the Inkatha Freedom Party (by now a political party in its own right), noting that the conflict had been going on for 15 years, spoke of 'the tears in our province [which] never dry'. Many on the ground started violence, she admitted, even though at the national level the IFP did not favour such an approach. Yet when families who had suffered knew the police would do little or nothing, 'people act on their own'.[80]

Nelson Mandela himself had written to Chief Buthelezi from Victor Verster Prison in 1989, urging national unity and hoping that cordial relations could be restored between Oliver Tambo and himself and between Inkatha and the ANC.[81] But after his release, he came to believe that the Nationalist Government, working through Inkatha, was responsible via 'hit squads' for violence against ANC activists. He reiterated this in December 1992, alleging that 'the state security services, using certain black organizations have been responsible for the death of no less than 15,000 people since 1984'. Though there were difficulties with MK as well, these were the result of 'infiltration by government agents'.[82]

Speaking in Mamelodi, near Pretoria, in April 1993, Mandela went further. 'I'm not going to blame the IFP and the Government only,' he confessed. 'We must face the truth – our people are just as involved in violence.' ANC supporters found guilty would be disciplined and even dismissed from the organization. There had to be political tolerance and organizations like the IFP should be allowed 'to do their political work'.[83]

His speech was made shortly after the murder on a school bus of six children on 2 March 1993, three of them sons of an IFP branch chairman. This event had caused Chris Hani to comment, 'We were jolted by the massacre of the children, the ten people in the minibus, as well as the armed ambush of a bus by ANC supporters.'[84]

Chief Buthelezi, too, was muted in his address at the funeral, urging supporters not to avenge the children's deaths, whereas only the previous year he had told the Inkatha Youth Brigade that unless they 'bugger up the ANC they are going to bugger up you and your future',[85] using the same kind of 'killing talk' he had accused the ANC earlier of using against his supporters.

The outlook was grim, not only in KwaZulu-Natal, but also in the rest of South Africa, for violence made potential investors uneasy and lack of investment from abroad would destabilize the country. 'I am not an apologist for the IFP,' Cosmos Desmond wrote in 1995, 'but I do believe that the ANC and its surrogates in academic and NGO circles must come to terms with the fact that Chief Buthelezi and the IFP have a rock-solid base in KwaZulu-Natal, particularly in the rural areas.' Indeed, he continued, Chief Buthelezi was seen as a defender of their Zulu-ness – 'what means he uses to achieve this is not their concern'. Moreover, Buthelezi was the key to the solution of KwaZulu-Natal's problems. If the ANC had made an accommodation with the Nationalists, 'why cannot they recognize the role that Buthelezi has played: a role they did recognize until 1984...'[86]

'What would forgiveness of the ANC mean for the IFP?' Craig McEwan has asked.[87] Here is the critical question for KwaZulu-Natal after so much bloodletting. Certainly Chief Buthelezi is aware of the issue of forgiveness, as Nelson Mandela is, too. 'I think that in many ways there was an element of compromise

STRUGGLING TO FORGIVE

inherent in the political rationale of previous generations of black (and white) activists that is rapidly becoming extinct within the breasts of today's young radicals,' Chief Buthelezi once wrote. 'Some have already lost these precious human qualities.' Yet he hoped the revered spirit of African humanism could be reborn and that Africans could 'learn to love' and to agree and disagree with intelligence and humility. There had been too much hate, distrust and betrayal. 'It has tainted us all and it is time we moved on.'[88] Moreover, the forgiveness which was required had to come from God.[89]

THE ROLE OF THE INDIAN COMMUNITY

The power struggle in KwaZulu-Natal between the IFP and the ANC affected others, too. There are many minorities within the province and the situation there highlights the complex relationships between Africans and Afrikaner and English-speaking South Africans, and African relations with the Indian and Coloured communities.

The Indians, as Bishop Rubin Phillip has commented, unconsciously remember the 1949 conflict in Durban,[90] a violence which left them 'in a state of insecurity that persists until today', according to Alan Paton. Some doubtless also remembered the injustices and inequalities involved in domination by 'a powerful white elite' who often behaved abominably.[91] Indeed one Anglican priest at the time saw Indians pursued and struck down as white onlookers jeered. The hall of his church, however, had become a haven. Another priest, the Rev. Alphaeus Zulu (later Bishop Zulu), also recounted a redemptive story of how a Zulu parishioner saved his Indian landlord and family by 'putting them in a truck wearing *doeks* like African women, with the men at the back shouting Zoo-loo-zoo-loo!'[92]

The Indian community, focused in Durban and Pietermaritzburg, also had Afrikaner pressures to deal with, for it, too, was uprooted under the Group Areas Act. Moreover, for decades Indian people had no adequate representation in Parliament. Some joined the ANC, many playing a prominent part, both in exile and within South Africa itself, as Fatimer Meer has explained.[93] By the 1970s the National Party itself was uneasy about its relationships with both the Indian and the Coloured communities, and so in 1973 appointed the Theron Commission which reported in 1976, recommending a Tri-Cameral Parliament.

The 1977 General Election therefore included in its programme three separate Parliaments, for whites, Coloureds and Indians, each with a Prime Minister and Cabinet. Common interest legislation was to be referred upwards to a Council of Cabinets, presided over by the State President, himself elected by a college of 50 whites, 25 Coloured and 13 Indians representing the three Parliaments, and assisted by an Advisory President's Council of white, Coloured and Indian experts.[94]

Earlier Indian communities had raised their own money for schools, though there were also subsidies. After the 1984 Constitution, however, the Tri-Cameral Parliament was able to alter the situation, though not supported by all. Indeed, as Mrs I. Gandhi, Gandhi's granddaughter, has commented, 'it was possible to make quite drastic improvements in Indian communities'.[95]

With the ANC in power, some Durban Indians now fear they will be denied business, education and commercial opportunities because of affirmative action policies, which favour appointments from the African community in an attempt to redress past discrimination and inequality. Consequently, in their attempt to protect their livelihoods, they are more likely to vote for the National Party, despite its record of racial oppression, or for the Democratic Party, or even for the IFP, because of its commitment to private enterprise.

Some Indians have personal stories to tell, of course, like Bishop Rubin, who experienced racial injustice when he was banned for three years. Later, as a priest in Pretoria, he narrated his experience to his congregation, tears coming down his cheeks as he spoke of Chris Hani's murder. A shift in attitude occurred among them as they listened. When he left for a new job in Durban, it took two and a half hours for the young people to say goodbye as they thanked him for helping them become more aware. Some, too, said, 'Sorry for what we've done.'[96]

'Throughout a 135-year chequered stay in South Africa,' Ram

STRUGGLING TO FORGIVE

Maharaj, Chair of the Hindu Development Trust, said at the time of Divali in 1995, 'we have largely remained true to Mahatma Gandhi's course of non-violence.'[97] In 1993 in the Diocese of Natal, where Bishop Rubin works, a final recognition of this tradition was given when a statue was erected in Pietermaritzburg in Gandhi's honour. 'Gandhi's moral force continues,' Fatimer Meer, the editor of *The South African Gandhi, 1893–1914*, has observed, 'and each year his birthday is celebrated. There is no single aspect of Gandhi's philosophy which was not crystallized here.'[98] There is also, besides Gandhi's Phoenix Settlement, near Durban, a Gandhi-Luthuli Peace Park, to remind KwaZulu-Natal (and South Africa too) of this part of their history, an inheritance likely to become high profile through the film of Gandhi's time in South Africa, *The Making of a Mahatma*.

Fatimer Meer is one of those who have supported the ANC for decades. 'There are,' she has observed, 'a handful of Indians who feel their destiny lies with the African people.' A veteran of resistance campaigns in 1945, 1952 and later (she was banned in 1954, 1976 and again in 1981), she feels that justice, not forgiveness, for apartheid's architects is the issue. Even though her house was bombed continually and in 1977 an attempt was made on her life, she is not interested in finding the culprits. 'I have forgiven these people,' she has observed drily, realizing they were just 'instruments of a certain kind of thinking'. It was important now for the Indian community, which was more privileged in the later apartheid years, to be willing to make sacrifices, along with others. 'All must suffer a little bit,' she says, so that the unemployment figures are equal for all communities. 'Is that restitution?' she asks.[99]

Few Indians will support Mrs Meer's view, however, but many will try to be forgiving in the Gandhian tradition. 'One's life is but a pendulum that swings between a teardrop and a smile,' Ram Maharaj wrote in 1995. 'Hate is too much of a burden to bear. While we may not forget, we human beings have the capacity to forgive.' 'Let us be good and do good,' he added, despite the rampant violence and crime, for non-violence provides the only path to peace and progress, based as it is on a conviction that the universe itself is on the side of justice and that those who struggle for it enjoy 'cosmic companionship'.[100]

THE CONTRIBUTION OF THE
COLOURED COMMUNITY

For the Coloured community in South Africa such a faith in the
future is most problematic because the community's identity is
so complex. With a San, Khoi, African, Malay and Afrikaner background, it can justifiably describe itself as fully Afro-European.
An indication of how Afrikaners themselves feel about the group
they too often shunned became clear in the Theron Commission
report, which was unhappy about both their status and the health,
housing and welfare facilities provided for them, making several
recommendations to improve their situation. This was a slight
step forward after their earlier loss of parliamentary representation, and the unsatisfactory nature of the Coloured Person's
Representative Council, which could so easily be manipulated by
the Government.[101]

Surprisingly, overall there was little revolt, especially among
the Coloured community in the Cape, though a number of its
leaders joined the ANC. When Nelson Mandela was first released,
crowds naturally came to hear him, but many were annoyed when
he spoke in Xhosa for they only understood Afrikaans.[102] In the
1994 elections many, indeed, voted for the National Party, no
doubt because scare tactics were used, but also partly because of
their dual identity and the link the ANC had with the South
African Communist Party. 'They would rather align themselves
with the pre-oppressor than with the pre-oppressed,' the Rev.
Simon Adams has observed of voters in the Stellenbosch local
elections in November 1995, when many voted NP, though overall in the Western Cape their support for it has declined.[103]

This identity problem and their minority status presents the
Coloured community with a difficult problem. Not surprisingly,
therefore, in 1995 a Coloured Liberation Movement was launched
to foster Coloured Nationalism. 'The Coloured people have been
humiliated for 300 years,' Mervyn Rees alleged, 'first by the
whites and now by the blacks. We must take our rightful place
again.' He then demanded the return of vast tracks of land taken
by Dutch and British colonialists from the Khoi and San and
claimed that the ANC-led Government's policies of affirmative

action excluded Coloureds because an application form for a job often stated that 'those applying must speak an African language'. 'The rise of Coloured Nationalism,' an ANC document warned in March 1995, could not be dismissed as 'racialism'.[104] Indeed, at an ANC rally in the Northern Cape in May, Nelson Mandela himself was at pains to reassure the Coloureds.[105]

Some members of the Coloured community have piercing insights into South African society, but many are still bitter about being dispossessed from District 6 in Cape Town. 'Whites,' says Simon Adams, 'are schizophrenic about other groups. They need to be educated in what it means to forgive and be forgiven. It's time for us to launch missions to white people now we've got our political freedom.' They feel superior, too, he feels, 'which makes it impossible for them to reach out to blacks and browns'. There is a problem with the African community as well, for 'when Mandela uses the phrase "our people" what does it mean to the Indian and Coloureds?'[106]

The poet and playwright Professor Adam Small also sees these complexities when he asks, 'What is the coloured identity?' The son of a Moslem mother and a Calvinist father, he became sensitized to the Coloured identity very early on. Not now worried about the use of the word 'Coloured' to describe himself, and influenced earlier by Black Consciousness, where the word 'black' covered any who were not white, he has become aware of a wider Afrikaner identity, which includes all for whom Afrikaans is a first language. 'There is, too,' he has observed, 'a coloured experience – intuitive, and not a white or a black or Asian experience.' 'What is forgiveness in all this?' he asks, for he sees a need for reconciliation between all those with Afrikaans links.

It is a theme he has tried to explore in his play *The Orange Earth*, which he wrote in English when he felt unable to use his own language because Afrikaans was the oppressor's language. It ends with an Afrikaans prison officer and a Coloured prisoner discovering that 'they are blood brothers'.

In real life Professor Small sees a similar reconciliation occurring, with F.W. de Klerk, an Afrikaner who 'left the Afrikaans house', but who, like the prodigal son, returned home. 'Therefore like the prodigal son he must be forgiven,' he comments. 'We've only started on that. We need time.'[107]

Adam Small has perhaps summed up his whole attitude in a poem he once wrote. In 'There's Somethin' , he lists everything that can be denied him – drinking pepsi-cola at the café; going to the theatre; boarding a carriage; or sitting at the front of a bus. He can be prevented from going to hospital in the same ambulance as whites, too, or from worshipping with them. But, he concludes, there is one thing no one could do: stop a person being loved however bad they have been.[108]

Three other people epitomize not only the variety of the Coloured community and its poetic qualities, but also the power minorities often possess to infect majorities with their attitudes. One is the poet, Dennis Brutus, who left South Africa in 1965 after a time on Robben Island. That same year he wrote that when people understand how fear undermines and corrodes, forgiveness is easier.[109]

More recently, Johann Magerman has shown how forgiveness can help a person reach out to wrongdoers, as on BBC radio he recalled the policeman he had seen inflict violence on fellow citizens during the period of the 1989 municipal elections, actions which included pointing a gun at himself. 'I believe you did that to kill me that day,' he said in a talk. 'We were both regarded as Coloureds. And yet you chose to align yourself with an institution that was morally bankrupt, made up of people who took pleasure in the death of their fellow South Africans.'

He hated the policeman after that incident, partly because he never apologized or asked for forgiveness. His grudge remained a burden until he saw a video of Father Michael Lapsley's response to the attempt to kill him with a parcel bomb. Now 'all I want to do is to forgive you', he has indicated to that policeman, not only in an attempt to rid himself of the burden of hate, but because he believes 'this is the only way for true and meaningful reconciliation'.[110]

Perhaps most astonishing of all has been the spirit of a mixed-race family in Cape Town, who were the last to be evicted from District 6. Interviewed on a BBC television programme, 'Last Supper in Hortsley Street', the father, a Moslem, said as his wife and family viewed their home disconsolately, 'I do not know what they do, and yet I do know what they do.' Then he added reflectively, 'May God forgive them.' Two thousand years ago Jesus said, 'Father, forgive them, they do not know what they are doing.' Amazingly, this man seemed able to reach similar heights of compassion for his tormentors.[111]

Chapter 5

Forgiveness and Healing –

The Role of the Churches

From the perspective of the churches in South Africa, healing has two dimensions: it is a gift of God, which is then mediated from one person to another or through the church as a whole. Without some transcendental aspect, words are too frail to enable adequate healing for all the brokenness. Wounds and scars there will certainly be for many years, and many painful memories and histories which will still scald. There will be guilt, too, on the part of those – some of them regular churchgoers – who committed dreadful crimes, for whatever motives.

The Christian churches (and the other world faith communities, too) have both a short- and a long-term role to play in assisting the healing process at the local and the national level. With their emphasis on penitence and the possibility of change through repentance; with the willingness on the part of some of the African churches to allow God to heal, clearly resources are available. Counselling and assistance for those who have been traumatized will be necessary, too, to help both victims and perpetrators work through their experiences. Such schemes, even if modest, can blaze trails, so that over the years more and more people can know a deeper healing.

The fact that the suffering of so many years has been acknowledged helps sufferers to feel support from and solidarity with others, particularly if it is offered locally. There is room, of course, for argument about which is more helpful – the vertical relationship with God, or the horizontal one between church members. What is incontrovertible is that countless stories have been listened to and many victims have refused to be crushed by what has happened to them.

Before the churches of South Africa, either individually or corporately, can act as agents of healing, however, they must first also address the fact that their own hands are not clean. There was far too much collaboration by the churches with apartheid's authorities, or at the very least silent acquiescence in evil doings.

THE CHURCHES AND LIBERATION

Christians, along with people from other faith communities, have been scattered through all the movements for liberation in South Africa, but the churches, as corporate entities, have also played a part. Many Christians, of course, watched from the sidelines, perhaps confused about the interactions between Church and society. Others – from Dominee J.F. Naudé, Beyers Naudé's clergyman father and one of the founders and first Chairman of the Broederbond,[1] to the Rev. Michael Lapsley, with his counselling work among ANC members in Harare – have taken sides and paid the price.

'I am in Congress precisely because I am a Christian,' Chief Albert Luthuli wrote in his autobiography. 'My Christian belief about society must find expression here and now and Congress is the spearhead of the struggle.'[2] He was but one of a number of Christians – like the Congregational minister the Rev. John Dube, the first President of the ANC, and the Rev. Z.K. Makgatho, its third President, a Methodist minister who was President of the Interdenominational African Ministers' Federation (now IDAMASA)[3] – who took seriously Christ's injunction to love God and neighbour and became committed to political affairs.

But it was one thing for individual Christians to become engaged in such action and quite another for South African churches themselves to be so involved as corporate bodies. Inevitably, of course, they were. Indeed, the seeds of the Dutch Reformed Church's attitude to the different races, which was then implemented by the National Party when it came to power in 1948, can be traced to a decision in 1878 to give in to those whites who objected to sharing a Communion cup with blacks. This was followed in 1881 by the establishment of the NG Sendingkerk for Coloureds as a separate missionary church.[4]

THE CALVINISTIC CHURCHES

'Do you know what the NGK is admired for most among our people?' Dr Piet Meiring once asked, citing a black NGK minister's remark. 'For the fact that at times of humiliation and hardship for the Afrikaners, the church associated itself one hundred per cent with the aspirations of the *volk*.' This was especially true after the Anglo-Boer War, when the Dutch Reformed Church actively opposed the attempt by Lord Milner to prevent the use of Afrikaans as a medium of instruction in schools, and in the 1930s depression when poor Afrikaners streamed to the cities for work. 'Can the NGK not now,' queried Meiring, 'when it is the turn of the blacks to go through the same process, stand behind them in the same way?'[5]

During the apartheid years Professor Meiring was one of a number of ministers who questioned the state's policies from within. Later, in June 1980, 22 Western Cape NGK ministers sent a letter to its highest executive, asking it to outlaw church council decisions which excluded blacks from the white church.

That September a 28-year-old minister told his conservative congregation in Boshoff, a small, rural town in the Free State, that apartheid was not needed 'because we are all children of God'.[6] His action sparked off months of discussion and argument in Church and press and he was reprimanded by the Moderator of the Free State Synod, though many supported his plea.

Earlier, in 1978, on his appointment as Minister of Health in the Bophuthatswane Cabinet, Dr Jacques Kriel and his family joined a DRC black daughter-church congregation when they moved to Mafeking, but his church refused to transfer his certificate of membership. 'It was liberating to experience the communion of the saints in such a manner in a black church,' Dr Kriel said when interviewed.[7]

In June 1982, 123 ministers and theologians of the white DRC churches published a letter in the official newspaper of the Church rejecting the Government's racial policies on scriptural grounds. This had a more profound effect than an earlier, less dramatic, 'witness' of eight theologians in November 1980, though this still caused a lengthy and bitter debate inside the NGK.[8] In August

1982 a meeting in Ottawa of the General Council of the World Alliance of Reformed Churches, to which the NGK and the NHK (Nederduitsch Hervormde Kerk) churches belonged (they had ceased to be members of the World Council of Churches much earlier), declared apartheid a heresy and suspended their membership.

They would be warmly welcomed back, the Council said, when black Christians were no longer excluded from church services, especially Holy Communion; when concrete support in word and deed was given to those who had suffered under separate development; and when unequivocal synod resolutions were made rejecting apartheid and committing the Church to dismantle such a system in both Church and society. Apartheid, they observed, was not only a political policy but a 'pseudo-religious ideology', depending to a large extent on moral and theological justification.[9] The Rev. Allan Boesak, who had been involved in these considerations, was made President of the World Alliance of Reformed Churches, later resigning from the post because of allegations about his conduct which cast doubt on his credibility.

The 1982 letter from the 123 NGK ministers had included a confession which spoke of their deep guilt before God 'because we ourselves do not sufficiently practise the unity of the Church of Christ'. Moreover, they were 'co-responsible for many of the social inequities' to which they had drawn attention.[10] 'I dare say the main reason why Afrikaner Christians have been so slow in confessing their guilt is precisely that others – for whom nothing was at stake – have tried so frequently to bludgeon us into it,'[11] the missiologist David Bosch, one of the few Dutch Reformed Church figures associated with the South African Council of Churches (SACC), has added, drawing attention to the individual and corporate confessions of guilt which were being expressed, some of them publicly.

On 29 August 1985 a regional NGK body confessed at its annual meeting that the personal and structural racism in society was contrary to love of neighbour and of justice. Indeed, apartheid had created misery, frustration and injustice, negative realities which the NGK had often uncritically tolerated. It was now prepared, it continued, to be critical and honest, with others 'to seek prayerfully for a meaningful alternative' and alleviate suffering wherever possible. David Bosch concluded:

At long last the process has begun. No longer dare we argue that the others also have guilt and that they, too, must confess their guilt and repent. Perhaps they have guilt. But that is of no consequence to us. We dare not make our confession of guilt and repentance subject to or dependent upon them. We dare not even demand forgiveness; we may not withdraw our confession of guilt if the other party fails to forgive us. Confessing our guilt is in itself a supreme blessing and a sign of grace. It opens up the fountains of new life and cleanses us.[12]

In Cape Town the following year the General Synod initiated a process whereby the church changed tack. In 1990 in Bloemfontein it presented a revised version of its document *Church and Society*. Here, whilst offering the right of freedom of expression in their own cultural milieu, the Church made it clear that not only must this 'not take place at the expense of others', but the Church itself had also not sufficiently understood apartheid. This had received an ideological and ethnocentric basis where freedom to remain true to one's cultural heritage had become a political ideology for 'the protection of the white minority's own interests to the detriment of others'. Attempts to defend this biblically were fallacious, it stated. Moreover, the system of migrant labour, because of its disintegrating effect on family life, should be eliminated or restricted to a minimum. Marriage between partners of different faiths and religion was not unscriptural but could cause much tension, it added, concluding that the DRC did not see itself as a national Church in the sense that 'church and nation are identified as one'.[13]

Thus in a clearly worded and balanced document – which also argued it would be unreasonable to 'brand as wrong and bad everything which took place within the political structure of apartheid'[14] – the DRC distanced itself from its past. By 1994, in response to an invitation from the Coloured and African churches, who had formed the Uniting Reformed Church and invited the Indian and white DRC churches to join with them, a bold proposal was put forward at the Synod not only calling for a firm commitment to unity, but also setting in motion a process which it was hoped would lead towards structural unity 'in the near future'.[15]

This was accepted by an overwhelming majority, though the implications would take several years to work out.

A further indication of the change which had occurred came when Nelson Mandela (speaking in Afrikaans) addressed the Synod for 20 minutes, the first head of state to do so. He did not mince his words, but also said he was gratified to know things had changed. At the end of his address the Vice-Moderator, calling him 'Madiba' (a term indicating great respect), finished with a phrase in Xhosa, the organ quickly gave a chord and all rose to sing Psalm 134, a custom normally observed for ministers.[16] Later a Synod committee set up procedures for the support and commendation of the Government's Reconstruction and Development Programme (RDP).

THE ENGLISH-SPEAKING CHURCHES

As far as the so-called 'English-speaking' churches are concerned, there is a long history of opposition to apartheid by their leaders, if not their congregations. For example, in 1957 Dr Verwoerd, then Minister of Native Affairs, introduced a clause intended to force racial segregation at worship in the 'non-racial churches', as they were termed. The churches, including the DRC, protested strongly, with Archbishop Clayton of Cape Town leading the way. The church clause was modified, only allowing the state to prevent black Christians from worshipping with white ones if there were complaints that they were a 'nuisance' or worshipping in 'excessive numbers'.

Successive Anglican Archbishops – from Joost de Blank and Robert Selby Taylor down to Desmond Tutu – all took similar stands, though in different ways. Selby Taylor, for instance, took the view that unobtrusive but firm influence was more likely to be successful in combating injustice and righting wrongs than stridency and courting overseas publicity.[17] Archbishop Bill Burnett expressed his opposition more bluntly in an open letter to Prime Minister Vorster in September 1976: 'Unless white Christians in particular admit the wrongs they have done to Black people and take action to redress them,' he wrote, 'there can be no possibility of healing in our land.'[18] In 1992, in a lecture commemorating the Roman Catholic Archbishop Stephen Naidoo, Archbishop Tutu called again for an apology for apartheid from the State President.[19]

Some Anglicans, of course, paid for their witness with their lives. Victor Afrikander, a priest in Imbali and Chair of the Pietermaritzburg Council of Churches, was shot dead driving the six-year-old daughter of a relative to school,[20] and Phakamile Mabija, a youth worker in the Kimberley Diocese, died when he allegedly fell from the sixth-floor window of a police station where he had been in detention.[21] Nyameko Barney Pityana, too, who had succeeded Steve Biko as SASO's President, was banned and restricted to Port Elizabeth from March 1973. Only his mother and doctor were allowed to visit him at home, to which he was confined from 6.00 p.m. to 6.00 a.m. on weekdays, weekends and holidays with few exceptions. He was also detained in 1977, under Section 6 of the Terrorism Act, one of the draconian pieces of legislation which existed to suppress opposition. He was kept naked for some time in his cell, though he was given blankets. His wife was also taken in under Section 10. In the end the family left South Africa for Britain, where Pityana equipped himself for the Anglican priesthood.[22] 'It is still too early for forgiveness. People still feel too raw,' he said in 1995, remembering not only his own family's experience but all the others who had been maltreated.[23]

Methodists and Roman Catholics also played their part. In 1976, 25 Methodist ministers appealed to the World Methodist Council for support, admitting the guilt of their Church, asking for help to challenge its apartheid practices and seeking financial help for detainees. Indeed, as the Roman Catholic Archbishop, Denis Hurley of Durban, has observed of the struggle for human and constitutional rights: 'The first in the field were the Methodists with pronouncements of their governing body, the Methodist Conference, going back to 1947, and reiterated and enlarged upon in 1948 and subsequent years.'[24] In fact even in 1926, when the Government was passing repressive laws, a Methodist magazine editorial had affirmed the equality of all people and attacked the British Government of the day.[25]

Nevertheless, it was only in 1963 that the Methodist Church had its first black President, and not until the 1980s that all its main office-bearers were black, although an overwhelming number of Church members were African. The Rev. Otto Ntshanyana, the Methodist minister in Khayelitsha, the large black city on the edge of Cape Town, is typical of several caught in the dilemma of many black Christians. When some wanted to take the law into their own hands he would ask: 'What is going to happen if you kill because of what has happened? The church should bring the peace of hope.'[26] As a Methodist preacher he felt that he could not go for military training. His brother took a different view and spent 25 years on Robben Island for his subversive activity.

With others, Otto Ntshanyana found himself caring for the families of those whose menfolk, and sometimes womenfolk, were either in prison or working with the ANC and other groups in exile. His brother was released in 1987, with no regrets about his actions and with a capacity to forgive what had been done to him. Now Otto Ntshanyana plays a new but mediating role in Khayelitsha, available to help in community conflicts but declining either to be an MP or Mayor.

White Methodists, too, were caught in dilemmas, some refusing to serve in the Armed Forces. Their Church urged members to vote 'No' to the proposals for the Tri-Cameral Parliament, because it was a way of continuing to exclude Africans from government. In the 1994 election, however, it advised members to vote as their consciences led.

The Roman Catholic Church also tried to affirm the multi-racial nature of South African society, seeking to ensure that its schools were open to all. But, from the time of the murder of Sister Mary Aidan during the 1952 Defiance Campaign right down to the 1986 pastoral letter, the Church sought to handle the conflicts circumspectly. 'We sorrow at the hatred which is abroad today in our country and we see to what terrible consequences it can lead,' Archbishop McCann declared following Sister Mary's death. 'But there can be no hatred in our hearts for the perpetrators. The African people mourn with us and join in common sorrow with the Europeans for the loss of a brave nun who loved and served them with true Christian charity.'[27]

Sister Mary, who worked in a church clinic in East London on the South African coast, had been caught one Sunday afternoon in the middle of a crowd, which had ostensibly gathered for a prayer meeting in a town square but was in reality a political meeting. Police tried to disperse it but were unsuccessful and Sister Mary, who was driving her car through the area on her way home, was stopped, attacked and stabbed to death and her car set alight with her in it. Her remains were cannibalized. Her rosary was found in the ashes of the car, her fingers burnt into the beads. Later, when the rosary was dropped on to a sheet of paper to be photographed, those who saw it were struck by a coincidence: it had formed the outline of the African continent.[28] 'Would the rioting in East London – and across South Africa – have ended had the Africans of East Bank location not recoiled in revulsion from her murder?' asks her biographer.[29]

By the time the young people of Soweto rose up in 1976, the Southern Africa Catholic Bishops' Conference accepted that it had been lagging behind 'in witness to the Gospel in matters of social justice'[30] and expressed a willingness to be more concerned about the struggle for liberation and development. At another time of violence, in 1986, the Bishops issued a pastoral letter which cautioned all and served as a warning to Catholics. They did not call for the oppressed to accept their situation but urged them to fight to abolish it by legitimate means, partly because of their 'very hope, their very love for those who oppress them'.[31] Motives must be kept in perspective, and vengeance repudiated along with any hope of power for power's sake or of dominating those who had dominated them.

During the State of Emergency declared by President P.W. Botha in June 1986, even the secretary of the Bishops' Conference, Father Mkhatshwa, was arrested and detained without trial, along with many others. In prison for a year, he was 'harassed, assaulted, insulted, humiliated and physically tortured'. Shortly after his release he wrote: 'I would never advise the clergy and religious to get involved in any activity which, though legal and peaceful, could result in their arrest and detention, and yet I feel disappointed that there were not more priests, bishops, sisters and brothers in detention.'[32]

STRUGGLING TO FORGIVE

Later becoming an ANC MP, Father Mkhatshwa feels he can look back on his experience without rancour, despite the extreme nature of his torture, because he considers there is a difference 'between remembering and wanting to be bitter'. 'It saps our strength and our energies,' he has added, 'which should be devoted to building for the future, even with our former enemies and former torturers.'[33]

Now the Regina Mundi Catholic Church in Soweto, which had been a focus for much opposition to apartheid, became even more involved in the struggles of the community against Afrikaner oppression. When, therefore, in 1995 the theologians responsible for the Kairos Document (which sided with the poor and oppressed) wanted to commemorate its tenth anniversary, it was in Regina Mundi's garden that they erected their simple memorial: 'In memory of countless known and unknown victims and martyrs of apartheid.'

THE KAIROS DOCUMENT

The Kairos Document was published only days after the launch in September 1985 of the National Initiative for Reconciliation, a fellowship of some 400 church leaders from a wide spectrum, called together by Africa Enterprise (later known as African Enterprise). The NIR had as one focus a belief that a new South Africa could emerge on a small scale through renewed relationships based on Christian conviction. But it gained little ground as many blacks responded more enthusiastically to the Kairos approach.

'Thus the NIR was forced to come to terms with the relation between reconciliation and social justice,' one of its leaders has explained. 'As it happened, the NIR moved to critical solidarity with the Kairos theologians: it shares their concern for structural justice but has reservations concerning some theological, analytical and strategic details of the Document.'[34]

'The crisis which gave rise to the Kairos Document,' Albert Nolan has observed, 'was not just apartheid. Nor was it the crisis which was created by P.W. Botha's declaration of a State of Emergency.' Rather it was caused by the fact that apartheid and the State of Emergency (involving tear-gas and maiming and killing) were being perpetrated in the name of Jesus Christ 'while the major Christian churches remained silent or responded with weak, unprophetic statements'.[35]

A group of Christians, mostly ministers, meeting in Soweto shortly after the State of Emergency declaration, described this crisis as *kairos*, a time when God called them both to choose and act. Gradually more became involved, aided by the staff of the Institute for Contextual Theology, one of several dynamic groups the South African situation had created.

'It would be totally unchristian to plead for reconciliation and peace before the present injustices have been removed,' the document considered. 'Any such plea plays into the hands of the oppressor by trying to persuade those who are oppressed to accept our oppression and to become reconciled to the intolerable crimes that are committed against us. This is not Christian reconciliation, it is sin. It asks us to become accomplices in our own oppression, to become servants of the devil.' There could be no reconciliation or forgiveness and no negotiations without repentance for the Bible made it clear that none could be forgiven and reconciled with God without repentance of sins. 'Reconciliation, forgiveness and negotiation will become our Christian duty in South Africa,' the Kairos Document concluded, 'only when the apartheid regime shows signs of genuine repentance.'[36]

As the issues it raised – violence, the legitimacy of the South African state, civil disobedience, reconciliation and forgiveness – were debated during 1986–7, several controversial statements were picked up by the press and focused on by critics. But elsewhere, especially in international Church circles, the document's stress on three types of theology – State, Church and Prophetic – were noticed. The first justified the status quo, described as an idol or false God. The second was the name given to opinions emanating from 'English-speaking' churches, with their emphasis on reconciliation, justice and non-violence. The third, the theologians observed, required careful social analysis and a biblically-based interpretation of the *kairos*, beginning with the people's suffering, spelt out in the context of the scriptural understanding of oppression and liberation.

At a press conference on 25 September 1985 at the SACC head-quarters, journalists attended in abundance, which meant that the material reached a wide public. In some townships there was wild enthusiasm, but in Government and white church circles there was great indignation, particularly where the churches were urged to support the campaigns of the people 'from consumer boycotts to stay aways'. They should, moreover, not only pray but mobilize members in every parish 'to begin to think and work and plan for a change in government in South Africa', said the Kairos theologians.[37]

Consciences were stirred within South Africa and outside, and the document was reprinted and translated into several languages. In 1989 Christians from nine Third World countries published *The Road to Damascus: Kairos and Conversion*, which told how they were applying to their own situations the insights they had learned from the South African document. Professor Bonganjalo Goba, a founder member of the Institute of Contextual Theology and by 1995 Chairperson of the United Congregational Church of Southern Africa (UCCSA) and Director of the Institute for Multi-Party Democracy, regarded the Kairos Document as 'the highlight of my pilgrimage as a Christian theologian'.[38] It is not surprising, therefore, that the UCCSA General Secretary of the time was one of the few church leaders to sign the Kairos Document originally and his Church one of those which tried to work out how to review and transform its structures and ministries.[39] John Kane-Berman, however, blamed the signatories for the intensification of the conflict in South Africa, which had led to an increase in violence, because of their support for the armed struggle.[40]

CHURCH–STATE TENSIONS

'The last twenty months since May 1986 have been the darkest part of the tunnel in the life of the people of South Africa,' the Rev. Frank Chikane, then secretary of the SACC, told a conference of church leaders on 2 February 1988. He reminded them of recent events – the scuttling of the Commonwealth Eminent Person's Group peace initiative; the violence of the state against any protests; the emergence of vigilantes and assassination squads; the deliberate creation of conditions for so-called 'black on black' violence; and the assault on the labour movement, including a sophisticated military attack on the building of COSATU. 'The list is endless,' he concluded. During the Christmas period of 1987, however, he had received a card from the Tutus which said: 'The light is shining in the Darkness and the Darkness cannot overcome it.' It was a message to cheer and strengthen what remained of him, 'which was almost at the point of death'.[41]

Considerable tensions now emerged between Church and state, precipitated on February 24 1988 by the Government's clampdown on 17 extra-parliamentary opposition organizations and leaders such as Albertina Sisulu and Archie Gumede. On February 29 the SACC drew up a petition for the State President and MPs and processed from St George's Cathedral in Cape Town to Parliament to present it. The 25 church leaders who took part were all arrested en route but released shortly afterwards. They declared that they would not be stopped by the state from campaigning for the release of prisoners, or from calling for clemency for those on death row, the unbanning of political organizations and the release of political leaders, or from urging negotiations. They also asserted their right to commemorate significant events and to ask the international community to apply pressure 'to force you to the negotiating table'.

Only the previous week, they added, they had issued a statement urging the oppressed – who would finally decide when apartheid died – to intensify the struggle for justice and peace and not to lose hope, for victory against evil was guaranteed by Christ.[42] The statement was signed by the President of the Council of African Independent Churches, as well as by Methodist, Roman Catholic, Anglican, Lutheran and Congregational leaders, the Moderator of the DRC's Sendingkerk and the Call of Islam Muslim Juridical Council. There followed an often lengthy and spirited exchange of letters between President P.W. Botha and some of the signatories. On 7 April, 44 university and seminary theologians sent a letter to the press supporting the church leaders. 'The church has a clear Biblical basis for its protest,' they maintained, 'and is in accord with the mainstream of Christian tradition in resisting injustice.'[43]

From the 1960s the churches grouped together in what became the South African Council of Churches had spoken out against the Government. 'When others inside the country were gagged and could not speak and could not travel and others were thrown in jail,' Nelson Mandela has said, 'it was the Church that kept the fire burning and kept the ideas for which they were suffering alive.'[44] With 10 of its 16-member executive black, in 1972 the SACC had been declared a black organization because its membership at grass-roots level was overwhelmingly African.

All was not plain sailing, however, for to make a stand against apartheid led to a fight on two fronts – against the Government and sometimes against one's own church. This fact became more evident when the contents of the 'Message to the People of South Africa', published in June 1968 and calling on the South African churches and population to reappraise the nature of apartheid society in the light of the Bible, was not taken up by the Council's member churches.[45] When it came to statements and exhortation, as Archbishop Hurley has observed, the churches were often very forward looking, but failed nevertheless to get the real gospel appreciated at the grass roots.[46]

Yet through the journal *Pro Veritate*, with its concern for economic justice and insistence that Christians should only give ultimate obedience to Christ not the state, and then through the Christian Institute, the nearest South Africa ever came to a Confessing Church on the 1930s German model (though there was much discussion about creating one), there were creative attempts to move South Africa beyond its constricted life. The Institute survived until 1977, sponsoring specific schemes and supporting individuals and groups, as well as playing a significant role in the SPROCAS reports on the future beyond apartheid society.

In the late 1970s, the state tried to clamp down, setting up the Eloff Commission to investigate the affairs of the SACC. This resulted in a court case in which the state tried to prove that the SACC, representing some 12 million people, was a front for the Communist onslaught against South Africa. The SACC was acquitted and it continued its work for victims of apartheid, as well as upholding its stance on particular issues like the right to conscientious objection to serving in the Armed Forces. The Baptist Richard Steele's experience gives an indication of how difficult this was. One of the first religious conscientious objectors in South Africa, he spent a year in military detention and, because he refused to wear prison uniform, suffered long periods in solitary confinement. Yet he could still say, 'I now believe more firmly than ever that the Christ-like way of forgiveness, love and servanthood, is right.'[47]

The difficult task of the SACC became clear again at the end of the 1980s when the member churches, despite target bombs which destroyed Khotso House (their head office) and Khanya House (the headquarters of the Roman Catholic Bishops' Conference), launched with others the Standing for the Truth Campaign in 1989. This involved defiance of segregated beaches, hospitals and buses, and in some areas there were marches which called for the release of Nelson Mandela.

At the beginning of the 1990s, with F.W. de Klerk as the new President, and Professor Johan Heyns as Moderator of the main Dutch Reformed Church, more constructive approaches became possible both in politics and in the relation of churches to each other and to society.

In an interview with his brother, F.W. de Klerk was clear. 'It is a matter of principle to see that the Church should convey the Biblical guidelines on politics,' he said. 'The vast majority of South Africans are Christian, and churches cannot escape their responsibility to motivate their members to strive for the principles of justice, fairness and communality in politics.' The same applied to the other faiths. But God's grace was needed to make a new beginning and work together for peace with justice as the lodestone. 'I am not asking for National Party rhetoric from the Church; what I am asking is the message of forgiveness and renewal also in politics,' he ended.[48]

De Klerk proceeded to invite Dr Louw Alberts, a noted Afrikaner physicist who chaired the Council of Scientific Research, to convene a meeting of Christians to consider what he had suggested. The churches of the SACC were not willing to respond, however, because the initiative came from the State President, whose predecessors had been in major conflicts with it.

After negotiations in June 1990, F.W. de Klerk withdrew and a new group emerged, made up of some of Dr Alberts' contacts and some from the SACC's constituency, chaired jointly by Dr Alberts and the Rev. Frank Chikane.

THE RUSTENBERG CONFERENCE

There had, of course, been church gatherings before – at Cottesloe in 1960, for example, organized by the World Council of Churches, the findings of which had led to the DRC churches leaving the World Council, and in Durban in 1973 and Pretoria in 1979, both organized by Africa Enterprise. At the former, blacks and whites had considered mission in South Africa[49] and at the latter, some 6,000 church leaders and members had met.

One of the most significant moments of the second gathering had been the testimony of a militant member of the Soweto Committee of Ten, who explained how she had been freed from hatred, a statement which reverberated across the country and in Soweto itself.[50] But there had never been anything to compare with the November 1990 Rustenberg Conference, as it came to be called. Here for the first time Charismatic and Pentecostal, Baptist and Dutch Reformed representatives joined with Methodist, Congregational, Anglican, Roman Catholic and African Independent Churches' delegates, as some 230 church leaders, from 80 denominations (some from abroad), and 40 para-church groups, met to work towards a united witness in changing South Africa.

Despite reservations from some participants, a consensus was reached. 'For the first time we condemned the system of apartheid together with those who supported it in the past,' the Rev. Frank Chikane has written. 'We have confessed the sins of our past together to our Lord Jesus Christ and to one another.'[51] At the heart of the gathering, during an address which explored how difficult it was to bring together two types of theology – those of resistance and of reconciliation – an unexpected confession was made by Professor Willie Jonker from the University of Stellenbosch, one of the most respected leaders in the Dutch Reformed Church. Some months before in the Church's inner councils he had been working on the text of a confession of sins which was later accepted by the Synod.[52] Now he shared the confession with a wider group, admitting that the DRC could do little more than acknowledge its guilt and ask for forgiveness and acceptance. Without it, mutual trust could not be restored, nor could they continue as though nothing had happened, for apartheid's wounds and racism were still present.

'The broken relations between the Churches cannot be healed by synodical decisions alone. An experience of reconciliation is necessary to enable us to come to a united witness,' he explained. 'I confess before you and before the Lord,' he continued, 'not only my own sin and guilt, and my personal responsibility for the political, social, economic and structural wrongs that have been done to many of you, and the results of which you and our whole country are still suffering from, but vicariously I dare also to do this in the name of the Dutch Reformed Church of which I am a member and for the Afrikaans people as a whole.'[53] He had the liberty to do this because at its Synod the DRC had declared apartheid a sin, confessing its own negligence for not distancing itself from it long ago, and warning against it.

His statement set the conference on fire. 'Professor Jonker made a statement that certainly touched me,' said Archbishop Tutu, 'and I think touched others of us when he made a public confession and asked to be forgiven.'[54] As he had explained earlier, when confession had been made, 'then those who have been wronged must say "We forgive you," so together South Africa could be re-built'. He made this present response, he continued, 'under pressure of God's Holy Spirit'.[55]

A dispute now arose despite the fact that the confession was by the white DRC leadership, citing decisions of their recent Bloemfontein Synod, but the black DRC remained unhappy. Tutu therefore made a further intervention, making it clear he had accepted the confession only on behalf of himself. He reminded the gathering, too, how people like Walter Sisulu had come out of a long prison sentence with an incredible capacity to love, no bitterness or longing for revenge, but a deep commitment to renew South Africa. 'I am humbled,' he went on, 'as I stand in front of such people.' Then he admitted that his own church had to

STRUGGLING TO FORGIVE

confess its racism and he, too, had to ask himself how often he had treated people as less than God's children and what his share was 'in our common sin'.[56]

Archbishop Ndumiso, from the Federal Council of African Indigenous Churches, spoke for many others when, after explaining how reconciliation and justice were linked, he pointed out how futile it was to throw stones at one another. Ways had to be found to build trust, but these could not prevail without 'repentance, confession, or forgiveness'.[57] The delegate from the Order of Ethiopia was, as it turned out, prophetic when he gave thanks at worship that God was calling white South Africans to give up 'the security of legislated and unlegislated privilege',[58] and black South Africans to forgive and embrace whites, so all might be ready to share socially, politically and economically.

During the conference there was a second unexpected confession, when Pastor Ray McCauley from the International Fellowship of Christian Churches said that the Fellowship, too, despite its short history, recognized its guilt: opposition to apartheid had not been effectively expressed, and convictions often had not led to practical action, while others had adopted a so-called neutral stance which resulted in complicity. 'We confess that our silence in these areas was in fact a sin,' he admitted, and failure to act decisively had made the Fellowship party to an inhuman political ideology. 'We ... repent of our sin and declare our complete rejection of all forms of racism and the evil, unjust system of apartheid. Please forgive us.'[59] The Fellowship, he said, was now resolved to play an active part in building a new South Africa.

When Beyers Naudé spoke, he maintained that no healing was possible without reconciliation which involved justice, but no justice was possible without 'some form of genuine restitution'. All churches needed to participate in an expression of guilt for apartheid, but the DRC especially, so could the DRC family of churches not consult widely in the black community 'and organize a gathering at, for example, Blood River, Bloemfontein or the Voortrekker Monument, to make their confession of guilt known'? This could be a deeply moving gathering where forgiveness could be asked for and received. He also wanted an apology to the World Council of Churches for the serious wrong which the

DRC had done to it after the Cottesloe Consultation. 'How easy it would be to say: "We are sorry. Forgive us", ' he concluded.[60]

A year previously, such a conference would have been unthinkable, as Archbishop Tutu had indicated in his opening sermon.[61] Now, at its end, 'The Rustenberg Declaration' was adopted, which included an extensive section on confession and restitution, more detailed than the explorations called 'Confessing Guilt in South Africa' which the SACC had recorded in the late 1980s. Though the South African situation owed much to Western colonialism, the Rustenberg Declaration focused on contemporary problems and remembered in sorrow apartheid's victims. To appropriate God's forgiveness, there must be practical restitution and genuine repentance, it continued, with reconciliation flowing from justice – a process which began with a penitent Church.

They confessed, therefore, that some had actively misused the Bible to justify apartheid and had later insisted that the motives were good, though the effects were patently evil. The churches' slowness to denounce apartheid as sin had 'encouraged the Government to retain it.'[62] Others had spiritualized the gospel, separating individual salvation from social transformation, and an allegedly neutral stance had resulted in complicity.

Yet more had been bold in condemnation but timid in resistance, and some churches had given no effective support to courageous individual protests against evil. Even when they had spoken out against injustice, their own structures 'continued to oppress'. Some were guilty of colonial arrogance and had allowed state institutions to 'do our sinning for us'.[63] Others had been more influenced by ideologies than the gospel, moving in separate worlds, yet claiming the Church was one body. The pain of black Christians had been insulated against while the culture of violence had remained unchecked. Faltering witness had led to the break up of families, lack of education for children and unemployment for millions.

Above all, the churches had been unwilling to suffer and even apartheid's victims themselves had contributed to the churches' failure 'as they acquiesced in and accepted an inferior status, and some became willing instruments of state repression'. Others had exhibited a desire for revenge, while those who had achieved privilege had exploited others, as indifference to suffering 'crept into our communities', where any who stood for justice and truth were ostracized. Yet more had allowed growing intolerance to go unchecked, or neglected to make theological contributions to the churches' renewal.

'With a broken and contrite spirit,' the delegates' statement concluded, 'we ask the forgiveness of God and of our fellow South Africans. We call upon the members of our Churches to make this confession their own. We call upon the Government of South Africa to join us in a public confession of guilt and a statement of repentance of wrongs perpetuated over the years.'[64]

The churches in South Africa were now urged to adopt the confession and pledge themselves to restitution.[65] Political leaders were called upon to set up a peace conference with those who could help end violence.[66] A National Day of Prayer was encouraged for the purpose of 'intercession, confession, forgiveness and reconciliation'.[67] A fresh agenda was needed in terms of a new economic order.

'Have we taken Rustenberg seriously?' Beyers Naudé asked about a year later, when nothing substantial had materialized, partly because of difficulties about follow-up. 'What have we done with the decisions and declarations made at Rustenberg?' Moreover, there were two large and growing groups of African indigenous churches who needed to be taken seriously. 'What has been the active, meaningful response by our members to Rustenberg?' he enquired. 'It has not been there.'[68]

One thing which did emerge from Rustenberg, however, were the decisions of the DRC to become an observer member of the SACC and of the Roman Catholic Church to become a full member. 'Anti-apartheid theologian Dr Beyers Naudé ... wept last Wednesday,' reported one paper, when the DRC was welcomed back to the SACC. 'This is a very deeply moving experience,' he said. 'This is the moment for which I have prayed and worked for so long.' Perhaps as moving was the fact that it was the Rev. Sam Buti, a former general secretary of the DRC daughter-church, the DRC in Africa, who had made the proposal to admit the DRC. 'This is the church that theologically supported apartheid,' he was quoted as saying. It had been courageous enough to say: 'We have been wrong, forgive us.'[69]

'In spite of our past – the albatross of apartheid around our neck,' Professor Piet Meiring observed, 'we found brothers again in the church ... But the DRC especially has to live with what it has done for many years and to show by deeds as well as by words its change of heart.'[70]

THE CHURCHES AND THE
NATIONAL PEACE ACCORD

Bishop Mogoba of the Methodist Church, who had led the final worship at Rustenberg, had taken the declaration with other church leaders and presented it to Nelson Mandela. Imprisoned for alleged PAC activities he had not engaged in, on Robben Island Mogoba had read the Bible, which had changed his life and led him into the Methodist ministry. For 30 years he had preached peace and reconciliation between blacks and whites, blacks and blacks and whites and whites, arguing that there was 'no earthly reason why we should choose to bleed ourselves before we sit down to work out a formula for peace'.[71] At Rustenberg he had mentioned his bad treatment on Robben Island and urged that the forces of hatred and racism be removed by God as they had been in him.[72]

Now in 1991 he found himself able to implement what he had been advocating as early as the mid-1970s for, with a business leader, John Hall, he headed up the National Peace Accord. 'When you are speaking about forgiveness in South Africa by church people who love, Mogoba comes first,' Chief Luthuli's relative Mrs Goba has observed. 'He is not speaking out of his head, but from his heart. Stanley surprises many, because he has suffered. His is a powerful testimony.'[73]

'On Robben Island it was difficult to forgive the people who were doing so much to you,' Mogoba admitted in a television interview when he was awarded the World Methodist Peace Prize in 1995. 'However feelings of anger eat you up more than the other person.'[74]

Aware that the black theology movement and the SACC's involvement with the Dependent's Conference (set up to help the victims of apartheid, especially families in distress), of which he was Vice-Chair, had helped to 'redeem the tarnished image of the Church,'[75] he now became an enthusiastic Vice-Chair of the Peace Accord. The Anglican John Hall, who chaired it, went through his own spiritual transition as the Peace Accord developed. He came to realize the importance of forgiveness, which became an important emphasis in many meetings,[76] as he often saw 'divine intervention in action, when mistrust and misunderstanding might have destroyed the path to a just dispensation for all.'[77]

Peace was given a new opportunity following F.W. de Klerk's speech on 2 February 1990 in which he announced the unbanning of the liberation movements and their leaders. Yet ironically there was even more fragmentation now than in the 1980s, with an escalation of violence in KwaZulu-Natal between the ANC/SACP/COSATU alliance and the IFP. By August of that year strife had been imported to the Johannesburg area, where single-sex hostels occupied by Inkatha-supporting migrant workers had become armed fortresses – though latterly the Rev. Mvume Dandala, from the Methodist Church in central Johannesburg and now the Presiding Bishop of the Methodist Church of Southern Africa, played a significant mediating role which helped the violence abate. Civil war also broke out in some black townships, between the inhabitants (usually ANC-supporting) and the hostel dwellers. Atrocities became normal, complicated by a shadowy 'third force' from within the Government which helped fan the flames by providing arms and training for Inkatha warriors.

The violence had different purposes in different places, but much was designed to halt or slow down the process of negotiation which was now in train. Sometimes fighting broke out when a party felt marginalized, or where an opportunity occurred to destabilize opponents. Self-Defence Units – 'rag-tag formations of armed youth', according to Bishop Peter Storey[78] – were created by the ANC, followed by the Self-Protection Units of the IFP, and when they clashed there was little mercy. The killings ran into thousands and were escalating further in 1991.

THE NATIONAL PEACE ACCORD

At this point major religious and business leaders said 'Enough!' In a clear display of moral and economic power through shuttle diplomacy, all the political leaders were finally 'pulled or pushed'[79] into accepting a code of conduct, to be monitored by civil society. Only in this way, they considered, could negotiations towards a new Constitution and the first democratic elections, which were in the offing, be secured. The result of these initiatives was the National Peace Accord, hammered out by all parties involved and signed on 14 September 1991.

Here were laid down codes of conduct for political parties and organizations; for the police; and the setting up of regional groupings to consider socio-economic reconstitution and development. There was also a section on the establishment of a Commission of Enquiry under a Supreme Court Judge, with a National Peace Secretariat to oversee the works. Once the Peace Accord had been signed by 29 groups – but not by AZAPO, the PAC, the Conservative Party or the far right-wing AWB (Eugene TerreBlanche's Afrikaner Resistance Movement) – the churches in their formal capacity receded into the background, and more so after the setting up of the National Peace Secretariat, the various peace committees across the country and the Goldstone Commission of Enquiry into the Prevention of Public Violence and Intimidation.

'In the local and regional peace committees in some areas the churches appeared to be left out because the politicians organized the meetings there with the police, representatives of the Government and business people,' Dr Mogoba has commented. So he told them they must invite themselves and when they did this, 'they immediately became leaders'.[80] Where churches stood back and waited, however, nothing happened.

Committees at every level were supposed to consist of people from all sections of society, including the churches. Not only were party relations very tense, but both the IFP and the ANC were at loggerheads with the police, accusing them of favouring one side or the other.[81] Because of the mistrust, committees were often chaired by business or church representatives, but as all parties were bound to attend, slowly atmospheres began to improve.

STRUGGLING TO FORGIVE

Team-building exercises were conducted at weekends, where some discovered that it was possible to conceive of non-violent ways to deal with conflict.

Bishop Storey, the Vice-Chair of the Wits/Vaal Regional Peace Committee and Chair of the Religious Bodies and Police/Community Relations Committee, went to meetings knowing that some present had been involved in fighting the previous night, yet he and his colleagues persisted.[82] 'After the Hani assassination, the country was poised on the edge of disaster,' he has reflected. 'It was then that the peace committees came into their own. Arrangements for the funeral were handed to the Peace Accord. Its structures handled the entire event and so won the confidence of all parties. From then on scores of events were organized in the same way.'[83]

A process of face-to-face discussions instead of fighting had to be accepted, as in the first Soweto meeting, where for several hours the IFP stuck to one point. People were so polarized they would not sit next to one another, but by the fourth meeting they were willing to do so. Val Pauquet, the Peace Trust secretary, has recalled that ANC representatives came in and greeted the police, whom they knew by name, and she makes an analogy between her ability to see Archbishop Tutu as a normal person after meeting him at Rustenberg, and how the militants from Soweto found the police General was normal, too.

Because of the mix of people in the National Peace Committee, 'the element of forgiveness was always there,' she has reflected, 'but not articulated as such – it was a thread running through the process'.[84] So it was in many local groups, though people were often more aware of the need for conflict resolution. This, however, always implied a certain way of looking at opponents. As the Rev. Liz Carmichael has observed, regional and local Peace Committees offered people in conflict-ridden situations the opportunity to resolve their conflicts in an alternative way.[85]

At its National Conference in July 1993, however, the SACC criticized the National Peace Accord for being tied to the Government through its funding relationship. It also accused white technocrats and business people especially of hijacking the Accord and so undermining its legitimacy and accountability at the grass roots. The National Association of Democratic Lawyers saw the domination of whites and business interests in leadership positions as being responsible for the Accord's inability to stop the violence. However, Jayendra Naidoo, formerly on the National Peace Secretariat, regarded this as largely unavoidable. By 1992 most black leaders were already committed elsewhere and as non-aligned personnel were sought to chair the peace committees, it was not easy to find others instead. Moreover, whites had skills which were much needed. 'These people were acceptable in black communities,' he has asserted, 'as people who would facilitate in good faith.'[86]

Not all situations were resolvable. Together with other members of the National Peace Committee, for example, Bishop Mogoba found himself standing between Ciskei soldiers and pro-testors, when without warning the soldiers opened fire. 'We hit the ground and lay there until the shooting ended,' he recalled. 'When we got to our feet twenty-eight people were dead and more than twenty injured.'[87] There were other problems, too. 'It is true,' observed Archbishop Hurley, who co-chaired a regional committee, 'that we were babes in the wood when the peace structures were formed. But we have learned.'[88]

'The peace structures have never really got to the root of the conflict in areas run by tribal authorities,' admitted Port Shepstone's local Peace Committee Co-ordinator, Bruce Walker. 'Most difficult of all is trying to mediate clashes between powerful IFP-supporting traditional leaders, who control many rural areas and ANC supporters, especially youths.'[89] Indeed, because of their peace work two local peace monitors were killed and two injured while patrolling Bhambayi, and the Rev. Richard Kgetsi, a member of the Port Shepstone Peace Committee, was assassinated in November 1993.[90] Although senior members of the ANC and the IFP seemed to want peace, factions on the ground disagreed, as has been admitted by the Rev. Danny Chetty, director of Practical Ministries, a church organization helping victims of violence, and Chair of the Port Shepstone local peace committee.[91]

Government funds for the Peace Committees ended on 31 December 1994, except in KwaZulu-Natal, where the provincial government funded them. 'People are saying we must run down.

But we have a tremendous contribution to make to the stability of the country,' the Rev. Chin Reddy, director of the Northern Transvaal Peace Committee, observed at the time. 'In terms of our activities very little has changed. There are still boycotts, marches and strikes, and we are constantly being called on to mediate or monitor.'[92]

Nevertheless, in March 1995 all peace structures officially ceased to exist. But once the Government of National Unity was in place, itself the custodian of the Peace Accord, John Hall was invited to address MPs. Dr Frena Ginwala, the Speaker, said the National Peace Accord had three important components – an awareness that South Africa was on the edge of a precipice; an ability to involve all sections of the population in monitoring and mediating through the structures created; and a perception that there was a clear link between peace and development.

'I want to say,' Dr Mogoba said, summing up the National Peace Accord's work, 'that the real failure has come, not from the Peace Accord or the Peace Committees, but from our political leaders. They have let us down as far as peace is concerned. They tended to politicize peace.'[93] At the time of the South African local elections in November 1995, he reflected: 'Human beings do not find it easy to be forgiving. But Christians have been forgiven and Christianity has forgiveness at its centre … That is why the Church is needed.'

'Reconciliation,' he added, 'will be very difficult. But reconciliation is an ingredient of peace.'[94]

THE AFRICAN INDEPENDENT CHURCHES
AND THEIR ROLE

Part of this peace process is bound to be more successful if it can involve the nearly 12 million Christians in the African Independent Churches, 80 per cent of whom belong to the Zion and Apostolic Churches and 20 per cent to the Ethiopian. Indeed, during the decade 1980–90, while mainline churches lost some 28 per cent of their members, the independent churches in townships and rural areas grew substantially, often through small-scale units which acted as an extended family. The Ethiopian Church, more overtly political than the others, may well hold one of the keys to the healing needed, for it has a holistic approach to living, and stresses the power of God's Holy Spirit to help churches care and share in fellowship.[95]

'The main line churches,' considers Professor Pippin Oost-huizen, 'need to ask forgiveness of the independent churches,'[96] aware that many westernized Christians have intellectualized their faith while the African traditional approach to religion has withstood such cultural onslaughts. Indeed, they have continued to emphasize healing, the wholeness of all life, the importance of ritual, especially cleansing and reconciliation rituals as in *Ukuthelalana amanzi* (to pour over water), a traditional Zulu ritual of reconciliation.[97]

The other part of the healing process will inevitably involve Christians in KwaZulu-Natal, where about one-fifth of South Africa's 40 million people live. Within the Province the Diakonia Council of Churches (for the Durban area), the Pietermaritzburg Council for Social Action (PACSA), and Africa Enterprise, as well as the KwaZulu-Natal Church Leaders' Group and the newly-formed KwaZulu-Natal Christian Leadership Assembly, are all trying to grapple with the immensity of the problems facing them, including the highest rate of political and criminal violence in South Africa. 'Each weekend,' said one pastor at an Africa Enterprise day seminar in October 1995, 'I know I will be burying people. What can I say to their families?'[98]

There needs to be, said another, both weeping and repentance, for they go together. 'South Africa must be made ungovernable', had run the slogan of the 1980s. Now KwaZulu-Natal was reaping the whirlwind. Any pastors who had supported the slogan should come forward, plead guilty, and ask for forgiveness before things could move on. Moreover, they needed to make it clear they were wrong as role models. One DRC pastor at the seminar, present at such a gathering for the first time, then admitted: 'We made lots of mistakes. And we are very sorry about that,' but he hoped people would not keep 'going on' about the past.

There had to be a recognition, too, another pastor suggested, that the achievement of liberation had come through the shedding of black blood. 'We must,' added a colleague, 'see and experience forgiveness in our province. Forgiveness means repentance, confession and restitution.' Moreover, the churches themselves had to put their house in order: transcend their divisions, admit they turned a blind eye when people were dying. 'How,' another asked, 'can those who have killed admit what they have done and seek forgiveness unless first the church leaders, and the politicians, too, confess?'[99]

'Are Quebec and Natal comparable?'[100] asked the Rev. Athol Jennings, one of those responsible for helping the growth of mediation and skills training, as well as conflict resolution work in the Province. If this is so, then all the peace and development work of the churches both nationally and province-wide, and all the fervent evangelical witness of groups like Africa Enterprise, will have been in vain. Once again, as before in South African history, Natal seems to hold a key position with regard to South Africa's future. The work of the churches in this Province is therefore crucial.

A start has been made with the KwaZulu-Natal Christian Leadership Assembly of March 1996, and the involvement of church leaders in brokering peace overtures between ANC and IFP leaders, which led to relatively peaceful provincial elections in the middle of 1996. Despite the IFP vote dropping to around 46 per cent, it remained the largest party and so formed the provincial government, though the ANC, with just over 33 per cent, and the NP, with nearly 13 per cent, indicate that in the Province there is a subtle balance of forces at work.

Perhaps the Africa Enterprise weekends held in the 1980s – when people as diverse as Carel Boshoff Jr of the Afrikaner Volkstaat and Vimleka Rajbansi, daughter of a veteran Indian politician, met and came to a deeper understanding of their respective viewpoints and histories[101] – are a harbinger of what can happen in KwaZulu-Natal as the violence abates. Yet greater concern for one another can come only through a deep forgiveness, for the scars and wounds in KwaZulu-Natal especially will not easily go away.

Chapter 6

Forgiveness and Justice –

The Role of the Truth and Reconciliation Commission

There is something within human beings which cries out for justice as a right. Indeed, one way to understand the phenomenon of revenge is to interpret it as a form of wild justice when real justice is not available. Yet eventually bloodletting, feuds and historic grievances must cease if communities are to live at all creatively.

It is remarkable that South Africa, well aware of the demands of justice, has set up the Truth and Reconciliation Commission as a way to handle the wrongdoing of the apartheid period. To opt for truth rather than strict justice (if, in fact, that were in reality attainable at all) shows a measure not only of wisdom but of courage.

Before an amnesty can be given by the State President, the details of the wrongs done have to be acknowledged and the person or people concerned have to accept that their actions will be publicly known. In that sense justice is done. In another sense, of course, that is the only punishment, except for one of inner conscience.

As the Truth and Reconciliation Commission has developed, Commissioners have found themselves in many complicated situations and have uncovered wounds that will remain unhealed long after the Commission's Report is completed in 1998. Such deep brokenness as the report will reveal will need addressing, perhaps by voluntary and professional groups, skilled both in trauma counselling and in the healing of memories.

There may well be unforeseeable consequences from the Commission's work, too, so all concerned for South Africa's future will need to watch the process carefully as it develops and be ready to give assistance as required.

This chapter was written, of course, before the Commission had finished its work and submitted its final report to President Mandela, but essentially the issues with which it deals have been covered, even if particular stories have not been detailed.

SOUTH AFRICA'S JUSTICE PROBLEM

'When our Nuremberg comes – and the trials go on in private, inside us, already,' Nadine Gordimer once said,[1] no one would deny that it was a legally elected white minority Government which had passed oppressive laws. The churches of South Africa, of course, had originally tried to alleviate the suffering caused but they, too, fell victim to some of the legislation.

'Mankind comes to this court and cries "These are our laws – let them prevail",' said Lord Shawcross, one of the Nuremberg prosecutors, in 1996 as he recalled the time when 10 Germans were hanged after a long effort to identify and punish the architects of the Third Reich's racial and military policies.[2] In the case of the Nuremberg trials, of course, one group of nations was victorious and one nation lost, so there was an inevitability about the result, as the international community established the concept of prosecutions for gross human rights violations and the principle of individual responsibility for illegal acts.

Dealing with human rights abuses in South Africa was very different from the German situation. Firstly, there had been an internal conflict with no victor or vanquished. Secondly, some in government after 1994 had held high office during the apartheid years. It had become clear during the peace negotiations that action was needed, the ANC calling in 1993 on those who had committed crimes against their people 'to break ranks with the past and expose the master minds behind these treacherous acts'.[3] But the National Party was determined there could be no Nuremberg-type trials.

THE MECHANISM OF THE TRUTH AND RECONCILIATION COMMISSION

The Truth and Reconciliation Commission (TRC) therefore emerged as a compromise approach and was legally established as part of the Promotion of National Unity and Reconciliation Act passed in 1995 after 200 hours of parliamentary debate. The Act, based on the principle that 'reconciliation depends on forgiveness and that forgiveness can only take place if gross violations of human rights are fully disclosed', offered amnesty to the perpetrators of 'acts associated with a political objective'[4] committed between 1 March 1960 and 5 December 1993, a date later extended to May 1994. Unless there had been broad agreement on how to deal with the past, one journalist commented, 'there would have been no settlement and no peace'.[5]

Amnesty International itself had suggested in 1994 that pardon be granted only after trial and conviction,[6] and in a speech prepared for the Commission, Professor Kader Asmal conceded that 'the Nuremberg approach would probably enjoy the support of most human rights organizations' but this would not be conducive to reconciliation 'and could be construed as a witch hunt'.[7] Forgiveness could come only after full disclosure of the facts, with reconciliation dependent on people coming to terms with the past. 'The generosity of the majority must not be interpreted as allowing the minority to believe in their collective innocence,' he warned.[8]

'The South African Commission will be unlike the Nuremberg trials in that it will be concerned with truth not justice,' Andre du Toit had said at a gathering convened by Justice in Transition to review its proposed activities.[9] It was with this end in view that President Mandela had signed the Act in May 1995, telling journalists later: 'Only by knowing the truth can we hope to heal the terrible open wounds that are the legacy of apartheid,' adding: 'Only the truth can put the past to rest.'[10]

There had, of course, been indemnities from prosecution already, through the Indemnity Act of 1990, which was amended in 1992 but later repealed, though the indemnities granted remained and temporary indemnities or immunities stayed in force for a year.[11] Under the 1992 Act, for example, 55 people had received indemnity 'in respect of acts with a political objective', including some who had refused military service, or deserted from the defence force in the late 1980s. Others from the right wing, the ANC, the IFP and the PAC, were released from prison and indemnified, but only a handful from the security forces had received similar indemnities.[12] Some, like Thabo Mbeki, had also received temporary indemnity from prosecution through a law allowing them to return from exile in 1990.[13]

However, pressure from the security establishment, which wanted blanket amnesties proclaimed, led the Government to introduce the Further Indemnity Bill at a special Parliamentary session in October 1992. It was rammed through the NP-dominated President's Council, despite opposition from white liberals and the majority Solidarity Party in the House of Delegates. Here it was blocked, with the Delegates arguing that criminals could not pardon themselves and that an ANC-led Government would repeal the indemnity, as had happened to a similar Act in the Argentine. The Bill had proposed secret hearings before a judge, presiding over a national council of indemnity appointed by the President, who had discretion over final decisions. Only the names of those pardoned would be made public, their crimes and their victims remaining secret.[14]

A further development occurred shortly before the 1994 elections when President F.W. de Klerk signed clemency orders for 3,500 policemen and two former Cabinet ministers, Adriaan Vlok and Magnus Malan. Knowledge of this only appeared in early 1995 when the matter came to the attention of the new justice minister, Dullah Omar, a leading member of South Africa's Moslem community. A Cabinet meeting held then considered that no indemnity from prosecution 'was acquired or granted in these cases,' the Cabinet Secretary reported, adding that the police named could still pursue their applications for indemnity through the courts, or through the TRC.[15]

During the ensuing controversy Pik Botha, the former Foreign Minister, said the indemnity applications had only ever been registered, never granted. It transpired that the collective application for the 3,500 policemen had not specified, as was legally necessary, the offences for which they were seeking indemnity. 'It was,' observed one commentator, 'an orchestrated thing. 3,500 applications in the space of four days, even by people who did not ask for it.'[16] ANC militants, on the other hand, *had* disclosed offences when more than 8,000 of them had won amnesties during the earlier negotiations.

The approach of the Truth and Reconciliation Commission was substantially different from what had gone before, though the NP negotiator, Danie Schutte, a member of the last white Cabinet, warned that any insistence on separate moral status for apartheid soldiers and guerrillas of the ANC's armed wing could undermine reconciliation.[17] Those who had argued for its establishment were influenced substantially by the experience of some 15 Truth Commissions, including those in Argentina (1984), Chile (1991), El Salvador (1993) and others in Uruguay, Zimbabwe and Ethiopia, as well as the experience of amnesties in former Eastern-bloc countries, but the process was necessarily tailored to South African needs.

The thinking behind the TRC, which could last for two years, after which a report with conclusions and recommendations would be sent to the President, led to the creation of three committees, one dealing with amnesty and indemnity, one with human rights violations and a third with reparations for victims. Each committee was to be chaired by a member of the Commission, aided by skilled colleagues. 'I could have gone to Parliament and produced an amnesty law,' Dullah Omar wrote, 'but this would have been to ignore the victims of violence entirely. We recognized that we could not forgive perpetrators unless we attempted also to restore the honour and dignity of the victims and give effect to reparation.'[18]

According to the Government Act establishing the Commission, it had no power of prosecution, or any juridical function, but could subpoena witnesses and had search powers and access to all documents. Only if perpetrators detailed their actions would they receive the amnesty offered, and their names would be published in the *Government Gazette*, together with information identifying the acts for which amnesty had been granted.[19] Those seeking amnesty had to apply by 15 December 1996, a date later extended to 31 May 1997. Amnesty Committee hearings, if necessary, would be held in public, unless its members and the Supreme Court Judge chairing it, decided otherwise.

The Human Rights Violations Committee, empowered to set up an investigating unit, had authority to record allegations and complaints, make recommendations and collect and receive articles relating to gross human rights violations. Information in its possession could be made available to the other committees. The committee dealing with reparations and the rehabilitation of victims was to consider matters referred to it by the other two, and gather evidence about the identity, fate and whereabouts of victims and the nature and extent of their sufferings. It could also make recommendations, which might include urgent interim measures of reparation. In consultation with the Justice and Finance Ministers, the President could set up a fund for such victims with money from Parliament and other donors.

Although the Commissioners were independent and had a full-time staff, it was acknowledged that they would need to cooperate with voluntary organizations. Indeed, human rights organizations, psychological and social support services, as well as religious groups, had the potential to complement the Commission's work. The 17 Commissioners were chosen from a list of nearly 50, selected by a panel chaired by President Mandela's legal adviser, from nearly 300 nominees from civil society, religious and other interest groups, with the public free to object to nominees.

Potential Commissioners were each asked the same questions – what was the role of a Commissioner; which of the three groups most suited their experience and interests; and, more personally, what obstacles might there be to their becoming a Commissioner. The very first interviewee, Professor Hendrik van der Merwe, who did not become a Commissioner, startled some by explaining that he believed in retribution as part of the process. 'My feeling is that some form of punishment is essential in a society like ours,' he told the panel. 'It is part and parcel of our moral code, our legal system and our theological belief, and I feel that the public embarrassment that would come with revelation to the Commission is a form of punishment,' though he added that forgiveness had to accompany such exposure.[20]

Archbishop Tutu, later appointed to chair the Commission, with the former Methodist minister and politician Alex Boraine as his deputy, was at pains to draw attention to a phrase he had noticed at Dachau: 'Those who forget the past are doomed to repeat it.'[21] He hoped, therefore, that the Commission would open wounds in order to cleanse them. Reconciliation, in his view, was not cheap and was based ultimately on forgiveness and repentance, which depended on confession.

When the final names were known – six of them women, including Yasmin Sooka, the President of the South African Chapter of the World Conference of Religion and Peace – it was clear that the President, with Cabinet approval, had opted for those with human rights records, psychological and social work backgrounds, and some from the world faith communities. He also appointed two who would enhance the resonances across South Africa's divides: a Methodist minister from KwaZulu-Natal and a civil rights advocate from Cape Town, who had been the selection panel secretary. Later more were added to the committees, though they were not in fact Commissioners. Not all were happy with the appointments, of course, one IFP spokesman worrying about the possible party-political affiliations of some members and the Democratic Party leader saying it appeared the Commission's representativeness had taken preference over its independence and impartiality.[22] However, because the legislation precluded people with a high political profile, it was probably inevitable that the emphasis would tilt towards those from the human rights arena, social welfare and religious constituencies.

'There is not a single person who has not been traumatized by apartheid – even the perpetrators. We have to pour balm on tortured souls,' Desmond Tutu had said in 1994.[23] Now he was presented with one of his greatest challenges, not only relating to 17 very varied Commissioners but also handling the complex dynamics the work of the TRC implied. 'He is determined,' wrote one reporter, 'that the Commission should focus not just on the apartheid regime but also on crimes committed by the liberation movement such as the ANC atrocities in Angolan detention camps,'[24] adding that Tutu favoured as broad a process of forgiveness as possible, provided those who perpetrated murders or torture could prove they acted politically.

By February 1996, by which time the TRC had begun its meetings (which opened with prayers suitable to its multifaith membership), Tutu was explaining that it was 'totally impossible' for the Truth Commission's Human Rights Violations Committee to hear evidence from a potential 100,000 cases – a figure worked out by human rights organizations – or investigate every single case. Instead they must discover the extent of the violations and if a pattern existed, and also recommend structures to ensure 'similar things do not exist again'.[25] A number of groups had promised cooperation and he had asked for a meeting with Chief Buthelezi.[26] In the end the ANC and the NP made two formal submissions and the Democratic Party, the IFP, the South African Defence Force (SADF) and its successor the South African National Defence Force (SANDF), and the South African Police (SAP), also made a submission. Later there were also submissions from the churches, the media and businesses.

The first visit of the Reparations and Rehabilitation of Victims Committee was to Port Shepstone, on the south coast of KwaZulu Natal, deliberately chosen because the wounds were 'still fresh' from recent massacres. Here it met with representatives of local communities, the churches, welfare and health organizations, the police and research bodies. Some, however, cautioned against individual financial reparations which might create dependency. Rather, reparations should be aimed at communities, since they had suffered as much. There was worry, too, that rural people might feel the process for gaining help was too cumbersome, as they had with the Government's 'victims of violence' fund which involved filling in complicated forms.[27]

As the hearings proceeded – which involved listening to the details of the horrific deaths of two Indian activists, Suluman Saloojee and Ahmed Timol, both of whom were alleged to have fallen from high buildings while in police detention,[28] and of Mapetla Mohapi, a Black Consciousness leader, who had also died in detention[29] – it was evident that the Commissioners themselves would need help. Each evening, therefore, debriefing sessions were arranged where they could talk about the work they were doing and 'process the feelings and emotions they go through', as Commissioner Glenda Wildschutt, from the Trauma Centre in Cape Town, explained. Journalists covering the Commission's work were also offered counselling facilities if required.[30]

PHILOSOPHICAL AND PRACTICAL DIFFICULTIES

Not all were convinced of the need for a Commission, of course, and some were uncertain about its role. 'At best the Truth Commission is likely to open deep wounds inflicted by the apartheid policies,' wrote the Rev. Buti Tlhagale. 'Once disclosure has been made surely civil litigation at least should be the order of the day. Disclosures cannot be made without a tinge of vendetta especially where the courts have failed to identify and prosecute individuals.'[31] Moreover, the Government of National Unity implied forgiveness – 'working with the murderers', as he expressed it forcefully.[32] The Roman Catholic Bishops initially had reservations, too, because they were acutely aware that hostilities had not ended. Might not reprisals and revenge be exacted from the public disclosure of perpetrators' names, they queried, especially in KwaZulu-Natal, where experience had shown revenge attacks were commonplace? Moreover, the possibility of witch-hunts on the part of relatives could not be ruled out.[33]

In the view of Rabbi Ivan Lerner, from the Claremont Hebrew Congregation in Cape Town, the Commission was 'a tragic mistake', for the investigation of past misdeeds could 'only be divisive'. If anything, the Commission would stir up the anger and animosity of whites and Zulus who were 'still uncomfortable with ANC majority rule'.[34]

Bishop Peter Storey, one of the panel of eight which drew up the list from which the final Commissioners were selected, responded immediately to this criticism. The Rabbi's view that South Africa's fragile miracle was in danger because the Commission would serve neither a healing nor helpful purpose, and should be disbanded, was what propagandists 'want us to believe', he wrote. They wanted people to believe that the TRC was an 'exercise in retribution and an obstacle to reconciliation'. Granted the Commission was risky and could go badly wrong, it was nevertheless a courageous attempt to deal honestly 'with the process of cleansing and forgiveness'. The heart of the matter was the Rabbi's confusion of forgiveness with forgetting. On the contrary, Bishop Storey explained, South Africa should not deny its past for the sake of its future, for the degree to which white South Africans could truly celebrate liberation and become part of 'our new nation' was in direct relation to their awareness of the suffering inflicted. However, unlike Nuremberg, or the Truth Commission in Chile, the South African Commission offered perpetrators the opportunity 'to come forward voluntarily and individually to confess. And then, if the disclosures are truthful and fit into the parameters of politically motivated crimes, it says they will be forgiven. That is amazing grace'.[35]

The families of Steve Biko and the Durban human rights lawyers Griffiths and Victoria Mxenge also disagreed with the TRC and tested the legality of the Commission in the Constitutional Court, saying they wanted justice and the chance for the law to weigh evidence in the normal way. The Court, however, ruled against them. In due course the killers of Steve Biko applied for amnesty, a move the Biko family instructed the Legal Resources Centre to oppose.[36]

Evidence in military and police files had been shredded, of course, so some legal experts asked how people could gain a verdict in their favour from a Court, though they also pointed out that violators of human rights who were not politically motivated could still be prosecuted. At the very practical level, moreover, could South Africa's prisons, already overcrowded, ever find space for the thousands who had violated human rights? In addition court cases were time-consuming, with appeals against verdicts involving lengthy procedures. If this route was travelled, would the agony of apartheid ever be over?

Yet if the Commission treated perpetrators from both sides of South Africa's civil war as equals, would it attain its primary objective – 'a restoration of the moral order', to quote Alex Boraine, who admitted that the TRC faced 'moral dilemmas', but was bound by the Act establishing it which made no distinction. A gross human rights violation was a gross human rights violation, whoever had perpetrated it.[37]

There was a further dilemma in the whole process. By using the concepts 'Truth and Reconciliation' the South African constitutional negotiators introduced words capable of many, especially theological, meanings. 'We should not blame the Nazis (alone) ... we should blame ourselves and draw logical conclusions,' Pastor Niemöller, who was imprisoned in Dachau for opposing Nazism, once said. And Charles Villa-Vicencio has remarked: 'In South Africa, certainly, most whites and some blacks need to hear such words.'[38]

The Commission is thus not only about the victims and perpetrators before it, but many others also. Yet it can never pronounce forgiveness. 'It can relieve,' Dr Wolfram Kistner has suggested, 'but it can heal neither the wounds of the victims nor the self-inflicted wounds of the perpetrators.'[39] Neither can it pronounce reconciliation. But it can help people face the truth, handle it so that it becomes creative and point to those who can counsel both victims and oppressors.

'It depends heavily on the churches and professional people to help build reconciliation, so it doesn't explode,' Fatimer Meer has observed.[40] Yet the Commission is not a Christian body as such, though it includes Christians. Politicians, however – and the Commission was set up by them – 'cannot forgive themselves', as the Rev. Robert Vithi has pointed out,[41] even if they have repented of misdeeds. Moreover, perpetrators of violence could argue that they were merely carrying out instructions from others and were not acting in an individual capacity.

Here then is the essential dilemma of the Commission, which may recommend memorials for the dead or liturgies of healing in its final recommendations as a way to handle the deep problems. Yet would such liturgies be Christian ones, use traditional African forms, or be multi-faith or secular in orientation? Such is the diversity of South Africa's multi-cultural life that it is difficult to see a way through such complexities – though neighbouring Mozambique quite successfully used public hearings involving perpetrators, with wrongdoers' names made public, in an attempt heal its wounds when Frelimo came to power.[42]

Once established, the Commission had a salutary effect on society as John de Gruchy noted. Had its opponents 'something to hide?' people asked.[43] It could, of course, implicate many people. Who, for example, really was behind the shadowy 'third force'? Who killed certain well-known people? What had the war-lords been doing? These were prickly questions, yet what was South Africa's long-term future if these sores and wounds were not dealt with?

The Afrikaner poetess, Antjie Krog, once suggested: 'Wasn't the mere fact that the abuses of the [Boer] War were never exposed not a key factor in the character that formulated apartheid's laws? Was the Boer veneration of Emily Hobhouse not a symptom of the desperate need for someone "from the other side" to recognize the wrongs that had been done?'[44] The implications for South African history now were clear: to ignore the past, even if the Truth Commission was the result of pressure from intellectuals and theologians rather than from the grass roots, as Hermann Giliomee had suggested,[45] might well leave a suppurating sore under the surface of South Africa's life for decades.

ENCOUNTERS BETWEEN VICTIMS AND PERPETRATORS IN THE COMMUNITY

Even before it had begun its operations, victims and perpetrators had started to reflect on the Commission's task and now and again confronted, or at least met, one another. Some victims, of course, like the Rev. Vuyani Nyobole, had already dealt earlier with the problems the Commission had to handle, when he had encountered the infamous policeman Charles Sebe, who had believed God had sent him to suppress Communism. Taunted and tortured while in jail, Nyobole was left maimed for life but was eventually released and one day encountered Sebe in the street. It was difficult to greet him. Perhaps because of his own struggle to forgive, however, he came to see that people must be 'led to forgiveness' and that 'it will not happen automatically'. Indeed, some were 'detained by the past even though their wounds have been healed'. Moreover, relations and neighbourhoods would be affected by the Truth Commission, so there must be a focus on communities as well as individuals.[46]

One Durban community worker, Ian Mackesie, had a different experience. Imprisoned and questioned for six months on three separate occasions in the 1980s, in 1993 he was near a car park in St George's Street, Durban, when he saw a car stop, its occupant get out and come over to greet him. Suddenly he realized it was one of his interrogators, whom he had not seen since his release. Hugging him, the man, who was in tears, said: 'I am so pleased to see you. You people were right and we were wrong. Will you please forgive us?' Ian Mackesie has commented since: 'We have to forgive the past, even if it means forgiving at a price, for no amount of retribution can pay back the harm that has been caused.'[47]

Not only Nelson Mandela but other victims, too, reached heroic heights in prison itself. 'I must admit that the first time I ever prayed seriously for the security police and the government was when I was in prison,' Tshenvwani Simon Farisani has written. 'Only then did I realize how much they needed our daily, serious-minded intercession.'[48] For others, like Bishop Peter Storey, forgiveness is a struggle. Once Bishop Storey found himself in a group with a policeman who earlier had harassed and watched him. Admitting to himself that he could not cope, the Bishop left the group forthwith.[49]

Tish White and Victor Mabuso have different stories to tell. One of Tish White's daughters was appointed to a community policing group, one of whose members was the colonel who had persecuted her parents for their work at the Wilgespruit Fellowship Centre at Roodepoort. Discovering who her parents were led to discussion with their daughter, which resulted in the colonel admitting he had now realized human beings should never do what they do not believe in. 'Once you have reached that point you are ready to receive forgiveness,' Tish has explained.[50]

Victor Mabuso's story is still unresolved. During the 1986 State of Emergency he was picked up by the police, who had been informed about his peace work, which had involved resolving conflicts between the township and a local hostel in the Benoni area. Held for 96 days, during which time he became ill, he was, he believes, given an injection which affected both his memory and general health for years. Why was he maltreated? Because of the

STRUGGLING TO FORGIVE

anger felt by the police at his peace work which prevented 'third force' activities from generating hostilities when other areas of Johannesburg were troubled. The experience haunts him yet as he asks continually: 'Why have they done this?'[51]

Rob Roberston, Frank Chikane and Nazipoh Plaatje are three others who have had contact with perpetrators.

Rob Robertson, a Presbyterian minister involved with conscientious objectors from 1963 onwards, was well known to the police as an activist. One night, when he was drafting material on how to assist ministers who helped people marry despite the Mixed Marriages Act, 'the window shattered and there were glass chips all over the desk'. It was the beginning of more than 12 assaults over the next two years.

In April 1984 Rob Robertson tackled the head of security in John Vorster Square, Johannesburg, indicating that he did not want the perpetrators of these acts prosecuted, but was concerned for their state of mind and sought a discussion with them. There was no immediate response, but one midnight in June 1995 he took part in a talk show with another guest, the former security policeman Paul Erasmus, who had been in charge of Robertson's file. He it was who had used a catapult, though he disclaimed knowledge of the shotgun which had also been used in an attack on Robertson.

'He reminded me of a midnight raid by three of them on an Indian member of my congregation,' Rob Robertson has recalled, 'so I could now place Erasmus. I was asked by the compère how I felt about all this. I indicated I had been under security surveillance since Sharpeville in 1960, of always being open about my activities, legal and illegal, and of my belief that if we maintain a friendly attitude towards those who don't like us then reconciliation is a "good possibility", as was now happening.'[52] Rob Robertson sent a letter to Erasmus after the broadcast, but no response had come by the end of 1995.

In April and May 1989 the Rev. Dr Frank Chikane, then General Secretary of the SACC, suffered strange attacks of sickness, first on a visit to Namibia, then during a trip to America, where he and other church leaders were due to meet President Bush and Congress members. In and out of hospital, he felt weak and nauseous, had difficulty in breathing and was, according to an American doctor, 'close to death'. After days in hospital he usually recovered. The illness seemed to be related to clothing he had brought with him and it was soon discovered that his luggage had been contaminated with a poison used in pest control and chemical warfare.[53]

In due course Paul Erasmus wrote to the *Mail and Guardian*, admitting it was he who had poisoned the clothes and that he had also been involved in the blowing up of Khotso House, the SACC headquarters. Frank Chikane wrote from America that the emerging information about his and others' poisoning came as 'a sign of hope that at least the truth about these brutal acts of the apartheid system shall be known', making a plea to those involved to 'disclose [confess] this information not only to free themselves from fear and a guilty conscience, but to relieve me as well from the pain of wanting to forgive but not knowing whom to forgive'.[54] For his part, as an indication that he was ready to break with his past, Paul Erasmus, urged on by his wife, was the secret witness 'Q4' in the Goldstone Commission of enquiry into violence in South Africa, submitted to the South African Government in April 1993 but not published.[55]

Later, documents seized at Brigadier W. Basson's home outside South Africa showed the country had both an offensive and defensive chemical war capacity, despite denials by the then head of the SANDF and the Surgeon-General. This enabled the TRC to call for a more in-depth report than the bland submissions of the SADC, which in 80 pages had never admitted wrongdoing during the apartheid years.[56]

Nazipoh Plaatje from Grahamstown had a different experience of being a victim from Robertson and Chikane. As a Christian she knew she had to forgive, partly because she expected forgiveness for wrong she had done. For her 'it's forgetting that's the problem'. In 1983 she had become very active politically and in 1985 was detained one morning at 3.00 a.m., when her children were very young and her husband on night duty. Twelve police, ten white and two black, were involved in breaking into cupboards in her home, stripping her of human dignity. She was then taken to prison. In 1987, she and her son were detained and kept in solitary confinement with weekly harassment and interrogation.

Released in 1988, for six months she had to have sessions with a psychologist to help her even to communicate with her family. Her subsequent involvement with the police through her community work presented her with a major difficulty, therefore, for she had to work with the major from the security branch involved in her earlier unhappiness. She wanted to work through her feelings with him, but could not because no platform was provided for them to do so. 'The police doubtless argue,' she observes, 'there was nothing they could do: they were only doing their work. Maybe it's very difficult for the police. I don't know.'[57]

VICTIMS, PERPETRATORS AND THE TRUTH AND RECONCILIATION COMMISSION

'I lost a brother in the war,' Tokyo Sexwale, the ANC leader, disclosed in 1995. 'He was one of our fighters and I trained with him in the USSR. I got captured but they destroyed his body. We signed the Geneva Protocol that governs the way that prisoners of war are treated. He did not have the protection of that treaty and his body is still missing.' As one-time Premier of Gauteng Province, and therefore technically responsible for the police at the top political level, he was not sure he could handle all the emerging truth. 'Can Nelson Mandela handle all the truth?' he asked. 'I don't know that either,' adding that 'the Church must assert its authority and teach us to handle the truth.'[58]

The ANC itself, of course, has not been above reproach, as Joe Seremane, himself severely tortured by the police,[59] found out when exiles from ANC camps were brought home by the SACC. Now he expected a reunion with his brother who had left South Africa in 1976. He was informed, however, that he would not be returning. 'Does he want to settle abroad?' Joe queried. 'No,' was the reply, 'He is dead.' He then discovered from two ANC victims, who had been in jail in Angola, that his brother had not died in combat. 'He died by – I'll call them my own brothers,' Joe has explained. Now all he wants is to have his brother's remains. 'It would make forgiveness easier if I knew where he is buried.'[60]

Chris Hani was at the time a persistent critic of these detention camps and the torture that sometimes went with them, as were several others on the ANC's National Executive, who argued that they could not expect the Government to release their political prisoners if the ANC continued to detain people without trial. However, the context in which they were living and working had to be understood – assassinations, poisoning, the destabilization of camps by South African agents. 'There were,' Hani explained, 'spies and government agents working among us.'[61]

Events had come to a head in a mutiny in 1984, after some cadres questioned what the ANC was doing fighting in Angola. Initially in favour of dialogue with the mutineers, Hani had reached the end of his tether when they had killed several key commanders in Bango camp, taking control of it as a result. The camp was recaptured, with lives lost on both sides. At this point Chris Hani withdrew and was not a member of the tribunal set up to try the mutineers, the outcome of which was the decision to execute nearly 20 of them. He rushed to Lusaka to get the ANC leadership to intervene, which it did, but it was too late.[62]

In due course the ANC itself set up an enquiry and the Motsoanyane Commission reported in 1993, presenting accounts of how 70 had been executed, beaten to death, committed suicide or died of natural causes in ANC camps. 'But,' one journalist commented, 'mystery still surrounds the whereabouts of 200 other ANC members who have been recorded as missing by organizations ranging from Amnesty International to the right-wing Aida Parker newsletter'.[63]

Nelson Mandela described the findings as a 'devastating attack' on the ANC, whilst challenging F.W. de Klerk to release the findings of an investigation he had ordered into accusations of 'dirty tricks' by the South African Military Intelligence.[64] The ANC, he maintained, had taken the international community into its confidence by exposing abuses by its own members.[65] 'It was,' commented Priscilla Hayne, 'the only example of an opposition group formally investigating and publically reporting on the dark side of its own past.'[66] The whole matter was scrutinized by the TRC when it considered the ANC submissions.

The Winnie Mandela episode – the courts convicted her of helping abduct Stompie Seipei, who was later found dead – was an incident which was not suppressed either, and was later investigated by
the TRC, along with many other allegations against Mrs Mandela
and the group around her in the 1980s, ostensibly designed to protect her. 'My deepest regret was that I was unable to help him
from the anarchy of those times,' Winnie Mandela admitted in
Parliament. 'He was taken from my house and killed.'[67]

'By accepting collective responsibility and letting the internal democracy take its course, the movement has been morally
strengthened and set a noteworthy example for handling aberra-
tions on the other side,'[68] one writer has commented on the ANC.
Nevertheless, it was only in August 1992 that Chris Hani and
Nelson Mandela admitted that some of their self-defence units
were out of community control, had fought among themselves,
flogged and 'necklaced' (i.e. set light to car tyres placed round the
victim's neck) opponents on trumped-up charges. They had also
imposed taxes on black businessmen and even fired indiscrimi-
nately on vehicles travelling on the Golden Highway.[69]

It is this suffering, too, which the TRC has also examined, especially 'necklacing', a method of killing which the women's protest
movement the Black Sash, with its strong human rights record,
refused to condemn outright. 'Joyce Harris tried,' wrote Ken
Owen of *The Sunday Times*, 'but, she told me, she was voted
down.'[70] 'Mac' Maharaj, for the ANC, promised the TRC he would
verify whether amnesty applicants who admitted necklace-
killings were ANC members as they claimed, for a message had
been sent by Oliver Tambo to Mrs Mandela and others asking
them to distance themselves from 'this method'.[71]

Perhaps the most striking case where issues of forgiveness and
justice occur revolved around the activities of the ANC activist
Robert McBride, both before and during the TRC's work. In 1986
he had planted a bomb in a Durban bar frequented by security
forces, which had killed three and injured 69 people. In the negotiations during the early 1990s McBride – who had been captured,
tortured and then given three death sentences, subsequently
changed to life imprisonment – was released. Barend Strydom,
who had walked down a Pretoria street and shot dead some 10

people, was also released after only two years in jail, even though he admitted he would do it again, unlike McBride, who had expressed remorse.[72]

McBride's mother and father, though finding it difficult to forgive the ANC for losing touch with its ideals, as they saw it,[73] nevertheless called for forgiveness for their son when there was an uproar on his appointment as Deputy Director General in the Department of Foreign Affairs. 'If Robert was accused of being a killer,' Derrick McBride argued, 'other government members should face the same accusations ... NP members can also be implicated in violent acts...'[74] To defend himself from NP attacks, Robert McBride indicated that it was Nelson Mandela who had said 'No McBride, no negotiations',[75] and drew attention to explosives assembled in the South African Embassy in London and allegedly used to bomb the ANC office in the capital, an event subsequently condemned by F.W. de Klerk.[76] (Craig Williamson eventually sought amnesty from the TRC for this act.[77])

'The ANC had never made noises to have the diplomats involved removed,' McBride added. 'The ANC was not an organization which only talked reconciliation.'[78] Hope Papo wrote: 'I find it contradictory for the NP to daily harp on the need for forgiveness and reconciliation but each time they continue to victimize McBride.' The destructive campaign by the NP, if followed to its logical conclusion, would leave 'no room for reconciliation'.[79]

The survivors of the bomb in the Durban bar, of course, believed McBride should not have been indemnified, let alone allowed to become an ANC MP and a diplomat.[80] When the story of the bombing was relived before the TRC in 1996, the issue was raised again and with it the general principle which the Truth Commissioners must address: whether to recommend that those who have taken part in atrocities should be barred from public service. 'We can forgive,' said Alex Boraine, citing the case of security forces whose promotion was not affected at the height of apartheid repression even though they had abused human rights, 'but it seems strange that with forgiveness may come reward.'[81] Subsequently the ANC, in one of its submissions, confirmed that it accepted moral and political responsibility for the operations of its armed wing, including 'mistakes' such as the Magoo's Bar bombing in Durban.[82] The TRC itself, having heard McBride's evidence in camera, then also subpoenaed the MK officer (by then a general in the secretariat of the SANDF) who had allegedly ordered McBride to commit acts of sabotage.[83]

People opposed the National Party's actions as strongly as others reacted to the ANC's. Winnie Mandela, for example, thought ex-Presidents F.W. de Klerk and P.W. Botha should be charged with apartheid crimes and punished if found guilty. 'To forgive them is for me equivalent to racism,' she told a student congress in 1995, arguing that the NP would make a mockery of the Commission. 'Reconciliation in South Africa,' she continued, 'will not come via the Commission, but by building houses and schools and improving the living standards of the masses.'[84] Undoubtedly her views were widely shared by others, as Professor Hendrik van der Merwe conceded. 'We cannot have healing in society unless we take into account there are millions of people who feel like that,' he has observed. 'Large numbers cannot forgive. The bitterness is too strong.'[85]

There is a further problem, too, for the Truth Commissioners: getting perpetrators of atrocities to come forward. However, by May 1997, 7,700 amnesty applications had been received, giving the 13-member Amnesty Committee just under 100 days to finalize their processing.[86] But allowing victims unlimited leeway to tell their stories, without application of the normal rules of evidence, had inherent problems, for the truth that emerged was only the witness's perception, and allegations were made without the checks and balances of normal courtroom procedure. Statements about the number of dead after shootings in Langa on 21 March 1969 proved the point, with one witness maintaining under oath that she had seen 175 bodies, while another witness simply said there were more than 20. Academics later pointed out the numbers quoted in this incident were part of an urban legend, which had proved to be without foundation when exhaustively investigated earlier.[87]

VICTIMS, PERPETRATORS AND THE COURTS

One perpetrator already found guilty by a court (though the sentencing was postponed) and who sought amnesty from the TRC was Dirk Coetzee. Earlier he had publicly admitted his involvement in the murder of Griffiths Mxenge. He explained that in 1981 he had been called to Durban and told to kill the civil rights lawyer, who had spent two years on Robben Island, and to make the killing look like a robbery 'because the police did not want another Biko case'. He asked for the help of two black colleagues who 'had the killer instinct'.[88]

Coetzee, however, is a perpetrator who defected, seeking out the ANC in exile and reporting what he had done, subsequently becoming an ANC intelligence employee. 'When I went to the ANC they were very friendly,' he has recorded. 'Hell, I mean I was so nervous telling Jacob Zuma about Griffiths Mxenge … he was a friend of Zuma, close friend. And Zuma didn't wink an eye … "We know, Dirk, we understand, you're a victim of the system, like thousands of other South Africans, black and white!" And that kind of attitude. Forgiveness. Forget.'[89]

It was not all as easy as that, as he discovered when he met Mxenge's brother, Dr Fumbatha Mxenge, who found it almost impossible to be with someone like Coetzee who claimed responsibility for 10 murders, where he and his accomplices 'were the judge, the law and the executioners'.

'We are not after Coetzee's blood,' Dr Mxenge explained, but he did not understand why he was free. 'You should be behind bars!' he exclaimed. 'We lost our parents afterwards of heart failure. We will be happy when justice is seen to be done.'

The meeting between the two, organized for a television documentary, showed Dirk Coetzee as a man now trying to live with his crimes, even though some had tried to eliminate him. He was not going to commit suicide, he explained, and was grateful Dr Mxenge had agreed to meet him. 'I really feel very sorry,' he confessed. 'I'd like to apologize for the grief and sorrow I created.' He hoped such events could lead to the start of understanding 'the absurdities of the past'.[90] For his part, however, Dr Mxenge had his worst suspicions confirmed.

'You can't forgive and forget the past if we don't know what the past was all about,' Dirk Coetzee observed in another context. Craig Williamson the former spymaster, for example, had written open letters to the newspapers.[91] Now, he suggested, he should admit he killed Ruth First and was implicated in the bomb which maimed Albie Sachs. In February 1995 Craig Williamson did make one admission: he had been part of a team involved in a parcel bomb attack in 1984 on Marius Schoon, then living in exile in Angola, which had killed his wife and six-year old daughter by mistake. Schoon had filed a 1 million rand lawsuit against Williamson, an action Williamson tried to stop by approaching the TRC. His case raised the difficulty of the Commission's work, for if Williamson denied the civil claim, this could be held against him in the consideration of his amnesty application, but if he admitted the allegations he might obtain judgement by default before the amnesty application was processed and thence be liable for damages.[92]

Often victims wanted to meet the perpetrators of their suffering, even though with some, like Dr Mxenge, it proved unhelpful. This was certainly true for Albie Sachs who lost an arm when a car bomb exploded as he was leaving his car for a swim while an exile in Mozambique. Later he said that if the bomber were caught he wanted him tried, but acquitted if there was insufficient evidence.[93] Once he even attempted to meet his would-be assassin, but this proved impossible. 'I did not feel any anger at all,' he has written, 'just a wish to let him see me and to personalize the relationship.'[94] Much later, he returned to the spot where the bomb had exploded and swam in the sea. 'The idea of an eye for an eye, a tooth for a tooth, an arm for an arm, fills me with anguish,' he wrote subsequently.[95] There was only one kind of vengeance which could assuage the loss of his arm: victory for the ideals for which he had stood.

Reflections such as these are at the core of the TRC's work, but they depend on a certain outlook from both victims and perpetrators. A measure of the complexity of the issues is indicated by a press report in 1994 headed 'Mandela discusses amnesty with the right', which suggested that, 'driven by the imperative to reconcile all South Africans',[96] he was risking the first serious controversy of his Presidency by meeting with South Africa's far right to discuss pardons for bombers who had killed 20 and seriously injured 45 in the run up to the 1994 elections.

The discussions focused on the situation of 34 supporters of Eugene TerreBlanche's Afrikaner Resistance Movement (AWB), arrested in connection with a bombing campaign. After the meeting Mandela said the question of amnesty for right-wing terrorists would be discussed further by the Conservative Party leader and the Justice minister, a comment which provoked considerable unease. Talking with the far right was good in principle, said one paper, but not if it meant 'rendering democracy hostage to the whims of a tiny minority'. The Chairman of the Lawyers for Human Rights wrote to Mandela to the effect that letting off the bombers 'would be to promote anarchy more than anything else. The time has come to try and foster law and order and the line has to be drawn now.'[97] In the event, five members of the AWB were sentenced to an effective 26 years each, two others to an effective eight years and three others received lesser sentences.[98] With the extension of the amnesty date to May 1994, however, the Freedom Front leader General Viljoen announced that he would seek amnesty for leading a plot before the 1994 election which, had it been successful, would have overturned the Government and established a *volkstaat* (a homeland for the Afrikaners who wanted one) by force.[99]

Two other court cases focused the TRC issues dramatically. One was the trial in Pretoria of Eugene de Kock, a white police commander, on more than 100 charges, including murder, theft, fraud and crimes committed for personal gain. In particular he was accused of heading a special police unit – Vlakplaas, named after the farm where it was based – which specialized in murdering anti-government activists and collaborated with ANC opponents to instigate political violence. 'Former members of the unit began disclosing its actions six years ago and an independent judicial commission led by Justice Goldstone last year uncovered evidence of Vlakplaas crimes,' one journalist reported.[100] De Kock, found guilty of 89 of the 121 charges against him, including six for murder, applied for amnesty for those crimes he had committed which fell within the TRC's frame of reference.[101]

STRUGGLING TO FORGIVE

The other trial, which reached to the core of the previous Government's life, concerned the arrest in Durban on 2 November 1995 of General Magnus Malan, Defence Minister from 1980 to 1991, along with 10 senior military officials, including other generals and an admiral, charged with the murder of 13 people in 1987, some of them women and children, who were attending a prayer meeting in a township in the Zulu heartland. The prosecution said it would not be referring the matter to the TRC because the accused had maintained their innocence. In the event, in a controversial decision, all were subsequently acquitted.

General Malan did, however, meet the TRC, telling them that in his view soldiers who committed unlawful atrocities should be prosecuted, but that he would accept moral and political responsibility for all their lawful actions, including cross-border raids when innocent people were killed. The sound judgement of SADF members had suffered in the battle, he explained, owing to the abhorrence generated by the deeds of terror committed by the liberation movements.

'If, however, moral blame is to be attached to the lawful actions of the SADF,' he stated, 'such blame must be levelled at the former governments and not at individual members of the SADF.' He said members of the previous Government were, on the whole, avoiding 'taking a clear, comprehensive, collective political and moral responsibility' for SADF actions, although he mentioned former President P.W. Botha as an exception. He hoped his explanation might be a spur to even the slightest understanding of 'former adversaries'.[102]

POLITICAL REACTIONS TO THE TRC

As the work of the TRC developed, it was clear that it did so against a backcloth of trials, like the one involving General Malan, as well as raising questions about what constitutes a politically motivated crime. Some perpetrators, of course, asked lawyers to weigh up for them the implications of the complex legislation. Others, like Pik Botha, the former Foreign Secretary, were either saying they had no need to confess, or waiting to see how the

Commission developed, or even trying to avoid the inevitable. Some in the former liberation movements reacted similarly. Though the former MK chief, Joe Modise, committed himself to going to the TRC, some comrades he had commanded were less keen to do so. The PAC MP, Patricia de Lille, said that some APLA members would not confess to the Commission.[103] By the closing date for amnesty applications, however, the PAC had submitted 460. On that day the ANC, too, delivered two batches, one of 56 and another of 300, which included 40 members of the ANC leadership, excluding President Mandela, but including Deputy President Thabo Mbeki, Defence Minister Joe Modise and his deputy Ronnie Kasrils. Only 20 former policemen and 30 defence force members sought amnesty then, and there was only one IFP applicant. There were, however, 21 applications from AWB members and some from former members of the Civil Co-operation Bureau, including Piet Koornhof, once responsible for forced removals, who delivered his application in person.[104]

Former State President P.W. Botha remained adamant about his role. 'I am not going to the Truth and Reconciliation Commission,' he stated categorically. 'I am not going to repent. I am not going to ask for favours. What I did, I did for my country, my God and my people and all the people of South Africa.'[105] His autobiography, published in 1997, contained all he had to say, his publisher stated, but the Commission itself wrote to him asking him a number of questions which they considered needed clarification, a step agreed between P.W. Botha and Archbishop Tutu at a meeting.[106] P.W. Botha's response was at one point contradictory, for like General Viljoen, he had asked President Mandela to put a moratorium on the prosecution of the trial of the generals so that they could approach the TRC instead. If he believed that those under him should submit to the jurisdiction of the Commission, he was, as one paper observed, 'showing a disappointing lack of loyalty by refusing to do so himself'. After all, he had been their commander-in-chief and, for a long period, also Minister of Defence when they had acted under his orders and policies.[107]

The IFP was likewise reticent, though in the middle of 1996 Chief Buthelezi presented a four-page memorandum to Archbishop Tutu during a 90-minute meeting in Cape Town. The IFP, whose national council had passed a resolution in July 1995 against participating in, or cooperating with, the TRC, objected to the combination of truth-finding with the administration of amnesty for politically motivated crimes, Chief Buthelezi explained.[108]

One of the Commissioners, Mary Burton, said she regretted F.W. de Klerk, P.W. Botha and General Malan had not applied for amnesty.[109] F.W. de Klerk, however, prepared a submission on behalf of the former Government, in which he drew a distinction between extraordinary actions that would normally be taken by any security forces to counter insurgence and terrorism and 'unacceptable, gross violations' such as murder and assassination.[110] 'When a person believes in his heart that he did not do anything wrong by acting legally against terrorism and armed insurgence, or forces intent on overthrowing a legitimate government,' he has observed, 'then no crime has been committed. As a result I do not intend to apply for amnesty in these circumstances.'[111]

In one NP federal executive, members had made it clear that 'the amnesty process should not be misused by any political parties for political ends'.[112] Rather the process was for individuals who were guilty of deeds which could lead to criminal prosecution and conviction, views which F.W. de Klerk conveyed to the TRC. On the question of whether the struggle to defend apartheid could be equated with the struggle against it, the NP statement maintained: 'It could be argued that in putting this question you are betraying your prejudice and a simplistic approach to your mandate.'[113]

Perhaps Desmond Tutu and Alex Boraine did step out of role when Tutu declared de Klerk's failure to accept that former NP policies had given security forces a 'licence to kill' was devastating, and when Boraine said de Klerk had contradicted himself when he first denied that the NP had abandoned the security forces and then distanced his party from gross human rights abuses perpetrated by them. 'The security police (who have applied for amnesty) tell us they were carrying out the orders of their superiors. The generals tell us they were following their policy of the day,' Boraine commented.[114]

Certainly the retired police commissioner, Johan van der Merwe, and the one-time Law and Order Minister, Adriaan Vlok, decided to seek amnesty. Van der Merwe admitted he ordered the booby trapping and hand grenades which killed ANC activists in 1986, and the 1988 bomb at Khotso House, the headquarters of the SACC, orders which had come 'personally' from the (then) State President, P.W. Botha, and had been relayed to him by Vlok. The grenade option had been sanctioned at Cabinet level, he indicated. Vlok himself would not comment on van der Merwe's allegations, but confirmed he would apply for amnesty for at least the Council of Churches bombing.[115]

The end result of the probings and questionings caused the NP to suspend involvement in the TRC, pending possible legal action. A spokesperson said Tutu and Boraine had indicated that they had found F.W. de Klerk guilty of gross human rights atrocities, which was a 'shocking' statement and a travesty of what was intended by the truth and reconciliation process.[116] The two Commission leaders, commented the *Pretoria News*, 'were unwise to comment, as they reportedly did, on the substance of de Klerk's evidence. Their remarks show that they have taken positions on the NP's contribution.'[117]

The TRC was bound, of course, to find itself in deep waters whatever it did or said, as when it received an ANC appendix to its final submission which contained the names of former government spies whose names it did not want revealed, partly, as 'Mac' Maharaj explained, because it did not wish to punish people for the rest of their lives. Alex Boraine, however, said transparency was fundamental and the Commission would 'weigh up' the ANC's secretiveness 'as a matter of some urgency'. Desmond Tutu said it was crucial 'for the integrity of this operation' that it was the TRC itself which made decisions about what was going to be disclosed.[118]

In one of its rulings the TRC Amnesty Committee accepted that the police and liberation movements were engaged in a 'direct armed conflict' and said police had been justified in believing they should act outside their normal line of duty in support of the apartheid government.[119] In practical terms this meant amnesty for a KwaZulu-Natal policeman who 'executed' two ANC members who had been transported to hospital after being wounded in a shoot-out with security police. It also granted amnesty to an ANC self-defence unit member who had wounded two policemen in a shoot-out, but refused the applications of two other members of the self-defence unit whose actions did not come within the parameters with which the TRC was working.[120]

The pardoning of Bruce Mitchell, a former policeman serving a 30-year sentence for the murder of 11 people in 1988, was, however, a decision likely to test the limits of national reconciliation, commented the *Guardian* newspaper.[121] A programme on BBC 2 on 27 July 1997 explained that Mitchell, a counter-insurgency agent, had mistakenly fired on Africans attending a funeral wake instead of the ANC activists he had been sent to find. At his trial he had not disclosed information he later gave to the TRC in an open hearing. He had become a Christian in prison and after his hearing visited the scene of his crime and met survivors, even praying with them, and visiting the graves of the dead. He reported that he had approached the Reparations Committee for help for the community which was in much poverty and that he himself would try to help.

Even more controversial, of course, was the application received by the TRC for amnesty from the killers of Chris Hani, Clive Derby-Lewis and Janusz Walus, both serving life sentences for the April 1993 murder.[122]

RESPONSES FROM THE CHURCHES AND CIVIL SOCIETY

Given all the complexities surrounding the TRC, it is not surprising that the churches have been exercised about both its theory and its impact. At the national level the SACC is clear that only after remembering and repenting, analysing errors and changing attitudes, can individuals and nations establish a new life. To proclaim a 'general amnesia' and bury memories was to plant psychological and social disorders which would yield a harvest of bitterness and a revenge mentality which could last for decades. In 1992, therefore, its executive committee urged Christians, and others of integrity in the security forces or related structures, with access to information relating to destabilizing policies or actions 'to come forward at once, and to tell the truth about what is taking place'[123] Brigalia Hlope Bam, General Secretary of the SACC, wrote in 1995: 'The most important task of the Church is that of helping the victims to voice their needs in the search for the whole truth.' It also involved, with the perpetrators, making the journey of acceptance, confession and forgiveness.[124]

The Dutch Reformed Church, like the Roman Catholic Church earlier, had reservations about the TRC, but as Professor Piet Meiring commented: 'Afrikaans churches have come to realize it is a must.'[125] Nevertheless, its General Synodical Commission, whilst acknowledging that from a biblical perspective truth was an important element of reconciliation, felt it was also important that 'the structure which is to serve truth does not compromise it'. Worried about possible negative consequences flowing from the TRC, it requested that the process be exercised free of party politics and not determined from an ideological point of departure and that all South Africans be properly prepared for its task. The Church would monitor the Commission, it added, for procedures 'that do not stand the test of Christian conscience'.[126] It also urged church councils and ministers to give pastoral care to those possibly unjustly accused and those found guilty, but resisted any suggestion that it should make a TRC submission, though its Western Cape Synod did make an apology to the TRC for its role in upholding apartheid. But it did, in a document published in 1997, admit to making a series of mistakes in supporting apartheid until the late 1980s and said it had not heard the Word of God correctly.[127] Dr Beyers Naudé, too, encouraged by others like Professor Nico Smith, published an open letter to the TRC in which he asked himself what had been lacking in his preaching that seemingly it had so little effect. He also asked other priests and ministers to add their names to the letter.[128]

Perhaps most surprisingly, the Salvation Army, which made its TRC submission on 7 June 1997, made a strong confessional statement admitting it had been insensitive to events and chosen to remain silent, partly because it had people of many political outlooks in its ranks, a sin of omission it deeply regretted. The

STRUGGLING TO FORGIVE

insensitivity, the statement added, was 'an affront to God and humankind'. It pledged itself to follow through the reconciliation process, to seek a just redistribution of resources and continue to offer pastoral care to victims and perpetrators.[129]

Professor John de Gruchy was concerned most of all for apartheid's victims rather than the danger of 'unfairly victimizing the perpetrators of past crimes', for the role of law was as important for democracy's future as 'the danger of alienating the military and the police'.[130] Yet he had to admit that even apartheid's opponents had 'also been tainted, compromised and even corrupted in the process'. The churches, therefore, had a pastoral role, parallel to the Roman Catholic Church in Latin America, where the rite of penance was being related by liberation theologians to structural sin (committed by institutions and organizations) and the creation of community. The churches' responsibility must be to help everyone recognize the nature and extent of their guilt and confess it appropriately, oppose false accusations, scapegoating and witch hunts, and help victims 'to exercise forgiveness rather than vengeance'.[131]

A first attempt to address some of these matters had occurred in 1994 when the SACC issued a booklet for wide circulation which provided resource material including two Truth, Healing and Reconciliation Liturgies, advice on trauma counselling, and a theological reflection on truth and reconciliation, as well as a sermon outline and explanations about the setting up of the TRC. Some, of course, like Denise Ackermann, considered that the churches themselves needed a Truth and Reconciliation Commission,[132] while others, like Nellis du Preez of Africa Enterprise, maintained that the churches in KwaZulu-Natal should make a public confession of their own guilt before pointing fingers at politicians both there and nationally.[133] Part of the transformation needed will certainly involve the letting go of past hurts for, as former Bishop Mogoba once pointed out, the suffering he experienced on Robben Island cannot be compensated for. The real compensation, and the greatest moment of liberation, was the 1994 election. In many ways, he considers, 'that was compensation enough'.[134]

Moreover, the whole truth about South African suffering would not be told by focusing on human rights abuses. In fact, the whole could not 'ever be told', and part of the churches' task was to point out that even the TRC would be unable to tell it. Of course, a joint public process when the President would announce that the door had been closed on the past, perhaps with a public, liturgical event, could play a valuable but symbolic role in the national psyche, yet despite good intentions this could still leave some victims high and dry. So the churches must remind society that the need to confess, to show contrition and be forgiven, would never be over.[135]

At the local and regional level, of course, many initiatives have started which deal with TRC issues. In the Anglican Diocese of Natal, for example, a task group on repentance and restitution for apartheid has been established, which has run workshops on reconciliation, emphasizing story-telling, thereby assisting the healing of memories. Similar workshops, sometimes involving both victims and perpetrators, and sponsored by the Religious Response to the TRC, a multifaith group in Cape Town, have been held, after the leaders have been trained in the counselling of victims. The World Conference of Religions for Peace, whose South African chapter is one of the sponsors, has even suggested that to conclude the Commission's work a national event should be held, for symbolic action and ritual was central to 'the process of National Repentance.'[136]

The Trauma Centre, also in Cape Town, plays a major role. Here Father Michael Lapsley, its chaplain – described as an 'icon'[137] of what the TRC stood for by Desmond Tutu when he testified to the Commission – makes a significant contribution because of his own experience in 1990 when a letter bomb, hidden inside two religious magazines, went off.

In hospital in Harare for three months, he was unable to do anything for himself, but he remembered Isaiah chapter 52 and the writer's lifting up of the disfigured suffering servant, as well as an Eastern Orthodox image of Christ on the Cross with one leg shorter than the other. As messages poured in, he realized that if he became filled with hatred or a desire for revenge, 'I would remain a victim for ever.' So he determined to get well and live life as fully and joyfully as possible. He realized, too, once attached to the Trauma Centre, that all his life had been a preparation for his current work. Memories mattered, but should not destroy. Forgiveness mattered, too, but how could the unrepentant be forgiven and South Africa be healed? 'Why did I survive a bomb that was supposed to kill?' he asked himself. 'Perhaps to be ... a sign that love and faith and gentleness are stronger than hatred and evil and death.'[138] 'If we are able to recognize our woundedness,' he has explained, 'heal our memories and move towards wholeness, then we have a much greater chance of breaking the cycle and creating a different type of society.'[139]

In Johannesburg there is an analogous organization, the Centre for the Study of Violence and Reconciliation, which started in 1988 and with other groups in civil society played an important part in lobbying Parliament when the TRC was being formed to ensure that it was heavily weighted in the favour of victims and hearings held in the open wherever possible. Indeed, at one point it took a group of apartheid victims to meet MPs, who spoke with moral strength to those in authority, thereby helping the Centre's leaders to realize the power victims had to help create a new South Africa.[140] There are now an increasing number of Khulumani ('tell your story') groups across South Africa as victims inform each other about these support groups which give psychological and, where possible, material help to hundreds.

The reactions of group members to the issue of forgiveness have been varied. 'Our President says we must forgive,' says one. 'Nobody has died from his family.' While another adds, 'We want the bones of our people here before we forgive.'[141] One of the leaders of the Centre, Paul van Zyl, is clear amid all the conflicting views that there cannot be a forgiveness and reconciliation philosophy in South Africa unless those who have suffered are mobilized and organized and the past confronted during the unique form of transition through which the country is passing.[142]

One community in particular which has come to terms with the problem of forgiveness is St James's Church in Cape Town. On the evening of 25 July 1993 its life was changed for ever when armed men burst into its worship, fired on the congregation and threw hand grenades attached to tins of nails. Eleven people died and 55 were injured, some maimed for life like Paul Williams, a teacher with two children, whose legs were badly hurt when a bullet went through his side. His mind, however, was not damaged, though he needed pain control therapy for a year. He is not bitter, he has said, and understands the political reasons which may have caused the atrocity.[143]

In the stressful days following the massacre, for which only one of the four gunmen was caught (and was subsequently converted in prison), the bereaved were able to speak of peace and strength and an overwhelming sense of God's presence.[144] Their pastor said: 'Members of the congregation were able to extend forgiveness to the perpetrators and face the future with calm assurance ... The sufferers at St James's were given the supreme privilege of presenting Christ as the true shepherd of the sheep.'[145] At Sunday worship and during prayer meetings the congregation asked God to bring the criminals not only to justice but also to repentance,[146] remembering that they, too, were offenders in God's eyes and in need of grace.[147] Strangely the effect of the massacre was to open the church to the community in new ways, both locally and nationally, as its pastor helped it with forgiveness first at the level of the will, leaving the question of feelings till later.

In one of the most dramatic encounters at TRC hearings, Dawie Ackerman, whose wife Marita was one of the 11 killed in the massacre, confronted for the first time Goinkhaya Makone and two colleagues from APLA, who admitted entering St James's Church in July 1993 and committing the atrocity. Asking the three men to turn and face him, he told them: 'I can forgive you the hurt you have caused me. But I cannot forgive you the sin you have committed. Only God can do that.'[148]

Another incident touches nearly the same depths. It concerns Father Smangaliso Mkhatshwa, now an MP, who invited two former security policemen who had once tried to murder him to his church to ask forgiveness from his congregation, saying this would contribute more to reconciliation than a confession and a handshake. The two, Captain Jacques Hechter and Warrant Officer Paul van Vuuren, who had applied for amnesty for the attempted assassination and other crimes, indicated they would accept the invitation.[149]

One African woman in Port Elizabeth perhaps epitomizes the many who have not lost their humanity despite their pain. Herself in exile from 1969, she discovered there were traitors at the top of the ANC itself. Indeed, a cousin, who as a freedom fighter had killed, was himself killed in 1989 after being betrayed by someone he thought was a friend. Nevertheless, as she reflected on the trial of Magnus Malan, whom she considered was unable to forgive because so many of his friends had been injured and nearly 20 had died in a car bomb atrocity – 'a terrible, terrible thing, a white man did that' – she concluded with words that may yet turn out to be prophetic: 'If Malan can forgive us, we are also going to forgive him,' adding, 'I think God is going to help us. God is on our side.'[150]

By February 1998, however, the TRC's path was as stormy as ever. With its final report due in June, there were still many amnesty requests unresolved, including those relating to the deaths of Steve Biko and Chris Hani. It was clear, therefore, that the amnesty committee's work would continue after June. Still unresolved, also, was the TRC's request for former State President, P.W. Botha, to appear before it, which he refused to do, despite his sub-poena.

Botha argued his long, written submission to the TRC was sufficient, whereas the TRC wanted to question him about border raids, the state's chemical and biological warfare programme and the murder of black activists. By now white society, and Afrikaners in particular, were suggesting the TRC was one-sided, especially when it had seemed to give a 'blanket amnesty' to senior ANC leaders.[151] Former generals started a fund for Botha, who had been summoned before a Western Cape magistrate, while General Viljoen, who himself had appeared before the TRC in response to his sub-poena, said Botha was becoming a 'rallying point for Afrikaner nationalism'.[152]

Some members of the NP, however, argued Botha should appear before the Commission, while the Justice minister maintained 'Nobody is above the law.'[153] The assistant editor of *Die Beeld* argued the TRC had no choice but to press charges against Botha, particularly after its nine-day public hearing (at her request) of charges against Winnie Madikizela-Mandela of murder, torture and kidnapping involving over 40 witnesses.[154] The results, however, were inconclusive, though she did, when prompted by Tutu, admit things in the late 1980s 'went horribly wrong' and that 'for those painful years I am deeply sorry'.[155]

Though the TRC heard allegations against Chief Buthelezi, too, it refrained from asking him to appear before it. Buthelezi had to respond latterly to suggestions by some, including Nelson Mandela, that the ANC and IFP should work closely together as, for the first time since animosities broke out in 1979 between them, the ANC invited a senior IFP representative to its conference.[156] Meanwhile, behind the scenes, 20 from each party prepared for a peace summit in KwaZulu-Natal in 1998,[157] a gathering which inevitably will have to deal with issues which had come before the TRC.

Nelson Mandela himself made two strong interventions in autumn 1997, one in a live interview on the eve of the ANC's 50th national conference, when he said he would be happy for Chief Buthelezi to become Deputy President of South Africa. At the conference itself, in his final address as ANC President, he startled many by a severe attack on white society and, as he perceived it, partly no doubt as a result of TRC submissions, its unwillingness to explain adequately its involvement in the maintenance and perpetuation of apartheid.[158]

While the Anglican and Roman Catholic Churches were among a number of English-speaking Christian groups to offer broad apologies at a special TRC hearing[159] and Pik Botha, the former Foreign Secretary, spoke at another of his failure to 'turn the tide of apartheid earlier', an apology Tutu described as 'courageous'[160], Mandela felt the institutions which supported apartheid had been less than candid in their responses.

'Please take this, the last but most generous offer of healing with the past,' Tutu had said in October 1997. 'Grab it, because once it is past it will not return.'[161] Clearly the healing results expected from the TRC's work will take some time to come to fruition.

Chapter 7

Forgiveness and Repairing –

The Role of Restitution

In the new South Africa citizens need to see clearly changes at all levels which indicate the repairing of past damage.

Land is a key issue, for it has not only territorial significance for Africans but symbolic power, too. Hence the land removals policy attacked both African rights in terms of tenure and African insights about identity. Whether the land redistribution and restitution programme will eventually work remains to be seen.

Another wrong from the past which is now being addressed is the unbalanced economy. Through its new policies the Government is seeking to redress previous imbalances, which favoured the white communities, in order to lessen or remove extreme inequalities.

The task, of course, is formidable, at one level relating to primary needs for water and light, at another level to jobs and housing. The arena is so vast, and the population of South Africa so large, that it will be difficult to see substantial results immediately, a fact bound to cause alarm and restlessness. Help will therefore be needed from the international community, especially from those Western nations who so profited from apartheid.

Concrete needs, of course, are often the most obvious. But all the legal changes in South Africa, with the new Constitution finally in place in 1997 (after certain alterations were made at the request of the Constitutional Court), are also important, as are the changes in how the police operate. 'We solemnly honour the pledge we made to ourselves and the world, that South Africa should redeem herself and thereby widen the frontiers of human freedom,' Nelson Mandela said on 10 December 1996 at a signing ceremony in Sharpeville, itself part of Vereeniging where, on 31 May 1902, the British and the Boers had signed a treaty which effectively disenfranchised the Africans for 92 years.

Changes must be made in all South African structures if the attempt at genuine repairing is not to be eroded. South Africa needs to make restitution in two areas especially, one external, the other internal. For many decades she destabilized the countries around her, causing them much loss of income and life. Her foreign policy must now play a constructive role across Africa and also a positive role globally because of her unique contacts with all continents.

At the internal level she owes it to her peoples to build up the democratic process, freeing their minds for involvement as citizens in local community action and decision-making. New and corporate histories need creating, too, to help people transcend lesser loyalties and outmoded views. Whether current attitudes and outlooks will overcome long and deep ethnic myths about one another in favour of a common South Africanness remains to be seen. Certainly it is naive to assume that the cultural conflicts which have always been evident before in South Africa's history will go away. Indeed they could even intensify if the economy does not pick up substantially.

Certainly there will be a testing time in the cultural sphere during the centenary of the Anglo-Boer War in 1999, a year which will also test the new democracy as the whole country goes to the polls again.

THE LAND ISSUE

'The aim of any truth commission or confession of guilt must always be forgiveness, healing and reconciliation,' John de Gruchy has observed. One further thing was needed, too: 'affirmative action on behalf of those who have been unjustly disadvantaged, including the just restoration of land.'[1]

This issue, of course, is being dealt with through the 1994 Restitution of Land Rights Act which aims to restore, or compensate for, land rights lost because of racially discriminatory laws passed since 1913. 'That's the white man's date,' says Joe Seremane's son,[2] arguing like many that the date should have been earlier, perhaps even 1652, when Van Rieebeck landed at the Cape. Yet to deal with complex questions of land ownership before 1913 might have created more difficulties than it solved, with the state finding itself with insufficient money for adequate financial compensation.

STRUGGLING TO FORGIVE

Four forms of restitution are possible: land can be restored to claimants, especially where it is state owned; if privately owned, the court can order its expropriation or purchase by the state; alternative state-owned land can be offered; or a financial compensation can be given for land lost, or alternative relief giving claimants priority access to state-funded housing projects.[3]

The form restitution takes depends on the circumstances of each claim, either from individuals or communities. Claims are investigated by the Regional Lands Claims Commissioner to establish if they qualify and then a settlement is negotiated. If all parties agree, the Commissioner involved recommends the proposals to the Land Claims Court for a legally binding court order. If there is disagreement, the case goes to the Land Claims Court for settlement.

Joe Seremane, the Chief Land Commissioner, who works in the Department of Land Affairs where the Commission is lodged, is typical of those determined to make the new South Africa work. On Robben Island from 1963 to 1969, he yet retains a strong belief in human dignity, drummed into him as a boy by his mother who would slap his mouth if he referred to other tribes disparagingly, insisting that 'those white pigs', as he called them, were also human beings.

Deprived of land in the Western Cape and Randfontein, where he was born, he was dumped in a rural area and later lived in one of the homelands. Far from making him bitter, however, his experience made him aware of the 'human frailty in every one of us', and how 'we need God to help us find the way'. His fellow South Africans, he adds, must 'stop crying by the waters of Babylon. It's becoming late – not only for South Africa.' Working now with civil servants who once implemented the draconian forced removals policies, he sees himself living out the atonement of Christ in a costly way, aware that 'when you walk the path of reconciliation and peace you will be lonely'.[4]

Emma Mashinini, the Commissioner for Gauteng, North West and Eastern Transvaal, who brings years of trade union organizing and negotiating experience to her job, has also worked with the SACC. Like Joe Seremane, she cooperates 'very peacefully'[5] with civil servants from the previous regime, who remained in office as part of agreements which led to the new Government. She enjoys listening to the stories people tell her, though she is pained if they break down when they describe their lost land. Often complex problems surround each claim, involving the history of the dispossession, the hardship caused, proof of ownership and notification of potential objectors. There is, too, a backlog of claims inherited from a previous commission on Land Allocation as well as over 11,000 new ones due to be investigated by 1997, with more expected before the closure date of 30 April 1998. Most are urban, and come from Gauteng, the Western Cape and KwaZulu-Natal, which has lodged over 5,000 claims, the largest response to date.

Views diverge about the likely outcome of the Land Commission's work. The Land Affairs minister, Derek Hanekom, who views the Land Act as one 'of enormous historical significance',[6] considers the actual expropriation or confiscation of land will be 'unnecessary', arguing that there is sufficient land available on the free market for the Government to buy, though officials argue that there is only about 1 per cent of land lying idle for redistribution.

Complications on the ground, however, may become formidable in some areas, particularly as younger and more educated people talk of 'regaining our ancestral land'. One commentator considers: 'Where dispossession was relatively recent and clearcut, they will doubtless get their land back. The problem comes when dispossession is lost in the mists of time.' Discontent could take the form of endemic rustling, or even attacks on farmers and their families. Indeed one farmer had to deal with land invasions when his Zulu neighbours either herded their cattle through his fences or tried to seize land for resettlement.[7]

Just off the main road to Ladysmith at Hermanskraal, the Amahlubi and Amantshe clans, both of whom have lodged land claims with the KwaZulu-Natal Land Commissioner, have already returned to claim their land. In 1995 this led to clashes with the police and the Amahlubi. Johan Geldenhuys, who manages two farms for an owner, does not object to the claim but thinks the tribes must wait for the Land Commission's investigation. Why should people seek a return to land offering very little prospect of a decent livelihood? 'Most of us grew up here,' one Amantshe

leader has explained, 'and despite the aridity, our livestock survived far better than in the places we have been to. Also it is the
only place we could call our own.'[8]

In urban areas, too, complications abound, though even where
large groups were removed, such as in Cato Manor near Durban,
individual claims often predominate – some 350 by autumn
1995. Others lodged with the Commission include Alexandra and
Sophiatown in Johannesburg, most claimants not favouring financial compensation for lost land rights. 'People see there is a lot of
goodwill in the Restitution Act, so they are willing to talk about
alternatives,' Joe Seremane has explained,[9] citing the Sophiatown
case and adding that even two white farmers had lodged claims,
which was a good sign. In Cape Town, those who lived on what is
now a grassy field opposite Kirstenbosch Botanical Gardens, when
it was known as Protea Village, have lodged 95 applications for
restitution with the Western Cape Commissioner, following a
reunion of the inhabitants when they vowed to reclaim land from
which they were forcibly removed in 1966.[10]

An even more striking claim is the one 30,000 Makuleke people
are putting together for 20,000 hectares of the Kruger National
Park, from which they were evicted in 1969 – but has the Government enough money to buy back land on such a scale? In
addition, the Government has pledged itself to respect communal
ownership, where the land is administered by a chief, yet how
viable is such a system where winning freehold rights or a patch
of land can rest largely on the whim of an unelected chief?[11] Some
land, of course, has already been returned. In December 1992, for
example, partly through international pressure and SACC help,
the community of Roosboom in the north of KwaZulu-Natal were
informed that land they had begun to reoccupy was to be restored
to them.[12]

Two years later the Government agreed to return land to
the Riemvasmakers, a stable, small farming community of 1,500
which had been built up over a century in the remote semi-desert
near the Namibian border in the Northern Cape, and dispersed
in 1973 to Northern Namibia and the Ciskei. The odds against
restoration were great. The land had been used by the Army and
also declared a National Park, with the black rhino now inhabiting

one part. The Commission on Land Allocation had been unhelpful, too, but the Riemvasmakers had persevered, submitting evidence which showed their forbears had lived there since precolonial times and their birthright was thus analogous to aboriginal titles accepted in Commonwealth jurisdiction. Moreover, as an economic report had concluded, the mountainous semi-desert had much potential for irrigation farming of high-value crops and eco-tourism. Though the South African Defence Force opposed the claim, the National Parks Board stated that it would stay on the land only if invited by the community, an unexpected source of support which helped to turn the Commission's views in favour of a return. The Army, however, still retained nearly a quarter of the original land and the Riemvasmakers say they will challenge this.

By the time of the Government of National Unity's mid-term report in 1997, the first 10 claims had been referred to the Claims Court, with the Elandskloof community having regained its land. Nevertheless, progress was slow, and Derek Hanekom's office recognized the need for a 'streamlining' Bill to bring more movement to the process. Problems and bottlenecks could only be solved by employing more Commissioners. Moreover, as land redistribution requests came in from those forcibly removed from residential areas and land now used for mining, claims were likely to rocket. The same applied to developed suburbs in former white areas.

THE RECONSTRUCTION AND DEVELOPMENT PROGRAMME

If compromises are inevitably necessary over land claims, it is also clear that those wishing for economic reparation to Africans will have to compromise, too, and come to terms with the implications of the ANC's acceptance of the market economy. For substantial Government intervention, however much some may wish it, can only occur if the economy, which is part of the worldwide capitalist system, expands quickly.

Between 1960 and 1974 the real South African economic growth averaged 5.5 per cent annually. Then for 10 years it was only 1.9 per cent. And while until 1974, the main source of foreign capital was investment, thereafter foreign loans decreased, leaving the country vulnerable.[13] By 1995 the economy was growing again but only by 3.3 per cent, though domestic private sector investment grew more than 32 per cent from early 1993.[14] It would, as Nelson Mandela warned, take years before the situation was radically turned around, largely due to the substantial inherited national debt.[15]

Such, then, is the context in which the Government's Reconstruction and Development Programme (RDP) must be seen – since 1996 no longer a separate ministry, but related to different ministries and under the central control of the Deputy President's office. It is now also seen in relation to a Growth, Employment and Redistribution Programme (GEAR) adopted in 1996. This aims to transform the South African economy and prepare it for a place in a competitive world economy by insisting on an overall framework of economic policy within which all major Government departments must work. It is hoped that this integrated economic strategy, which aims for a 6 per cent growth rate by the year 2000 without rejecting fiscal discipline, will lay the foundations for an enhanced RDP. By restructuring and developing the economy – especially in areas of growth like tourism and through some 20 mega-projects, including the development of the Maputo Corridor and Richards Bay in KwaZulu-Natal, each costing half a billion rand or more – there is an expectation that such a growth rate can be achieved.

However, it is a cruel fact that since 1975 the poor have become poorer. Indeed, in 1991 almost half of South African households lived below the poverty line, with an average annual income in 1975 of nearly 5,000 rand becoming in 1991 3,400 rand (in 1991 prices). To add to the graph of misery it has been estimated that one quarter of all households live on less than half the poverty line figure,[16] many in the former Bantustans, though within white communities poverty has also risen overall from 3 per cent in 1975 to 7 per cent in 1991. In terms of the nine new provinces, the Gauteng area is the wealthiest with only 23 per cent below the poverty line, compared with 72 per cent and 77 per cent in the Eastern Cape and the Northern Transvaal respectively. The rest, except for the Western Cape with 26 per cent poor, are all in the 50 per cent bracket. Often the poorest live in rural areas where women and children are the most exposed.[17] Vulnerable, too, is the 50 per cent of the black population under 25 years of age.[18]

By 1995, when the new Government produced its first full budget, the policy trend was clear: to attract foreign investors and also gently shift wealth and services from mainly white upper-income groups to the poor black masses.[19] It was announced, too, that spending on housing would more than double, though it would still be only 3.4 per cent of non-interest outlays. Health spending would also go up to 13.4 per cent and education costs to 26 per cent. Yet as one businessman observed in 1994, 'You can't make a success of the RDP on a 3 per cent growth rate,' adding that he thought the potential existed for between 5 and 6 per cent.[20]

According to the theory, the Government's RDP programme integrates 'growth, development, reconstruction and redistribution in a unified programme',[21] linked to a policy aimed at providing access to electricity, water, telecommunications, transport and health, education and training services. Broken down into human terms, these figures bring hope for the 12 million without access to drinking water and the 21 million with inadequate toilets and refuse removal.[22] Escom, with excess generating capacity, has begun the task of providing more than the 36 per cent of South African households currently supplied with electricity,[23] its programme reaching 400,000 more in 1996 and 1997.

The RDP hope is to build 2.5 million new homes as part of an economic and human development which would lead to the greater empowerment of citizens. Such development, however, has to be attempted in a climate where 70 per cent of the population receive only 11 per cent of the rainfall and where drought is an imminent possibility, thereby making substantial developments exceptionally difficult.[24] Moreover, as the Rev. Demetris Palos has observed, 'Politicians made promises which are unfulfilled and unfullfillable.'[25] Indeed, after only nine months in power, President Mandela himself was admitting there was insufficient money to meet housing demands, higher wages and better living conditions, and warning that demonstrations and violence could not alter the fact.

By the end of 1995, however, there were 300 new water projects, progress which suggested that the target of bringing water to millions within five years would be met.[26] Indeed, by the end of 1996, 700,000 had been supplied with water, with 1.7 million supplied in 1997. Also in train were 489 RDP projects employing 28,000; the upgrading of 614 municipal service projects, which could benefit 3 million; free health care for children, pregnant women and breastfeeding mothers (though this may well put too much strain on the medical services), as well as 3.5 million free school meals, 2.7 million benefiting from electricity projects and 4,100 families from 64 million rand earmarked for land reform programmes, with another 24,000 families benefiting from land redistribution programmes worth 31 million rand. By the time of the mid-term report of the GNU, the National Nutrition and Social Development programme had reached 1.3 million in 1996 and 1.5. million in 1997, and the Primary School Nutrition programme, though initially plagued with administrative problems, had increased from helping 3 to 5 million. Also by 1997, 2 million trees had been planted across South Africa, involving over 2,000 community forestry projects.

Crime, however, would not stop, as residents of Bloemfontein argued, unless all basic human needs were met. 'The socio-economic factors, which are at the roots of the problem, must first be addressed or we will be fighting a losing battle,' Teboho Tekesi, from the Free State ANC Youth League, warned.[27] It was a vicious spiral, for if South Africa's crime and violence escalated, outside investors would be cautious, which would affect the growth rate, thus slowing down development considerably.

There are, of course, countries outside South Africa anxious to help, including the European Union, which in November 1995 set aside 593 million rand for projects involving education and training, urban development, health, rural development and water provision, trade investment and the promotion of good governance and democratization.[28] In effect this meant supporting groups like the Kagiso Trust, the largest black-led national and independent development agency in South Africa, with its network of community projects, and also the Human Rights and the Cato Manor Development Programmes.

In December 1995 a gala event in Soweto attended by more than 50 ambassadors and high commissioners, as well as local and international business and political figures, sought support to complement local government initiatives. 'Upgrading is the responsibility of municipalities, but for Soweto, with millions of inhabitants, it would take decades to do that,' said Walter Sisulu, speaking for President Mandela. Sponsors were sought, it was explained, for projects such as paving sidewalks or sinking boreholes, a challenge Water Affairs minister, Kader Asmal, responded to by announcing that his department would contribute 500,000 indigenous trees for Soweto to help in its upgrading.[29]

Many other non-governmental organizations and groups have also made development a priority. They range from the Quaker-sponsored reconciliation and reconstruction programme in Cape Town, with its conflict-handling, mediation, peace and reconciliation work, to the Vuleka Trust, based in Botha's Hill, Natal, with its emphasis on training programmes to empower people through interpersonal skills. In the Diakonia Council of Churches in Durban, too, there are teams for development and reconstruction, democracy and justice, community resources and peace. In particular, many groups across South Africa spent their energies in 1995 on voter education programmes aimed at the first-ever local elections that November, though in parts of the Cape and KwaZulu-Natal they were held in 1996 due to unresolved political conflicts.

'The achievement of ordinary South Africans in joining hands after being forced apart for many years, has been astonishing,' one paper commented. 'What was unthinkable a few years ago is now taken for granted.'[30] However, the need for reconstruction to be more tangible was becoming ever more urgent, for too few were seeing improvements in their lives.

Problems were particularly evident in housing, where many different types of homes were needed, with the Government admitting in Parliament in 1995 that only about 10,000 homes had been built in its first year, 50 per cent fewer than in apartheid's last year. Basically a housing backlog of 1.45 million needed eradication by building annually 250,000 houses for new families. In addition, 400,000 migrant workers in 200 hostels had been promised better accommodation. Worse still, delivery targets estimated in 1994

STRUGGLING TO FORGIVE

and advertised as part of the RDP, were unlikely to be met. Indeed, delivery had effectively ground to a halt due to soaring costs for building materials and other difficulties, though ironically funds to build the homes existed, with the housing budget for 1995 boosted by 80 per cent. The situation looked more positive by 1997, however, with 200,000 homes in line for construction and a policy firmly in place to build, or have started, 1 million homes in the first five years of democratic government.

The 70 per cent of the population whose income was less than 1,500 rand monthly stood no chance of securing finance from the private sector and were completely reliant on government capital subsidies of 12,500 or 15,000 rand for housebuilding. But after providing 7,000 rand for a service site, the remaining money was perhaps sufficient only for the foundation and roof. Not surprisingly, many, including politicians, were wary of this approach, yet few of its detractors came forward with alternatives. Crucially, in 1995 the National Housing Finance Corporation was looking at ways to raise wholesale funds for low-cost housing which would make the incremental approach workable.[31]

Effective local government structures were vital, too, for delivery of houses. The success of the Masakhane project, which aims to get tenants (who had withheld payment for local services under apartheid) to begin paying, as in Gauteng, where a 50 per cent improvement rate was registered, was also vital to obtain large-scale private sector housing funds. There were further problems: an underestimation of the housing backlog, changing household patterns and mass migration both from rural areas and neighbouring countries, which have led to the enormous growth of informal settlements on city edges.

The politics of restitution, therefore, could well be blown off course by such structural difficulties. As anger, frustration and disappointment escalate, the patience and tolerance of millions could evaporate with unknown future consequences. The assumption of the Government has been that it can attract major foreign investment and through economic growth address these social needs with minimal international borrowing. Many believe this unrealistic because of the nervousness of foreign investors concerning South Africa's prospects for stability. Moreover, if South

Africa's economy runs into trouble, it could be forced to borrow heavily to appease expectations.[32]

THE HUMAN RIGHTS ISSUE

Human rights in South Africa is a topic which has absorbed the minds of many because of the gross violations which have occurred. Yet, because of the poverty, some argue that without proper attention being paid to social and economic rights, South Africa will have only 'a new order that works for the already advantaged and works against the poor'.[33] Indeed, when the final Constitution was passed in May 1996, though one section of the Bill of Rights contained references to equality, human dignity, and the right to life (the death penalty abolished earlier remained abolished), with equal emphasis on the freedom of political and religious belief and opinion, the economics section stated only that 'the state must take reasonable and progressive legislation and other measures to secure adequate housing'. It took a similar approach, too, in the section on health, food, water and social security. Only after agitation, and a nationwide strike against proposed lock-out rights for employers against striking workers, were trade unions and their right to strike guaranteed.

Agreement was easier about creating a Gender and a Human Rights Commission, the latter launched on the 36th anniversary of the Sharpeville Massacre. Financed through the Justice Department and responsible to Parliament, the Commission was given wide-ranging powers of investigation, search and seizure, and the subpoena of witnesses. At the ceremony where most of its 10 members, including the chairman, Dr Barney Pityana, were sworn in by the Constitutional Court, Deputy President Thabo Mbeki emphasized that freedom for individuals meant nothing unless it included freedom from hunger, poverty, ignorance and fear.[34]

'My own feelings as I followed the evidence at the inquest ranged from amazement at some of the statements made by the security police, or at least amazement that anyone could be expected to believe them, to disgust at the behaviour of doctors who treated Biko during his last days,' wrote one lawyer in 1980.[35] It is the memory of incidents like this which has led to the emergence of groups determined to promote a human rights culture, backed up by legal bodies and the courts and undergirded by the new Constitution. Often the necessity for this becomes clear at the local level, as in the Bellville Police Station in Cape Town, where many former torturers are now involved in community policing.[36] 'The process of turning around,' Dr Pityana has observed, 'is nowhere near finished. Human rights work is for now – and for the future.'[37] Indeed, in his own office he has to work with those who have dealt with indemnity appeals from exiles and others and with civil servants who earlier had implemented banning orders on people like himself.

The police in Bellville and the civil servants in Pretoria are only two of the many groups caught between the past and the future. Within a politics of restitution they raise the vexed question of forgiveness and remembering and how reconciliation can emerge as some form of justice develops. For unless there is a clear change in the police and the military, it is useless to expect forgiveness to be exhibited. For this reason, if for no other, the new user-friendly police uniforms, replacing their paramilitary olive jackets and severe battledress trousers, are welcome. 'It is extremely important and very significant because it's part of the effort to demilitarize the police,' Laurie Nathan, head of the Centre for Conflict Research, has stated. 'But it does not in itself achieve that. I am optimistic it will, but it will need a substantial change in both attitude and conduct as well.'[38]

There has also been an attempt to change senior police titles. Initially some 200 were entitled to use the new names, as uniformed generals and colonels lost their military rank and became directors, superintendents and commissioners, changes which a police representative welcomed, indicating that most police favoured the changes.[39] Since the 1994 election local police, too, have come closer to communities which once despised them, though sometimes they are pressurized towards change through police community forums which the Government has established. But just one bad action will immediately tarnish the newly polished image. Police have also been experiencing changes inside themselves, like Brigadier Steve Van Rooyen who met with Chris Hani, Jacob Zuma and Thabo Mbeki. 'You know what?' he has admitted. 'They were completely different people from what they had been made out to be. It goes to show that perceptions can change when people get to meet and know one another and the reverse is also true.'[40]

At the community level, the Policy Research Project of the Centre for the Study of Violence and Reconciliation in Johannesburg has been involved in disseminating the results of its studies to both regional and national Government, holding workshops on community policing and setting up the first police management training course for middle-level managers with the South African Police. In 1994 the Gauteng Community Policy Project was established under the joint management of the Policy Research Project and IDASA, bringing together a large group of non-governmental organizations from the region, the South African Police and representatives of the metropolitan government's office. Its task was to build community–police relationships; to promote debate around the issues of community policing; and to gather information and develop policy for future use by policy makers within the Ministry of Safety and Security, in the longer term helping communities to be actively involved in policing in their areas.[41] Despite these new approaches, there were reports in 1995 that police torture was still being used, three groups noting that continued human rights violations were 'still the single greatest threat to the successful transformation of the old South African police'.[42] This led the National Safety and Security Minister to promise an independent directorate for investigating complaints.

In the Army the integration of the South African Defence Force, two homeland armies and former MK soldiers, which began in early 1994, was fraught with difficult dynamics, though by the middle of 1995 nearly 10,000 from the former MK and Azanian People's Armies had become part of it.[43] By 1997 over 20 thousand former MK or APLA members had been integrated into the new force or demobilized. Some former Government soldiers, of course, were defensive about their role and anxious for a collective forgetting, while others, who wanted to confess, were concerned about how they were being judged. Only a few were outraged at

STRUGGLING TO FORGIVE

the Magnus Malan trial, although anxiety levels were raised by it as professional soldiers wondered who else might be tried, undermined as they saw themselves to be by a small group in intelligence and other special task groups. In addition there were tensions between their professionalism and the outlook of the former MK guerrillas.[44]

With the prisons, too, South Africa has a long way to go. In 1993, for example, prison violence claimed 44 lives and some prisons were 50 per cent overcrowded. One prison, however, adopted a novel way to reduce tensions, helped by a former stockbroker jailed for fraud, who obtained the support of the authorities to create a soccer field. Soon the Krugersdorp Inmates Football Association was running a league, with reserve sides. Using former connections, the stockbroker also raised money to enable the prison to have a modern, well-equipped gym. Half the inmates were in prison for armed robbery, but all agreed that sport had made life bearable and transformed the atmosphere.[45]

In May 1995, a year after Nelson Mandela's inauguration, a special amnesty was granted for prisoners. Sentences were reduced by a quarter, with a maximum remission of six months, excluding sentences for child abuse. A second remission applied to all charged solely with arms possession, ammunitions and explosives offences associated with political conflicts before 6 December 1993. 'We hope,' said President Mandela, 'we are sending a message to all prisoners that they should mend their ways and make a fresh start. We appeal to society to help them re-settle in communities as responsible and law-abiding citizens.'[46] Patently South Africa's prison population presents an enormous challenge to reformers, for 80 per cent return to prison and conditions can only improve very slowly. 'We should be thinking in terms of building more schools, places of entertainment and more medical institutions,' Nelson Mandela said after visiting Pollsmoor Prison in Cape Town, 'but we have to do something about the overcrowding which is beyond words.'[47]

THE NEW CONSTITUTION

If at the micro level of the prison service there are problems with turning in more positive directions, equally there have been problems at the macro level of the laws and procedures for the overall governance of the country. The legacy of the past has been formidable, but the final Constitution, shaped in part by over 2 million submissions, was agreed in May 1996 by nearly all the main parties, though not without some reservations. IFP boycotted the whole constitutional dialogue, saying it would challenge the result in the courts,[48] though ultimately it accepted the final text.

Immediately the Bill was law, the NP announced its decision to go into opposition.[49] Superficially the NP gained by this, but as one commentator observed wryly as he thought of the TRC's hearings: 'The tears of the good cleric (among others) guarantee that the National Party will be anathema to the present generation of black South Africans, at the very least.'[50] In the Constitution the ANC had opted for 'a simple form of majority rule, despite the complexities of our society', F.W. de Klerk explained,[51] so it was unnatural to continue in Government when all the principles it stood for had been discarded. As the news spread, the rand plunged but later recovered somewhat, though for a long period before the announcement the currency had been in trouble, the country's foreign reserves falling in April 1996 to only 1.73 billion.[52]

The Parliament voting for the new Constitution was very different from all previous ones, with South Africa now united as one country in nine provinces. President Mandela, when defending the appointment of his former wife to a Government post, explained that it should be understood in the context of the GNU which had in it 'all sorts of people whose hands are dripping with blood'.[53] One observer added: 'Half the Parliament is people who have had to learn to forgive. They do it with greater or lesser graciousness.'[54]

One who played a considerable role in the transition was General Constand Viljoen, the Freedom Front leader, who in the main kept a consortium of conservative Afrikaner groups within the parameters of constitutional politics. Chief of the Army from 1976 to 1980 and thereafter head of the SADF until his retirement

STRUGGLING TO FORGIVE

in 1985, General Viljoen showed pragmatism, concerned mainly to represent Afrikaners who said 'they had no party in which they had enough confidence to guide them through the transition'.[55] Understanding that political change not consolidated by economic development would result in political instability, he considered that one Afrikaner task was to help boost the economic development of Southern Africa as a whole. Indeed, the Freedom Front went ahead with settling white farmers in neighbouring countries without waiting for foreign policy approval.

In the November 1995 local elections the Freedom Front obtained well over half the Afrikaner vote, which the General interpreted to mean that most Afrikaners accepted co-existence but had also expressed a wish to be self-reliant. Rejecting comparison with the IFP (despite its Zulu nationalism it is federal, while the Freedom Front stands for territorial self-determination), General Viljoen believed Afrikaners would exercise their political power through a *volkstaat* (a homeland reserved for Afrikaners alone). 'There are areas that can be established now,' he observed, 'though the process will cater for Afrikaners dispersed throughout the country.'[56]

With the conservative Zulus in the IFP on the one hand and the Freedom Front led by a General who, though preaching peaceful co-existence, has rejected assimilation and the 'melting-pot principle'[57] on the other, those attempting to create a non-racial democracy will find that ethnicity issues will not go away, especially as the Constitution safeguards 11 languages. Hence the National Assembly and the National Council of the Provinces will have to come to terms with the relation between Presidential Government in Cabinet and the other groupings, which now includes the National Council of Traditional Leaders, and the indigenous ways by which they govern areas under their authority.

By rejecting a substantial federal solution for South Africa's problems – the major point of disagreement between Chief Buthelezi's party, the IFP, and other groupings – South Africa has opted for a strong central Government, albeit with built-in checks and balances such as the Public Protector, the Constitutional Court and the Commissions, with clear lines of demarcation between national and provincial responsibilities. Yet have these divergent forces really been contained in the new structure, or has South Africa slipped almost inevitably into a one-party democracy, where the support for the ANC-led alliance will always make it the party in power for a decade at least and maybe longer?

SOUTH AFRICA'S NEW EXTERNAL RELATIONSHIPS

South Africa has to redress the past externally, too, by building new and creative relations with all continents, especially her own. Already she has begun to find a new role in Africa, handing over Walvis Bay to Namibia and scrapping its debt, and developing a new relationship with Mozambique which became clear during President Chissano's 1995 state visit. Like Angola, Mozambique paid a heavy price for supporting the South African and Namibian freedom struggles, so Speaker Frene Ginwala felt some apology was due, even though a previous Government had been the destabilizer. Drawing attention to the aggression, economic sabotage and the fomenting of a civil war, which resulted in the deaths of thousands of Mozambicans, with many more maimed, Dr Ginwala addressed the President and said: 'Here before the elected representatives of the South African people, and on their behalf – I want to apologize for the terrible crimes my country committed against the people of Mozambique.'[58]

While Dr Ginwala's statement prompted calls from opposition MPs for her resignation – some even left the debating chamber – the Mozambican President said he accepted it, but 'only in the context that you are encouraging a brother to proceed further in the co-operative alliance with all those who stand for democracy and peace. Your apology has touched my heart and the heart of the whole Mozambican people,' he added. For her part, Dr Ginwala said later that her statements had been based on facts well documented internationally. Some of them had even been admitted by the National Party, including members of the previous Government.[59]

Dr Ginwala's apology was, of course, only the beginning of South Africa's new relations. Now back in the United Nations and the Commonwealth, and a member of the Organization of African Unity, she is also forging new links with Asia and Latin America and with North America and Europe. 'Our role in Antarctica is pivotal,' Harvey Tyson has said, 'as it is in non-proliferation, environmentalism and the new kind of international blocs that are emerging.'[60] Others look out and see a more creative future, too. Barney Desai of the PAC visualizes 'South Africa leading another economic community for Southern Africa' in the middle 'between the rich and the poor; between the first and third world'. Pik Botha, as the (then) Foreign Secretary, even believed South Africa could help forge prosperity for the 100 million people in the 10 nations around her. 'If we succeed,' he has added, 'then in fifteen or twenty years time we will be able to help the rest of Africa.'[61]

South Africa's return to global politics may prove to be a tougher, more complex matter than some imagine, for to balance the competing influences of continents and meet her internal needs at the same time could prove extremely difficult. Already, however, Escom is rehabilitating power grids in several countries and South African railways are upgrading ports in Mozambique, as South African Airways boosts its ties with other African airlines and many companies make Johannesburg their African focus.[62] Yet with Johannesburg being on the shortest route from Singapore to Rio de Janeiro, South Africa also needs links with Asia and Latin America. Two other possibilities also emerge: a new relationship between the countries bordering the Indian Ocean basin, and the development of the Zone of Peace and Cooperation in the South Atlantic, which South Africa has now joined.

SOUTH AFRICA'S NEW INTERNAL RELATIONS

If South Africa's external democratic relations are changing, so are her internal ones, at both local and provincial levels. This is all part of making amends for the past, but clearly it will take a long while before democratic procedures are fully lodged in the minds and hearts of local communities. It is the function of IDASA (the Institute for Democracy in South Africa) to help the country mature as it adjusts to this new life. Originally set up in 1986 to find a democratic alternative to the politics of repression and black–white polarization, its earlier work of facilitating meetings between banned political organizations and prominent white South Africans has been superseded by workshops, seminars and training courses promoting the theory and practice of democracy, including the understanding of good government and informed civilian participation in public life.

In the Free State, for example, IDASA has played a constructive role with its projects at the student level, taking blacks and whites from different universities to Zambia and Zimbabwe, and at the family level offering courses in conflict resolution. At the provincial level it facilitated a negotiation forum out of which emerged the Free State Skills Training Programme. A Rural Development Forum was also set up and education and training forums, too. Now IDASA is involved in community policing issues and forums and workshops for police personnel and communities to help them understand their responsibilities. 'We need more IDASA building-blocks to hold things together,' Teboho Loate, from Bloemfontein IDASA, has observed. 'We need a strong non-governmental organization environment.' Indeed, there are those who think that the real, effective criticism and evaluation of the Government will come from civil society. For Teboho Loate the critical question, however, remains how you reconcile your experience and need as an individual and as a South African, whilst recognizing that society has 'not got to the point where we can identify a South African culture'.[63]

This, of course, is the key task as the ANC and its allies seek to develop a national culture which requires the education of people in 'principles of non-racialism, non-sexism, human rights and democracy',[64] and the NP tries to develop as a multi-racial grouping, though in effect it is based on an Afrikaner identity as much as the IFP is based on a Zulu identity, with which others are invited to associate. The indications are that there will be attempts to forge new alliances and even new parties to get round some of these difficulties.

To date the only unifying memories most South Africans have are ones of conflict. 'There are no common heroes ... no statues or symbols of joint accomplishment,' W.L. Nkuhlu has observed. 'Instead we have the memory and scars of the suffering we have inflicted on each other.'[65] Moreover, as Albert Nolan has remarked, 'European culture has been largely distorted and African culture nearly destroyed',[66] though clearly *ubuntu* (the quality of human-ness) is inherent in many communities, even though severely eroded by apartheid and damaged further by rapid urbanization.

There is much goodwill and energy behind the attempt to build a nation, but fears, too, about possible destinations. One thing is clear: both left and right were taken by surprise by the swift changes which required compromise and lateral thinking because of South Africa's diversity. Indeed, the 50-member ANC National Executive itself reflected this diversity with seven whites, seven Indians and seven Coloureds serving on it.[67]

PROBLEMS OF NATION-BUILDING

South Africans are not agreed about what constitutes nation-building. 'The "new South Africa" I visualize is that of a society ... transcending racial, ethnic and tribal barriers,' Joe Seremane has indicated. 'A society responsive to cultural cross-fertilization which will minimize tensions in human relations.'[68]

Neville Alexander backs this up, arguing that if South Africa rejects the nation-building project, 'we have to accept some sort of ethnic project – because identity is inescapable'. He disagrees pro-foundly with the political philosopher Johan Degenar, who argues that South Africa's inherent contradictions make it vital to give priority to creating a just and democratic society rather than a nation. Building democracy and a nation must not be juxtaposed, he maintains, conceding that because the Broederbond project of separate nationhood failed, many are afraid of nation-building, even though it need not be chauvinistic and can run in tandem with the redistribution of wealth and rights.[69] Building-blocks for such a task have two essential elements: consciousness-building and institution-building, the former revolving round the idea of non-racialism, the latter around institutions of the state and civil society widely regarded as legitimate.

From his Marxist perspective, Neville Alexander does not con-sider a non-racial capitalism historically possible in South Africa. Rather, nation-building must be internationalist and rooted in the poor, in contrast (as he sees it) to the PAC and Black Consciousness attitude which implies struggle to destroy the system, after which the non-racial society will appear. A non-racial project inevitably uses non-racial methods, just like democracy, which cannot be brought about 'by authoritarian means'. There is a big conflict, he concludes 'between these two concepts'.[70]

Professor Degenar sees two contradictory models, too, the National Party's broader view of nationhood, which accommodates ethnicities, differing from the ANC's model of a nation-state, seen as a territorial nation transcending ethnic divisions, yet expected to be 'strongly African nationalist in its sympathies and myths'. Thus the NP's model of cultural diversity would seem to clash fundamentally with the ANC's model of cultural homogeneity. But can a nation be defined by a broad South Africanism and expressed through a renewed National Party? Alternatively, will the ANC's non-racialism ever be supported by more than a few of the Afro-Europeans and Asians as well as most blacks? There is one further complication: an ethnic culture, which adapts itself most successfully to modernization and its conditions, inevitably becomes dominant. What then is the status of cultures with less adaptive skills? If the concept of nation inevitably entails homogeneity in an impersonal culture, would it not be advisable, as Professor Degenar has suggested, to counter the formation of a South African nation 'in favour of a democratic society which can accommodate a plurality of cultures'?[71]

It is these issues, and the effects of affirmative action, whereby more blacks are gaining access to the power structures, which make South Africa such a challenging place. What is clear in all the ambiguities is one thing: no move forward is possible without the development of a culture of tolerance. As has been clear in KwaZulu-Natal, intolerance will lead inevitably to violence and death. For these and other reasons, Professor Degenar refers to the 'myth of the nation', talking instead of 'the sovereignty of justice', to which each citizen owes the highest political loyalty. The goal must therefore be a constitutional, pluralist democracy, with a sense of common belonging and mutual respect for different cultural traditions, where the need to belong is met both by communal cultures and common citizenship replacing a common national feeling.[72]

Further, the word 'national' in both the National Party and the African National Congress needs evaluation, the former burdened with its link with Afrikaner Nationalism, even though the party is now multi-racial (though whites still predominate), the Afrikaner Nationalist ideology being taken over by the Conservative Party. The ANC is likewise afflicted because the word 'national' has been linked with the African liberation struggle. 'This problem of sectionalism,' Professor Degenar has written, 'and the tension between the Charterist position and the Africanist approach within the movement bears witness to this.'[73] To what extent, therefore, is the ANC a genuinely democratic, non-racial movement and to what extent an African nationalist one?

Such complications will remain and may even escalate in importance as a black bourgeoisie emerges and perhaps leaves behind millions of black dispossessed. What will happen, too, if the Asian and Coloured communities eventually feel sidelined? To whom will they turn? Those who will mobilize the poor have not yet emerged, Professor Villa-Vicencio considers. 'But they will ... Even trade unions are developing into bourgeois trade unions – they speak for the employed.'[74]

THE CONTRIBUTION OF THE CHURCHES

Some politicians, of course, are aware of the forces with which they are dealing and know they need help. The former Premier of Gauteng, Tokyo Sexwale, declared: 'The challenge of the churches is to stay with us. If you forsake us, if you abandon us – we will sin; we are just human.'[75] Politicians had sought reconciliation because the churches had formerly taught this concept. Now the Church must help them handle truth, because many could not cope with it. 'It is not given to everyone,' he indicated, 'to be a Nelson Mandela, suffer twenty-seven years in jail and come out full of forgiveness.'[76]

Part of that truth must include raising white consciousness, though this will be difficult for, as Peter Storey has commented, 'Trying to find apartheid supporters is like looking for a Nazi in Germany in 1946'[77] – though in District 6 in Cape Town words have been inscribed on a church wall urging passers-by to recall with shame those forcibly removed because of their skin colour. Yet such statements are rare, as Dr Emilio Castro and colleagues from the World Council of Churches noted after a visit: 'We have often heard the word reconciliation used without any sense of repentance or any offer of restitution.'[78]

Commending any spirituality able to receive the load of the past and not 'transfer hate and revenge into the future', Dr Castro suggested that because all churches saw Christ's cross as God's final attempt to overcome human alienation, 'and, from the side of the victims and in identification with the oppressed, pronounce the words of forgiveness: Father, forgive them, they do not know what they are doing,'[79] South African Christians *should* be able to explore the theme of penitence and restitution, both within church structures and beyond.

Some work has already been done in this field as the Black Anglican Forum has shown, with its emphasis on the need for Africans to find and learn from traditional approaches.[80] 'The whites in so far as they have incarnated their spiritual genius in the South African economic and political institutions have sabotaged and eroded the power of Christian love,' Dr Manas Buthelezi has commented, urging emphasis on black theology 'outside the limitations of the white man's institutions'.[81] But to seek a black theology takes South African Christians not only into new realms in their multi-racial life, but also poses the question: what do the African independent churches with their millions of members have to contribute as South Africa struggles to forgive?

Certainly some consider that too many have turned to liberation theology – which in a sense starts from a negative emphasis on oppression instead of a positive premise – rather than African theology because there is a distinct touch of tribalism about that which they distrust.[82] Dr Frank Chikane, too, has added a caveat to black theology, for in the 1970s and early 1980s a disturbing God reminded him to 'question the very answers of Black theology'. Even though it had freed him from 'the God of the white oppressors', he discovered also that those 'who talked about a black liberation theology could ourselves be oppressors'.[83]

Can the churches, who share in 'the guilt and glory and grandeur of South Africa's conflicts now three centuries old',[84] ever heal such deep wounds? One thing is certain: unless they develop a true understanding of Christ's personal and corporate atoning work, the effect of Christ's crucifixion is in danger of remaining mere theory.

'What is a new agenda for the churches?'[85] is the question which some, like Canon Mcebisi, have asked. Surely it must be to teach South Africans to live neither with utopian fantasies, nor with hopelessness because change is slow. Rather they need a critical solidarity with the Government, to encourage the growth of democracy and underpin it with a theology of empowerment, which enables ordinary people to feel they have some control over their lives. But they must also remind society that it needs continual repentance, as Chief Luthuli realized many decades earlier when he discovered that someone he thought was a transformed Afrikaner had regressed and was now secretary for Bantu education. 'Can it be that he has repented of repenting?' he asked.[86]

Another aspect of the churches' work is concerned with the place of minorities. Of course the Church must speak for the voiceless, and work in the interests of the poorest, but sometimes tasks can change. 'If, for example,' Dr Frank Chikane, now in a senior Government job associated with Deputy President Mbeki's office, has observed, 'at any time in the future a situation were to emerge where injustice was meted out by blacks against whites, I should be obliged to defend the underdog. Indeed, if I were not prepared to return to prison in so doing the gospel I preach would be without integrity.'[87] The churches, too, can aid the birth of a culture of tolerance, especially through the Dutch Reformed family of churches, for within them many of South Africa's main conflicts are visible.

If, as Professor W. Jonker has suggested, 'the quarrel with the English is over', and there is 'a cross-cultural movement',[88] then at another level Afrikaans and English-speaking churches can also become more mutually accepting, which in itself will have further repercussions on society. Moreover, if the Dutch Reformed Churches can recover the authentic Calvinistic tradition which said that 'the sense of revolt which is born in the hearts of the oppressed comes from God',[89] then a sharper theological thinking may emerge as contact between Calvinism and black liberation theology deepens.

Maybe, too, the Pentecostal tradition can contribute a richer insight. Certainly one of its world leaders, David du Plessis, has given a personal example, which could well be emulated more widely, when he described how he was led as a Pentecostal to forgive what he held against Protestants; then to look at Roman Catholics with the eyes of love, which made it easier to forgive; and finally to forgive history itself, for God was lord of history. 'My friends,' he once told a congress in Durban, 'my life was completely revolutionized from the day I began to practise forgiveness.'[90]

CHANGING HISTORY

History, however, is not so easily forgiven, as became clear when Queen Elizabeth II visited South Africa in 1995. Earlier, in 1994, the (then) Prime Minister John Major had addressed the Cape Town Parliament and referred to conflicts where 'right and wrong mingled on each side in the Boer wars and left a bitter legacy'.[91] Now, as Queen Elizabeth started her tour, the issue of Afrikaner suffering again surfaced as leaders of the HNP (Herstige Nationale Party) and the Boerestaat made it clear that the Queen was not welcome. In a letter dated 14 February 1995 addressed to the Queen in London , and also published in South Africa, Jaap Marais (the leader of the HNP) demanded that she kneel before the monument to the dead Boer War women and children. The Freedom Front suggested the Queen should lay a wreath at the Women's Monument,[92] a suggestion supported by the ANC MP Carl Niehaus, who argued that as the Queen was to lay wreaths at memorials for the dead of two world wars, she ought to do the same in Bloemfontein. 'That would be in the spirit of her speech to Parliament,' he added.[93]

In that speech Queen Elizabeth had drawn attention to the spirit of reconciliation evident in the new constitutional arrangements in South Africa, adding that the country had an essential role to play as a new force for regional stability. Though Britain's relationship, 'like that between many old friends, has been at times a tempestuous one,' she commented, 'nevertheless the two countries have much to offer one another. Let us make the most of the affection between us.'[94] At a State Banquet later she referred directly to 'the pain and suffering which [the Boer War] entailed for so many, especially the Afrikaner people'.[95]

F.W. de Klerk later remarked that Afrikaners had overcome past bitterness and, just as they and the British had been reconciled 30 to 40 years ago, there was now a reaching out to all South African communities in order to build a new nation together.[96] 'Britain over the years had had its differences with almost every one of the peoples of South Africa – be they Afrikaner, Zulu or Xhosa,' one newspaper commented,[97] adding that the British and the Zulus at any rate 'seem to have forgiven each other for past clashes'.[98]

Kaiser Nyatsumba was more reflective when he drew attention to those who urged that the past should not be dragged into the present. 'There is a lot of merit in that argument,' he wrote, 'for a country with the kind of history ours has.' But there were things that ought not to be forgotten. Knowledge of the past could enable people to appreciate the present better and to know what 'pitfalls and temptations' to eschew.[99]

As Queen Elizabeth discovered, reparation for past events can suddenly be demanded. Even though General Smuts believed that since the Boer War 'Britain has made ample amends for her sins and South Africa has no truer friend',[100] others remained unreconciled, still feeling that an explicit apology is needed, perhaps to be given during the 100th anniversary of the Anglo-Boer War in 1999. Such an apology, however, would have to be to both blacks and whites, which might then open up once more the controversy over a formal apology for apartheid itself.

Certainly, for a new friendship between South Africa and Britain to be properly pursued, past events need to be transcended, perhaps by acts like that between the Zulus and the British regiment which lost 153 men in the battle at Rorke's Drift last century, whose cadets are raising £200,000 to build a community hall at a school situated on the battlefield.[101] Sometimes, too, symbolic meetings can help to move history on, such as the occasion in 1996 when Chief Buthelezi, grandson of the Zulu leader of the time, met at Rorke's Drift with Brigadier David Bromhead, whose ancestor Gonville Bromhead had received a Victoria Cross for bravery in the battle.

These issues also need dealing with on an individual level, which is where the South African Nobel Laureate Peace Park and Academy, launched in March 1996 at the Wilgespruit Fellowship Centre, can play a part. One of its most creative aspects is the Peace Trail, starting with the Anglo-Boer War, and including counselling opportunities, a meditation area, a flame of forgiveness and an area where individuals have to walk over hard and stony ground to reach their destination. Chief Albert Luthuli's family donated his pass book, so it could be burned and its ashes interred in the Peace Park. Archbishop Tutu has given the Cross of Nails, originally presented to him by Coventry Cathedral.[102]

When it comes to building new relationships within communities or between groups, however, such approaches are more difficult, as some cry out for justice and others cannot forget. All the issues raised in this book – forgiveness in relation not only to restitution but also to justice, healing, love, repentance, remembering and reconciliation – had to be confronted in the township Mpophomeni, for example, where the conflict between the IFP and the ANC had been very intense but had subsided by 1995. Clifford Mabaso, a low-profile ANC community leader, who had lost his own son in Imbali, had earlier floated the idea of a reconciliation memorial for the township which would bear witness to the community's desire to end its strife.

His idea caught on and plans were made for its erection. The Nokulunga Gumede Reconciliation Memorial, in memory of the girl who had been killed by an army vehicle, was opened on 16 June 1995 – Soweto Day. The names of others who had died were put on the memorial only at the express wish of their families, even if their names were known, as an indication that the families themselves wanted reconciliation. At the unveiling the police and the main political parties were all represented. So, too, was the community which had suffered. The Rev. Dr Khoza Mqojo attended from the SACC, and the Bishop of Natal, Michael Nuttall, said prayers, blessed the people and asked for forgiveness. English farmers from the neighbourhood also came to the event. Next to the memorial, itself a unique symbol of reconciliation in South Africa, a cross was erected on the spot where Nokulunga Gumede had died.[103]

Other incidents across South Africa are also a cause for hope, ranging from a Soweto pastor who encourages people to bring back stolen goods which he refuses to surrender to the police, saying they represent 'people confessing',[104] to the Afrikaners who bombed the house of Cas Human, because of his anti-apartheid activities, now greeting him in the street.

The story of Frank Erasmus, who once petitioned his town council to build a Berlin Wall to keep blacks from a nearby squatter camp out of his suburb, is also instructive. Realizing they had come to stay, he made contact with the leader in the nearby black township, and one Sunday night he drove with four others to a church where they were welcomed by a singing, cheering crowd of 400. More meetings followed and soon the two communities removed the litter from a stretch of land between them and planted a tree of peace, as a watching crowd held hands and sang 'Come together, people of Africa', after which everyone sat beside the wall for a beer and barbecue party. Later, as hard-line whites moved away from the suburb of Boksburg where this minor miracle had occurred, the area became multi-racial.[105]

Three other stories also point to a constructive future. One concerns Neil Alcock, an English South African, who once farmed in a prosperous area in Natal before throwing up his comfortable existence in the 1970s to start a land reclamation scheme in Mdukatshani, an impoverished part of Zululand. While there, Neil and and his wife Creina lost all their possessions when their hut burned down, but soon Zulus began to converge on them, some offering cash, others promising help with the rebuilding.[106] It was a triumph for the love they had both shown during their time in the region.

Sadly, worse was to come when in 1988 Neil Alcock and five Zulus with him were ambushed and killed. It seemed as though all his work against desertification, and his identification with Africa, had come to nothing. 'Creina and Neil Alcock were the only whites I knew who had lived for decades among Africans on more or less African terms.' Rian Malan has commented. 'They arrived in Africa years ahead of the rest of us, and it was hard not to see their experience as some sort of foretaste of what awaited the rest of us there.'[107]

But Neil Alcock's love was not unrewarded. There is grass where before there was none and the *dongas* (steep-sided gullies) are slowly silting over, aided by the Zulus Neil Alcock had trained. There is less tension between the Zulus and the white farmers on the border, too, though they say this is because Neil Alcock no longer stirs things up with his radical proposals.

There is one further fact to note. In the winter of 1988 two age-ing Zulu men stood on the spot where Neil had been killed and asked his spirit to enter their sacred stick. They then returned to the mud hut by the river where his widow still lived. Next day a vast Zulu crowd gathered, wearing old clothes so the returning spirit would recognize them and not be startled. Several *sangomas* (witch doctors) were in the crowd, with their traditional beads and totems, inflated pig bladders in their hair. Two cattle were slaugh-tered and their carcasses butchered and hung in Creina's bedroom so there was blood everywhere, to wash away past sins. 'After that,' writes Rian Malan, 'the ceremony became a celebration and Zulus came from far and wide to join in ... In the end the sun went down and the celebrants went home, leaving the horns of the sacrificed cattle nailed to the roof of Creina's home.'[108] Neil Alcock had finally become an honoured ancestor.

The second story concerns Mama Mabala, a woman in Soweto, who with her husband has given over her home and garage to more than 70 of the thousands of street children who inhabit South African cities, often with no remaining link with their homes. 'We tell them to forgive everybody,' Mama Mabala has explained. 'Some are calling to see their sisters and fathers; some did not want to see them before ... They can stay here but they must go to the others and forgive them ... There is no peace for them until they forgive everybody and make a new feeling in their hearts.'[109]

The third story is just as intimate and concerns Sylvia Collier, a Roman Catholic in Cape Town who went on a weekend retreat and found she was sharing it with Dr Mamphele Ramphele, now Vice-Chancellor of the University of Cape Town. At the final meal

STRUGGLING TO FORGIVE

Sylvia Collier broke the usual silence and asked Dr Ramphele if people in the townships would respond to contemplative prayer. Dr Ramphele replied positively, encouraging Sylvia Collier to persevere in her aim of introducing such prayer to the townships. 'At this stage of the conversation,' Sylvia Collier has remembered, 'I felt so much pain welling up in me because I was aware of my life and her life and how different they had been ... With the awareness of the pain I found tears running down my face uncontrollably.'

Dr Ramphele was astonished and asked what the tears meant. Sylvia Collier explained that she felt anguish about what people had done to one another. Dr Ramphele replied that all South Africans needed to 'let go of the past and forgive each another'. Sylvia Collier reflected, 'I went away from the retreat encouraged by her attitude regarding the prayer and her attitude towards me as a white South African.' She then made links in Nyanga with a group of women who had started a crèche for pre-school children, attending one of their meetings to explain contemplative prayer. 'The quality of the silence was deep as the eight women responded,' she observed of the small initiative which she continues to develop.[110]

Sylvia Collier is just one of the many who have discovered that the suffering endured by black South African men and women has ennobled them, enabling them to enrich others. 'Suffering either destroys you or makes you,' Donald Cragg, the secretary of the Church Unity Commission, has remarked. For him, it was the example of Robert Sobukwe which made an impact as great as Dr Ramphele had on Sylvia Collier.[111]

ROBERT SOBUKWE, NELSON MANDELA AND THE POLITICS OF FORGIVENESS

Like Chief Luthuli, whose image is now to appear on all new South African passports, Robert Sobukwe was rooted in his Christian conviction. He had, as many have noted, an astonishing personality and was respected by everyone. 'He took all people on the same level,' says one of his colleagues. 'How did he do it? We don't know.'[112]

Critical of the far-left tendency in the ANC, his African nation-alism was never narrow and even his guards on Robben Island, where he spent nine years, came to respect him. Released when he became ill and sent to Kimberley, he was put under house arrest and further humiliated by not being allowed to take up a profes-sorship in America, because the Minister of Police would not relax the banning order, thus preventing him from travelling to the airport. His last chance of making 'a healthy and happy family life', as Aelred Stubbs has remarked, was gone.[113]

He did manage to practise as an attorney in Kimberley, how-ever, but earned little as his clients were poor, his lawyer's office being more like a doctor's consulting room. But in 1977 he became ill with lung cancer. While he was waiting for his operation, Steve Biko died. Robert, under sedation but still fully conscious, saw the headline in a newspaper which had been left in a corridor,[114] so attempts to conceal Biko's suffering from him proved futile.

Despite the purgatory of his life, he remained triumphant. When the Rev. Joe Fourie met him in Kimberley, for example, his capacity to forgive was already evident.[115] Joe Seremane confirms this spirit, describing one occasion when he was with Robert Sobukwe and they came across a police truck on its side, sur-rounded by a crowd of blacks who were teasing the officer in diffi-culty. Robert Sobukwe took off his jacket and as the crowd opened up, he went to help the policeman lift the wheel and deal with the punctured tyre.

'Why do you help these dogs?' Joe asked.

'If you want them to be loving,' Robert Sobukwe replied, 'you must help them to love.'[116]

Sobukwe's spirit of forgiveness was one of the most striking things about him, transcending his intellectual prowess and political wisdom, illuminating the very fibre of his personality. Once, recu-perating in Cape Town after serious surgery, he was visited by Alex Boraine, who asked him how he saw the future and looked at the past. Sobukwe, 'gentle with a strength that was very humbling', said he felt 'sorry for the Government', blind to the situation and its seriousness. 'And then,' Alex Boraine continues, 'he used this phrase "We must forgive them because they really don't know what they are doing. We must pray for them that their eyes will be opened."'

STRUGGLING TO FORGIVE

Boraine says, 'He then asked me: "Will you pray for them now?" So I knelt next to him, although he hadn't asked me to. I also prayed for the government. Then he prayed and said: "Father, forgive them." He also said: "Take away all bitterness from us and help us to work for a country where we will all love each other, not hate each other because hate will destroy us all."'[117]

'You could see forgiveness in him,' the Rev. Arthur East has observed, adding as he contemplated the emergence of a spirit of forgiveness in South Africa: 'Maybe Robert Sobukwe started all these things.'[118] Such people, in the view of the poet Don Mattera, need no spot which marks the place where they lie. Rather, Robert Sobukwe should be set to rest on a high mountain to enable him to see the land he loved and for whose people he died.[119]

If Robert Sobukwe's death had a transcendental quality about it, so, too, has Nelson Mandela's life. 'God's providential gift to South Africa', as Archbishop Denis Hurley has described him,[120] he is exorcizing South Africa's history in a profound way. He is also having a global impact as the world looks to South Africa now with hope, a fact which was clear during his state visit to Britain in 1996.

'President Mandela forgives 200 years of injustice' read one newspaper headline commenting on his address to both Houses of Parliament. 'He did not dwell on the colonial past,' its reporter explained, 'but stressed the help some British leaders, from William Wilberforce to Harold Macmillan, had given to bring about a change for the better in South Africa. But if he did not dwell on the underside he made it clear he was aware of it, also.'[121]

'Eight decades ago,' Mandela reminded his listeners in Parliament, 'my predecessors in the ANC came to these venerable houses to say to the Government and the legislators of the time that they, the patricians, should come to the aid of the poor citizens. With no pikes to accompany them, because British armies had defeated and disarmed them, they spoke eloquently and passionately of the need for the colonial power to treat them as equal human beings, equal to the 1820 settlers and others who wafted down from Europe before and after 1820.' But the delegation was rebuffed. Despite this and 'the terrible cost we had to pay as a consequence, we return to this honoured place neither with pikes, nor a desire for revenge, nor, even, to assuage our hunger for bread,' he continued.[122] Rather he came as a friend to all the people of the native land of Archbishop Trevor Huddleston, though, of course, behind the scenes he urged the keeping of promises to help South Africa's economy, for apartheid had taken a terrible toll.

'The symbol of Mr Mandela's state visit is immense,' wrote one journalist. 'Today, apartheid's most prominent political prisoner, once reviled by British government leaders, will be received with a 21-gun salute and will ride in a State Carriage down the Mall with the Queen.'[123] A chapter lasting two centuries was being closed, Mandela asserted, as a new millennium approached. He hoped that for both Britain and South Africa it would herald the advent of a 'glorious summer of a partnership for freedom, peace, prosperity and friendship'.[124]

Certainly the words 'Nelson' and 'Trafalgar' would never mean quite the same again. As this latter-day Nelson – who was a peace-maker rather than a successful victor in war – surveyed Trafalgar Square from the balcony of South Africa House, outside which anti-apartheid campaigners had kept vigil for so many years, he knew that he and South Africa had this century made the politics of forgiveness uniquely their own.

Epilogue

South Africa's legacy of conflict – English–Afrikaner; Black– white; African–Indian; Indian–white; Black–black, with the Coloured community not yet sure where to focus its primary identity – presents post-1994 South Africans with a complex set of shared, and often bitter, memories which need to be overcome. But history cannot easily be transcended, either by communities or individuals, and can indeed remain alive in a mythical or a political way, sometimes in a subtle combination of them both.

Moreover, groups in South Africa see the same history entirely differently, which makes the task of forgiving extremely complicated. Add to this cocktail the fact that certain policies were pursued because of forces outside the country – Communism this century and the rise of Johannesburg as a commercial centre last century – and the problems become compounded.

It is important, therefore, to work creatively on the relation of forgiveness to remembering. To forgive does not mean to deny or cast aside the wrongs done. Forgiveness in history does, however, mean that the sting is taken out of past events. As the Welsh Nationalist Waldo Williams has said, forgiveness is finding the way through the thorns to the side of the old enemy.

THE GERMAN EXPERIENCE

The process can be seen clearly by considering how Germany sought to heal wounds and relate to the international community after 1945, though she was helped by the rise of the Cold War which meant she was needed as an ally. Her financial reparations to Israel, albeit forced on her, played a key role along with other reparations, an indication that in great conflicts there is a relation between forgiveness, remembering and repairing or reparation.

Essentially, of course, time had to elapse before any form of reconciliation could be effective, especially between Germany and France, though this was ultimately achieved, as was reconciliation with Britain and with all the north European countries. Reconciliation with Poland, Czechoslovakia and Russia took longer because of East/West tensions and conflicts, but here, too, a process was at work which culminated in Chancellor Willy Brandt's *Ostpolitik*. Nevertheless, some after-effects of Germany's actions remain unresolved to this day.

If timed properly, formal apologies can help the process, for genuine repentance eases situations and makes new beginnings possible. But repentance alone, which does not issue in deeds, can do more harm than good, because there are bound to be doubts about the genuineness of the repentance if there are few changed attitudes or policies. Thus the Stuttgart Declaration – issued just after 1945 by leading pastors, who themselves had fought Nazism – controversial though it proved to be because it only talked about Germany's guilt, paved the way for the world Church, through the ecumenical movement, to come to Germany's help. The Nuremberg trials were also a key ingredient in bringing what many felt to be a measure of justice to the resolution of the conflict, though only selected leaders were tried and sentenced to death.

Also helpful on specific occasions were visits and statements from charismatic figures, such as when Chancellor Brandt knelt in penitence in Warsaw and President Richard von Weizsäcker visited Prague after the collapse of Communism and sought forgiveness from the Czechoslovak people on the very spot where Hitler had announced the annexation of their country. In addition, he did not shrink from reminding the German people of what they had done in a speech to the Bundestag on 8 May 1985, the 40th anniversary of the end of World War II in Europe.

The allies could, of course, have left a defeated Germany to solve its own problems, but it was against their self-interest. Altruistic forces, too, compelled a more forgiving approach which perhaps amounted to love – exemplified on the personal level by Save

Europe Now, which sent food parcels for individuals in distress, and on the corporate level by Marshall Aid, set up by President Truman to help reinvigorate Europe. Perhaps some of these responses also contained a dim apprehension that Germany's disaster was in part related to the severe reparations imposed on the country by the Treaty of Versailles at the end of World War I.

SOUTH AFRICA'S STRUGGLE TO FORGIVE

Such reflections highlight the seven main themes of South Africa's struggle to forgive after a long period of colonialism and a protracted (but contained) civil war. They point to reconciliation as an overarching goal, the theme which has preoccupied two of the country's main charismatic figures, Desmond Tutu and Nelson Mandela. They also highlight how significant remembering is as a human experience, and how it can overwhelm those who do not deal with it. Repentance in South African terms must come not only from Afrikaners but also from other white communities who, by their silences and sometimes by their active support, froze the society in a time warp. Love and forgiveness in terms of politics are less easy to discern, but they must always find their pivot in the tension between majorities and minorities, where by restraint all-powerful groups deliberately do not trample on those who have little significance in their eyes.

Healing, perhaps uniquely the task of the churches and other world faith communities, if first they reform themselves, can come through all manner of activities and therapeutic works, as well as through discerning the signs of the times – in South Africa's case the effects of the world monetary system with all its complications on the young democracy.

Justice, always to be sought and never fully attained, hopefully will now find some fundamental base in South Africa through its Constitutional Court, which will serve as a bulwark against future tyranny. Yet justice in human rights terms will mean little if economic development fails to materialize and corporate restitution is experienced as a pale shadow of the original intentions of the negotiators of the new future.

In South Africa reparation is probably the key which will open the doors leading to all the other themes, affecting both individuals and communities. However, in so far as apartheid was sustained by the international community, though there were always those who opposed it, countries such as the United Kingdom now have a moral responsibility to act not only in their own interest, but also to redress what the West has taken out of South and Southern Africa for so long.

It is indeed in no one's interests to have South Africa in flames because expectations cannot be met. South Africans, on the other hand, cannot expect the international community to invest in their country if crime does not subside and the democracy is not run with care. There must be neither cheap triumphalism, because now there is majority rule, for example, nor naive romanticism which thinks that if only certain obstacles to economic growth were removed all would be well.

FORGIVENESS ELSEWHERE IN AFRICA

South Africans should take heart, however, when it comes to national reconciliation, because they are following in the footsteps of a fine African tradition. In Kenya under President Jomo Kenyatta, for example, a similar policy was pursued with much success. 'I myself suffered for long,' he once wrote, 'but I promise you I am not bitter. I ask those of you who still have hatred in your hearts to cast it aside.'[1] A happy and prosperous nation could not be built, he felt, while people harboured ill feelings about the past. He developed this idea in a speech in 1963 when he said: 'One thing I want to make clear is this. We must learn to forgive each other. There is no perfect society anywhere. Whether we are white, brown or black, we are not angels. We are human beings, and as such we are bound to make mistakes. But there is a perfect gift we can exercise, that is to forgive one another...'[2]

Robert Mugabe in Zimbabwe preached in a similar vein at the start of the new nation,[3] and in Mozambique, of course, President Samora Machel conducted a five-day 'trial' of 1,000 representatives from among the 100,000 collaborators with the former

STRUGGLING TO FORGIVE

Portuguese colonial rulers. Here forgiveness in politics was a necessity, for how could so many be imprisoned, even if tried and found guilty? Instead, representatives from the secret police, the army, and so on, were made to come out and recount their stories of spying, massacres and betrayal in front of Frelimo leaders. Then Samora Machel 'pardoned' the perpetrators, though earlier their names had been made public in the places from which they came. The guilty could then take down their name tags and go free, provided they committed themselves with other Mozambicans to building the new country. 'There are,' Machel said finally, 'no secret police or traitors any more.'[4]

SOUTH AFRICAN COMPLEXITIES

Such responses are not dissimilar to the actions taken in South Africa. But South Africa differs radically from other African countries because of the complexity and numbers of its multi-cultural mix. There can, therefore, never be such a straightforward solution as in Kenya, Zimbabwe or Mozambique. This irritating fact brings South Africans up with a start and makes them understand more than most the imperfections of nation-states and indeed the imperfect nature of politics itself. Perhaps, too, it teaches them their need to learn how to forgive the fallibilities of history and not itch for utopias as some among them have in past decades.

There has been little acculturation (or assimilation) yet in South Africa, of course. 'The cultures of the different groups and a growing cosmopolitan culture are in sharp contrast,' as W.A. de Klerk has observed, 'as are rural and urban cultures, white and non-white cultures, and Afrikaans and English cultures,' adding that in his view, 'ethnic cultures draw lines in South Africa. Ours is not an ordinary pluralism; it is a conflict pluralism.'[5] If this is true, it may well present South Africans with serious problems. Alternatively they may be the world pioneers of a multi-cultural, multi-faith society. What is clear is that without love nothing can develop – love of diversity and a tolerance of the complexities of society. Indeed, any attempt to give precedence to one group, or to downgrade another, will put the new democracy in jeopardy.

There is one further problem and that is the number of conflicting forces impinging on South African society: international capitalism; fundamentalist Islam from North Africa; American and British media styles and approaches; radical socialist hopes and aspirations; Africanization and in some cases a strengthening of tribalism; the enlightenment tradition versus traditional African models of leadership; and so many forms of Christian expression that it is almost impossible to itemize them. Such forces can make for a rich and creative society, but they can also lead to some groups feeling threatened and overwhelmed, enabling clever leaders to play on incipient fears.

All South Africans are affected by these influences, either becoming incorporated into them or revolting against them. They are affected, too, by the subtle interactions between the various histories, different for all sides. This, however, may well elude the unseasoned observer, for they range from the Coloureds 'who have to stretch both ways and across'[6] to those who side with the Africans and 'live on the frontiers of life'[7], and to those whites who recognize that South Africa has always been a partnership between black and white, but who know now they must be prepared for a drop in standards so that many more can have a stake in health and education.[8]

NEW ROLES FOR SOUTH AFRICANS

At every point in South African society, therefore, roles have to change, sometimes dramatically, sometimes more slowly and imperceptibly. On the one hand Afrikaners need to find a new place in society if they are not to remain 'on the political sidelines for ever', as Nelson Mandela has warned Afrikaner intellectuals.[9] On the other hand young Moslems, like Ebrahim Rasool, have to wrestle with the meaning and significance of compromise in post-1994 South Africa, even if it means that some of the cherished convictions held during the struggle years have to be modified.[10]

Futhermore, it is inevitable that opposition will emerge as in all multi-party democracies. Yet, as the ANC-led alliance with the South African Communist Party and the trade union movement,

COSATU, is likely to be the dominant political grouping national-ly for the forseeable future, it is most probable that any major opposition to ANC policies will come from within its ranks, espe-cially if the Government allows, or is unable to prevent, a new underclass from developing. Inevitably, therefore, the struggle in politics will be again and again to forgive the imperfections, alliances and temporary arrangements of democratic life, in the face of appalling sorrows and needs. Nonetheless, political con-structions which are anything less than fully democratic are likely to be worse for South Africa, both in the short- and long-term, in view of all the international pressures on her.

Such maturity in a young democracy demands much from its leaders, but already there are many who understand these compli-cations. If, then, the international community – which was mobi-lized during the apartheid years to support the struggle against it – wants to be constructive, it must show a fresh solidarity with South Africa in all her complexities and can perhaps also learn from her new explorations and her attempts to build 'a rainbow nation'.

In the dynamics of groups, whether large and small, one person can be made by the processes at work to play either a negative or a positive role. In the same way a nation can be singled out by the others to be a focus for strands in international life which either trouble or excite. This is what has happened to South Africa in the past, when anger was expressed towards Pretoria by the Western nations, perhaps because of an unconscious guilt, itself the legacy of slavery going back centuries as a result of European encounters with Africa. Now, with the tables turned, hopefully South Africa can demonstrate for America and Europe how to struggle success-fully with issues so familiar to them: relations between rich and poor both within nations and between north and south; between majorities and minorities, whether of faith, race, culture or gender; creative handling of land questions and how to balance, within this mix, traditional and enlightenment insights and perceptions.

THE ROLE OF RELIGION

South Africa's expectations, which are being worked out by many differing groups, can ultimately only be made effective by putting forgiveness into politics, indeed by allowing religion itself to have a legitimate and public role. This will be difficult for South Africans, for in the past it has been religion which has played such an ambiguous role in establishing apartheid, both formally and informally. Nevertheless, religion is crucial to the South African experience, for it pervades the country – partly because of the African awareness of the supernatural, partly because Calvinist theology in particular takes God seriously and seeks to allow God's reign among both individuals and groups. Indeed, over 80 per cent of South Africans claim adherence to some form of Christianity and there are also small but vigorous Hindu, Jewish and Moslem communities.

Forgiveness, of course, is not solely the prerogative of Christianity, though it is pivotal to it, nor indeed is it the prerogative of religious people alone. It is rather a state of mind and heart which recognizes that life on earth can never be utopian, and that the checks and balances which democratic societies have carefully established, sometimes over centuries, are important. South Africans have to wrestle theologically with this experience and interpret it religiously as well as culturally, personally and politically. They will need especially to explore the hinterland between forgiveness and repentance and which comes first, as well as the vexed relation of justice to forgiveness. They need to ask themselves, too, if there can ever be healing for millions if there is no restitution or reparation for past wrongs and if a more caring society is not created.

For the Christian community in South Africa specifically, forgiveness stems from the teaching of Jesus Christ, through whose life and death God reached out to humanity with forgiveness, demonstrated again and again by Christ in parables and through actions which often involved healing. This came to its inevitable climax in the crucifixion, and in the Book of Acts the stoning of Stephen confirms this central fact of Christ's ministry, for Stephen is presented by the early Christians as dying a martyr's death, like Jesus, with words of forgiveness for his tormentors on his lips.

To use the classical theological word 'atonement' is, perhaps, to sterilize God's dramatic action of healing and reconciliation through Christ, as human sin is set aside. But in effect that is what South Africans are being led to explore in their own histories, as some struggle to repent, others to forgive or make restitution, and yet more to find liberation through remembering in a new way. They struggle, too, to understand how God's justice and love intermingle in atonement so that God's final act of justice is to forgive – which is both the final justice and the end of justice.

In the Christian tradition God blots out transgressions, but as contemporary South Africans know only too well, memory sears and scars and threatens to ruin both present and future. Add to this the fact that few South Africans have in common any positive memories of the past, except the 1994 General Election, and you have a society very much in transition, almost on a pilgrimage to a new destination, the map routes for which are not always clear.

THE FUTURE

What, then, can happen? Surely there must be a growth of consciousness which leads to a realization that all have suffered. The Africans have suffered by being oppressed for so long. But the oppressors have suffered, too, for it was their very fear of the numerical strength and power of a culture alien to them which made them so grotesque in their behaviour. In such ferment the temptation to use violence on the one hand, or revert to lethargy on the other, becomes overriding. Some leave South Africa for good, of course, but few can take that route, so another option is to refuse to act responsibly, the effects of which can be just as damaging.

If, however, South Africans can seize their destiny and find deep meaning and significance in their experiences, they may well be given the courage to go forward in faith together despite the ambiguities, paradoxes and contradictions of their history. Here religious faith becomes paramount and for the Christian community at least there are theological, liturgical, sacramental and spiritual resources, as well as the wisdom contained in the Bible itself about the way God acts in history and in both personal and communal living, which can bring new life and possibilities.

One thing is certain, for South Africans as for others: there can be no let up on forgiveness, for when one issue has been dealt with, another inevitably occurs. Forgiveness in politics, therefore, just as in personal life, must continue to be understood as a process, rather than something to be applied temporarily, like a poultice. It must also, however, in any given situation be related to the other ingredients of atonement. The Truth and Reconciliation Commission, for example, involves reparation, remembering, love and repentance, with justice being given a low profile. The South African authorities offer financial help to victims as a form of repairing, and the victims are encouraged to forgive, though their memories still hurt. The perpetrators of wrong, if they acted politically and can prove it, are encouraged to remember what they did by recounting the details to the Truth Commission, and are implicitly asked to repent. They are then given a formal pardon by the President. Their names, however, and what they have done, are made public to satisfy in part the need for justice. The great spirits will, of course, be reconciled, but this will not be the experience for most, who will live with their scars and stains for the rest of their life.

In terms of the Land Commission, healing for the dispossessed will come through reparation and justice, when they either get their land back, or receive some other land, or are at least awarded financial compensation as of right. The state accepts responsibility for doing this, for it was the state which took land away in 1913 and in 1936 and now desires to make restitution as far as this is practical. By telling their stories to the Land Commissioners – remembering – the victims will experience some form of catharsis. Repentance here comes not so much from individuals but from the body politic, which has set these legal processes in place, at the end of which some form of reconciliation might be experienced by the aggrieved. Again, however, there will be no perfect solution in the arrangements and negotiations themselves are bound to be protracted.

As far as the churches are concerned, the Dutch Reformed Church is the group which can most creatively follow a path of forgiveness in politics. For healing to occur, however, it needs to show more love for the churches it has established. This is what is now occurring in part through the pressures on it from the Uniting Church. Reconciliation is in the air, albeit slowly. The DRC daughter-churches, of course, remember their past treatment, but hopefully will be able to put it aside as the uniting process for the whole DRC family in South Africa develops, no doubt with false moves and dawns.

Perhaps surprisingly, one of the most conservative of the DRC group of churches – the NHK – in July 1997 amended its 200-year-old constitution to allow blacks to become members. But the main DRC stumbling block to better relations with its daughter-churches has been the adoption of the Belhar Confession, which broadly maintains that apartheid was a sin. Two DRC black churches which accepted Belhar insist that the main Dutch Reformed Church, the NGK, must also adopt the confession if unity is to be established between them all, and in 1997 pulled out of a joint committee working towards a united Church. Within the main DRC family there are clearly deep divisions, too, between conservative and liberal members on the issue of unity, with many in the Western Cape clearly wanting unity soon.[11]

In the 1980s many South African theologians declared that it was a time of *kairos* in South Africa. Now it is a time of new *kairos*, in which South Africans are certainly involved, but which affects the entire planet. The world is being tested at all levels as the millennium approaches, when drastic policies will be needed to cope with global problems. South Africa has already moved into this future with one big leap forward, developing a politics of forgiveness in a more sophisticated manner than any other country. She now needs to show how citizens can be empowered to join in that process at the grass roots and help create a multi-faith and multi-cultural society across all the former divisions. If South Africa can begin to do this, she could become one of the key players in the 21st century.

Notes

Prelims

1. Nokukhanya Luthuli in Peter Rule, with Marilyn Aitken and Jenny van Dyk, *Nokukhanya: Mother of Light*, The Grail, South Africa, 1993, p. 166.
2. Professor Adam Small, *The Star and SA Times*, 10 April 1996, p. 9.
3. Moses Mapalakanye, in *Let's Reconcile*, Quarterly Journal of the Reconciliation and Reconstruction Programme of the Quaker Peace Centre, Cape Town, 1995–6, p. 8.
4. Mmutlanyane Stanley Mogoba, *Convicted by Hope*, (ed) Theo Coggin, Department of Public Relations and Communication of the Methodist Church of Southern Africa, September 1994, p. 75.
5. Jan Gruiters, Secretary for Africa Affairs, Pax Christi, Netherlands, in Pretoria to author, 4 December 1995.
6. Rev. Arthur Blaxall, *Suspended Sentence*, Hodder & Stoughton, 1965, p. 125.

Chapter 1

1. Miriam Makeba, interviewed on the South Bank Show, ITV London, 9 April 1995.
2. Nelson Mandela, *Long Walk to Freedom*, Little, Brown and Co, 1994, p. 604.
3. Lord Walston, letter, *The Independent*, 15 June 1988.
4. *Mission to South Africa, The Commonwealth Report*, Penguin, 1986, p. 73.
5. Ibid., p. 137.
6. Fatimer Meer, *Higher than Hope*, a biography of Nelson Mandela, Hamish Hamilton, 1988, p. 22.

7. Ibid., p. 25.

8. Mandela, *Long Walk to Freedom*, p. 106.

9. Ibid., p. 147.

10. Julius Nyerere, in Kenneth W. Gruchy, *Guerrilla Struggle in Africa*, a World Order Book, Grossman Publishers, New York, 1971, pp. 30–3.

11. Nelson Mandela, *No Easy Walk to Freedom*, Heinemann, 1965, p. 109. The letter was dated 26 June 1961.

12. Ibid., p. 164.

13. Mandela, *Long Walk to Freedom*, p. 350.

14. Mandela, *No Easy Walk to Freedom*, p. 189.

15. 'Mac' Maharaj, interviewed in London in 1978, in Nelson Mandela, *The Struggle Is My Life*, International Defence and Aid Fund, London, 1990, pp. 249–50.

16. Mandela, *Long Walk to Freedom*, p. 474.

17. *SA Times*, 16 February 1994.

18. Mary Benson, *Nelson Mandela, The Man and the Movement*, Penguin, 1994, p. 148.

19. Mandela, *Long Walk to Freedom*, p. 65.

20. *SA Times*, 18 May 1994, p. 6.

21. Mandela, *Long Walk to Freedom*, p. 559.

22. *SA Times*, 14 December 1994, p. 8.

23. Mandela, *Long Walk to Freedom*, p. 617.

24. *The Spectator*, 19 November 1994.

25. Nelson Mandela, *Nelson Mandela Speaks, Forging a democratic, non-racial South Africa*, David Philip in association with Mayibuye Books and Pathfinder Press, Steve Clark (ed), South Africa, 1994, p. 237.

26. Nelson Mandela, Address at the opening of Parliament, May 1994.

27. Mandela, *Long Walk to Freedom*, p. 566.

28. Ibid., p. 582.

29. Ibid., p. 545. Earlier Nelson Mandela had written to the ANC in Lusaka echoing Mrs Margaret Thatcher's comment about Mikhail Gorbachev.

30. Reported on SABC News, 8.00. p.m., 27 November 1995.

31. *Daily Mail*, 21 January 1995, p. 12.

32. Mandela, *Long Walk to Freedom*, p. 573.

33. *SA Times*, 2 October 1993.

34. Carl Niehaus, quoted in *Time* magazine, 3 January 1994, p. 36.
35. Ibid., p. 37.
36. *SA Times*, 22 September 1993, p. 3.
37. Ibid., 15 December 1993, p. 1.
38. Mandela, *Long Walk to Freedom*, p. 604.
39. *SA Times*, 2 March 1994.
40. *Saturday Star*, 25 November 1995, p. 2. Nelson Mandela was addressing a Black Management Forum in Johannesburg.
41. SABC News, 23 November 1995.
42. *SA Times*, 21 June 1995.
43. Ibid., 2 August 1995, p. 1.
44. Ibid., 23 August 1995, p. 3.
45. Channel 4 News, United Kingdom, 15 August 1995.
46. The incident was confirmed to me by one of Dr Verwoerd's grandsons, Dr Wilhelm Verwoerd, in an interview in Stellenbosch, 22 November 1995.
47. *SA Times*, 19 July 1995, p. 18.
48. Dirk Coetzee, in Hilda Bernstein, *The Exile Experiences of South Africans*, Cape, 1994, p. 213.
49. Benson, *Nelson Mandela, The Man and the Movement*, p. 214.
50. Nelson Mandela, interview with Nicholas Bethell, 27 January 1985, ibid., p. 197.
51. *SA Times*, 23 February 1994, p. 4.
52. Nelson Mandela, *Mail and Guardian*, 10–16 November 1995, p. 4.
53. *The Independent*, 4 May 1995, p. 13.
54. Alec Russell, *Daily Telegraph*, 8 June 1995, p. 10.
55. *The Independent*, 8 June 1995, p. 13.
56. Alec Russell, *Daily Telegraph*, 8 June 1995, p. 10.
57. The Rev. Theo Kotze, interview, Cape Town, 10 November 1995.
58. Benson, *Nelson Mandela, The Man and the Movement*, p. 231.
59. From the opening address to the ANC National Conference, 2 July 1991, in Philip, *Nelson Mandela Speaks*, p. 102.
60. George Alagiah, interview with Nelson Mandela, *Newsnight*, BBC, 8 May 1995.
61. *SA Times*, 3 August 1994.
62. George Alagiah, interview with Nelson Mandela, ibid.
63. John Carlin, interview with Nelson Mandela, *The Independent*, 29 April 1993, p. 13.

64. Nelson Mandela, interview with John Carlin, ibid.

65. Nelson Mandela, interview in *Time* magazine, 14 June 1993., in Philip, *Nelson Mandela Speaks*, p. 260.

66. Nelson Mandela, 'Liberation Not Power', in Charles Villa-Vicencio (ed), *The Spirit of Hope, Conversations on politics, religion and value*, Skotaville Publishers, n.d., p. 147.

67. Ibid., p. 148.

68. Desmond Tutu, *The Church and Human Rights in South Africa*, University of Pretoria, Centre for Human Rights, 18 May 1992, p. 2.

69. The Eloff Commission of Enquiry presentation was on 1 September 1982.

70. Bishop's Enthronement Charge, St Cyprian's Cathedral, 21 September 1991, in *Highway*, October 1991, p. 2. *Highway* is the journal of the Diocese of Kimberley and Kuruman.

71. Shirley Du Boulay, *Tutu, Voice of the Voiceless*, Penguin, 1989, p. 26.

72. Recounted in *Time* magazine, 29 October 1984, p. 2., at the time of the award of the Nobel Peace Prize to Bishop Tutu.

73. Archbishop Tutu, contribution to Paul Alberts (ed), *The Plight of South Africa's Children*, National Children's Rights Committee and UNICEF, 16 July 1995.

74. Du Boulay, *Tutu, Voice of the Voiceless*, p. 55.

75. Desmond Tutu to Martin Kenyon, 19 December 1966 in *Tutu, Voice of the Voiceless*, p. 69.

76. Martin Dennis, 'A Life in the Day of Desmond Tutu', *Sunday Times* magazine, 1994.

77. Desmond Tutu, 'Spirituality and Fear', article prepared for Elmarie Otto (ed), *Christian leadership in South Africa*, 30 November 1994.

78. Desmond Tutu, *The Rainbow People of God*, John Allen (ed), Doubleday, 1994, p. 21.

79. Dirk Coetzee, in Bernstein, *The Exile Experiences of South Africans*, p. 213.

80. Du Boulay, *Tutu, Voice of the Voiceless*, p. 163.

81. Ibid., p. 168.

82. Ibid., p. 136.

83. Desmond Tutu, 'What It Means to Be Human', contribution to a book for the Anti-Barbaric Coalition (ABC) in America, 14 June 1995.

84. Desmond Tutu, to World Council of Churches' Central Committee, Kingston, Jamaica, January 1979.

85. Archbishop Tutu's archives, in review of Mandela, *Long Walk to Freedom*, for *The Tablet*, 12 January 1995.

86. Du Boulay, *Tutu, Voice of the Voiceless*, p. 233.

87. Ibid., p. 166.

88. Ibid., p. 168.

89. Archbishop Tutu, Oxford Union Address, 'Why I Am Still Hopeful', 17 January 1994, p. 2.

90. Archbishop Tutu, 'Tearing People Apart', address in Durban, March 1980, published in *South African Outlook*, October 1980, p. 155.

91. Tutu, *The Rainbow People of God*, p. 208.

92. Archbishop Tutu, speech on receiving National Civil Rights Museum Award, Memphis, Tennessee, 1992.

93. Tutu, *The Rainbow People of God*, p. 100.

94. Father Buti Tlhagale, in introduction to Desmond Tutu, *Desmond Tutu, Hope and Suffering*, Collins/Fount 1984, p. 21.

95. Letter, 8 April 1988, in Tutu, *The Rainbow People of God*, p. 149.

96. Father Buti Tlhagale, ibid., p. 18.

97. Desmond Tutu, quoted in Charles Villa-Vicencio (ed), *The Spirit of Hope*, pp. 266–7.

98. Ibid., p. 277.

99. Ibid., p. 278.

100. *SA Times*, 5 April 1995, p. 4.

101. Ibid.

102. Ibid.

103. *SA Times*, 26 July 1995, p. 2.

104. Ibid., 10 August 1994, p. 5.

105. Archbishop Tutu, sermon, NGK Suid-Oos, Pretoria, 12 November 1995.

106. Tutu, *Desmond Tutu: Hope and Suffering*, p. 182.

107. Sermon, NGK Suid-Oos, ibid.

108. Archbishop Tutu, *Highway*, October 1991, p. 2.

109. Archbishop Tutu, inaugural address to International Symposium, Caring for the Survivors of Torture – Challenges for the medical and health professionals, Cape Town, 15 November 1995.

110. Archbishop Tutu, sermon, Human Rights Day, 21 March 1995, to a congregation including Queen Elizabeth II and two witnesses of the Sharpeville Massacre 35 years earlier.

111. Archbishop Tutu, homily, St George's Cathedral, Cape Town, 27 March 1991.
112. Ibid., 24 April 1994, in Tutu, *The Rainbow People of God*, p. 258.
113. Ibid., p. 222.
114. Ibid., p. 223.
115. Archbishop's Charge to 28th session of Provincial Synod, in *Highway*, November 1995, p. 3.
116. Oxford Union Address, 27 February 1990.
117. President's Report to All Africa Conference of Churches' General Committee, Kenya, 4–8 March 1995.
118. Archbishop Tutu, address to Foreign Correspondents' Association Annual Dinner, 13 November 1995.
119. 28th Session of Provincial Synod.
120. *SA Times*, 27 April 1994, p. 4.
121. Archbishop Tutu, charge to Diocesan Council, 12 August 1995.
122. Desmond Tutu, foreword to Brian Frost, *The Politics of Peace*, Darton, Longman and Todd, 1991, p. ix.
123. Archbishop Tutu, 'The Secular State and Religion', Archbishop Stephen Naidoo Memorial Lecture, 8 July 1992. 'I call yet again on the State President in a representative capacity on behalf of those who spawned apartheid and who benefited from it to say "We are sorry for all the hurt we have caused you. Forgive us." Then those who have been wronged must forgive.'
124. *SA Times*, 12 October 1994, p. 17.
125. Du Boulay, *Tutu, Voice of the Voiceless*, p. 269.
126. Ibid., p. 101.
127. 'Liberation as a biblical theme', Pretoria University, March 1981, in Tutu, *Desmond Tutu: Hope and Suffering*, p. 77.
128. Archbishop Tutu, after introducing Nelson Mandela to the crowd after his inauguration as State President in 1994, in Tutu, *The Rainbow People of God*, p. 262.
129. Archbishop Tutu, 'Civil Society and Freedom', *Sunday Times* and Alan Paton Literary Award dinner, 2 June 1995.
130. For *Odyssey*: Tony Grogan, 8 February 1994, published by Tafelberg.
131. Archbishop Tutu, speech, 'Freedom and Tolerance', Cape Town Press Club, 6 June 1995.
132. Archbishop Tutu, 'Against Racism', The Shoki Coe Memorial Lecture, Tainan, Taiwan, 13 June 1995.

133. Villa-Vicencio (ed), *The Spirit of Hope*, p. 283.

Chapter 2

1. John Fisher, *That Miss Hobhouse*, Secker and Warburg, 1971, pp. 269–70.
2. A.C. Martin, *The Concentration Camps, 1900–1902*, Cape Town 1957, p. 6.
3. Hope Hay Hewison, *Hedge of Wild Almonds, South Africa, the 'Pro Boers' and the Quaker Conscience, 1890–1910*, James Currey, London, 1989, p. 316.
4. Black Concentration Camps section in the Boer War Museum in Bloemfontein.
5. Allister Sparks, *The Mind of South Africa*, Heinemann, 1990, p. 128.
6. Alexander Hepple, *Verwoerd*, Penguin 1967, pp. 165–6.
7. J.C. Smuts, *Jan Christian Smuts*, Cassell, 1952, p. 47.
8. Thomas Pakenham, *The Scramble for Africa, 1876–1912*, Weidenfeld and Nicolson, 1991, p. 45.
9. Quoted in Sarah Gertrude Millin, *General Smuts*, Faber and Faber, 1936, p. 223.
10. Thomas Pakenham, *The Boer War*, Futura/Macdonald and Co., 1982, p. xxii.
11. David Harrison, *The White Tribe of Africa*, BBC, 1981, p. 23.
12. Canon Farmer, 29 March 1901, SPG Series E (Ref 47) Pretoria, in Pakenham, *The Boer War*, p. 573.
13. Emerson Neilly of the *Pall Mall Gazette* in *The Boer War*, p. 408.
14. Ibid., p. 410.
15. T.R.H. Davenport, *South Africa, A Modern History*, Macmillan, 1991, p. 200, quotes an official figure of 14,154.
16. See J.L. Hattingh 1968 Thesis for University of Pretoria, published in *Archives Year Book of South African History*, Pretoria Government Archives, quoted in Hewison, *Hedge of Wild Almonds*, p. 202.
17. Hope Hay Hewison gives a figure of 21,942 (out of 448,435) British dead, including 5,774 killed in action and 16,168 who died from wounds or disease. 400,346 horses, mules and donkeys also died and there were over 100,000 casualties, *Hedge of Wild Almonds*, p. 232. Thomas Pakenham in *The Boer War*, p. 572, gives a figure of 7,000 Boer deaths among the 87,365 fighting, including 120 foreign

volunteers and 13,300 Afrikaners from the Cape and Natal. From the beginning, under military control, there were camps for the black women and children from the Boer farms, 29 of them housing 100,000 Africans. In December 1901 the deaths in the Transvaal camp were officially 13,315 (*Hedge of Wild Almonds*, p. 152).

18. Pakenham, *The Boer War*, p. 571.

19. John Fisher, *The Afrikaners*, Cassell, 1969, p. 204.

20. Pakenham, *The Boer War*, p. 571.

21. Smuts, *Jan Christian Smuts*, p. 83.

22. Quoted in Boer War Museum Pamphlet, Bloemfontein, n.d.

23. Pakenham, *The Boer War*, p. 569.

24. Will Hutton, *The State We're In*, Vintage, 1996, p. 124.
'The Boer War was fought to prevent the Transvaal gold reserves, then 25% of the world total, falling via the Boers to their German backers and so permitting the Reichsbank to challenge the supremacy of the Bank of England.'

25. *Bywoners* were those who had 'squatted' on land, but who had no right of possession.

26. Hewison, *Hedge of Wild Almonds*, p. 229.

27. Davenport, *South Africa, A Modern History*, p. 205.

28. Rudyard Kipling, *The Complete Verse*, Kyle Cathie Ltd, 1990, p. 173.

29. William Plomer, quoted in Pakenham, *The Boer War*, p. 572.

30. F.S. Crafford, *Jan Smuts, A Biography*, Allen and Unwin, 1946, p. 71.

31. Quoted in a leaflet on the concentration camps published by the Boer War Museum, Bloemfontein, n.d.

32. Thomas Pakenham, introduction to Denys Rietz, *Commando, A Boer Journal of the Boer War*, Jonathan Ball in association with Faber and Faber, Johannesburg, 1990 (first published by Faber and Faber, 1929).

33. Ibid., p. xviii.

34. Hewison, *Hedge of Wild Almonds*, pp. 251–2.

35. Nellis du Preez, interview, Pietermaritzburg, 26 October 1995.

36. Patrick van Rensburg, *Guilty Land*, Penguin, 1962, p. 10.

37. Pakenham, *The Boer War*, p. 491.

38. Peter Walshe, *Black Nationalism in South Africa*, a SPROCAS publication, Ravan Press, 1973, p. 5.

39. W.A. de Klerk, *The Puritans in Africa*, Penguin in association with Rex Collings, 1976, p. 102.

40. Fisher, *The Afrikaners*, p. 233.

41. Ibid., p. 102.
42. C.f. Selections from W.K. Hancock and Jan van der Poel (eds) *Smuts Papers, Vol IV*, Cambridge University Press, 1966, pp. 201 and 209.
43. De Klerk, *The Puritans in Africa*, p. 103.
44. Crafford, *Jan Smuts, A Biography*, p. 222.
45. De Klerk, *The Puritans in Africa*, p. 113.
46. Ibid., p. 115.
47. Leo Marquard, *The Peoples and Policies of South Africa*, Oxford University Press, 1952, pp. 69–70.
48. Recounted by Dominee George Daneel, interview, Pretoria, 15 October 1995, of a Moral Re-armament meeting he attended.
49. Alan Paton in Edwin S. Munger (ed), *The Afrikaners*, Tafelberg, 1979, p. 25.
50. Hepple, *Verwoerd*, pp. 59–60.
51. Paton, *The Afrikaners*, p. 25.
52. Ibid., p. 32.
53. E.G. Malherbe, *Education in South Africa*, Vol 2, quoted in Harrison, *The White Tribe of Africa*, p. 142.
54. Thomas Jones (ed Keith Middlemas) *Whitehall Diary, Vol 3, Ireland 1918–1925*, Oxford University Press, 1971, p. 7.
55. W.K. Hancock, *Smuts, Vol 2, 1919–1950*, Cambridge University Press, 1968, p. 525.
56. *The Cape Argus*, 8 June 1963, quoted in de Klerk, *The Puritans in Africa*, p. 227.
57. W.K. Hancock, *Smuts, Vol 1, 1870–1919*, Cambridge University Press, 1962, p. 232.
58. Fisher, *The Afrikaners*, p. 344.
59. Millin, *General Smuts*, p. 225.
60. Smuts, *Jan Christian Smuts*, p. 32.
61. M.K. Gandhi, *The Selected Works of Mahatma Gandhi, Vol 3, Satyagraha in South Africa*, Ahmedabad, 1966, p. 56.
62. Louis Fischer, *Gandhi, His Life and Message for the World*, a Signet Key Book, 1954, p. 27.
63. M. Gandhi, *Satyagraha in South Africa*, Ahmedabad, 1928, reprinted edition 1972, quoted in Jay Naidoo, *Tracking Down Historical Myths, Eight South African Cases*, Ad Donker, 1989, p. 139.
64. Fischer, *Gandhi, His Life and Message*, p. 36.
65. Ibid., p. 47.

66. *Satyagraha in South Africa* in Naidoo, *Tracking Down Historical Myths*, p. 139.
67. Fischer, *Gandhi, His Life and Message*, p. 48. Contrary to what many writers have said, General Smuts did not send his sandals back in 1939. See Hancock, *Smuts, Vol 2*, p. 347.
68. Smuts, *Jan Christian Smuts*, p. 498.
69. Speech to members of the Indian Community, Northdale, Pieter-maritzburg, 12 March 1993, in Philip, *Nelson Mandela Speaks*, p. 223.
70. *The Indian Opinion*, 4 September 1904, quoted by Ebrahim Sulaman, Islamic Arabia in Dawal Centre International, Durban, *Daily News*, 31 October 1995, p. 17.
71. Oliver Tambo, *Preparing for Power, Oliver Tambo Speaks*, compiled by Adelaide Tambo, Heinemann, 1987, pp. 186–7.
72. S.V. Mvambo in Karis and Carter, *From Protest to Challenge*, Vol 1, 1971, p.12, in *Oliver Tambo Speaks*, p. 187.
73. Hancock, *Smuts, Vol 2*, p. 113.
74. Davenport, *South Africa, A Modern History*, p. 247.
75. Luthuli, *Tribute to a Hero*, Leader Press, 81 Sparks Road, Overport, p.3. n.d.
76. Eddie and Win Roux, *Rebel Pity*, Penguin, 1972, pp. 186–7. First published in 1948.
77. Ibid., p. 82.
78. Ibid., pp. 187–8.
79. Ibid., pp. 105–7.
80. Jackie Probler, *A Decisive Clash? A short history of black protest in politics in South Africa 1875–1976*, Acacia, Pretoria 1988, p. 82.
81. Harrison, *The White Tribe of Africa*, pp. 119–20.
82. Ibid., p. 213.
83. Nokukhanya Luthuli in Peter Rule, *Nokukhanya, Mother of Light*, with Marilyn Aitken and Jenny van Dyk, The Grail, South Africa, 1993, p. 97.
84. Walshe, *Black Nationalism in South Africa*, p. 28.
85. Dr H.F. Verwoerd, Senate Debates, 3 September 1948, in Hepple, *Verwoerd*, p. 111.
86. Philip, *Nelson Mandela Speaks*, p. 278.
87. Sparks, *The Mind of South Africa*, pp. 236–7.
88. Benson, *Nelson Mandela, The Man and the Movement*, p. 23.

89. Albert Luthuli, *Let My People Go*, Collins/Fontana, 1967, p. 103.

90. Hepple, *Verwoerd*, p. 123.

91. Mrs Goba, interview, Durban 27 October 1995. When young, Mrs Goba lived in the Luthuli household for a number of years.

92. Fatimer Meer, in Villa-Vicencio (ed), *The Spirit of Hope*, p. 179.

93. Rule, *Nokukhanya, Mother of Light*, p. 56.

94. From a Public Statement by Chief Luthuli when dismissed by the Government in November 1952, issued jointly by the ANC and the Natal Indian Congress, in Luthuli, *Let My People Go*, Appendix A, p. 207.

95. Ibid., p. 102–3.

96. Ibid., p. 118.

97. Mrs Goba, interview, 27 October 1995.

98. Helen Joseph, *Tomorrow's Sun*, Hutchinson, 1966, pp. 171–2.

99. Z.K.Matthews, *Freedom for My People, The Autobiography of Z.K. Matthews, Southern Africa 1901–1968*, memoir by Monica Wilson, Rex Collings, London, with David Philip, Cape Town, 1981, p. 173.

100. The full text can be found in Luthuli, *Let My People Go*, pp. 210–14.

101. Ibid., p. 141.

102. Ibid., p. 142.

103. Ibid., p. 143.

104. Mandela, *Long Walk to Freedom*, p. 189.

105. Ibid., p. 248.

106. Matthews, *Freedom for My People*, p. 195.

107. Aelred Stubbs, C.R., eulogy preached at Requiem Mass, Priory Chapel of the Society of the Precious Blood, 1 March 1978, in *South African Outlook*, August 1978, p. 117.

108. Mandela, *Long Walk to Freedom*, p. 260.

109. Joe Slovo, *The Unfinished Autobiography*, Hodder and Stoughton, 1996, p. 147.

110. Mandela, *Long Walk to Freedom*, pp. 260–1.

111. Ibid., pp. 272–3.

112. Totius (J.D. Du Toit), in *The Penguin Book of South African Verse*, edited with an introduction by Jack Cope and Uys Krige, Penguin, 1968, pp. 194–5.

113. Sparks, *The Mind of South Africa*, p. 129.

Chapter 3

1. Sparks, *The Mind of South Africa*, p. 326.
2. Alan Paton in Edwin S. Munger (ed), *The Afrikaners*, Tafelberg, 1979, p. 76.
3. Davenport, *South Africa, A Modern History*, p. 412.
4. Professor B. Keet, *Whither South Africa?*, translated by N.J. Marquard, Grahamstown, 1956.
5. J.H.P. Serfontein, *Apartheid, Change and the NG Kerk*, Taurus, 1982, p. 106.
6. Dali Tambo, *People of the South*, South African TV, 8 October 1995.
7. Serfontein, *Apartheid, Change and the NG Kerk*, pp. 2–3.
8. The Rev. Dr Beyers Naudé, *Challenge*, June/July 1995, pp. 2–3.
9. Ibid.
10. In Peter Randall (ed), *Not Without Honour, Tribute to Beyers Naudé*, Ravan Press, 1982, p. 92.
11. *Challenge*, June/July 1995, pp. 2–3.
12. Ibid.
13. Hlope Brigalia Bam, 'Crossing the Frontiers', in Charles Villa-Vicencio and Carl Niehaus (eds), *Many Cultures, One Nation, Festschrift for Beyers Naudé*, Human and Rousseau, Cape Town, 1995, p. 36.
14. Horst Kleinschmidt, interview, Johannesburg, 18 October 1995.
15. The Rev. Dr Carel Antonissen, interview, Stellenbosch, 21 November 1995.
16. Professor Pippin Oosthuizen, interview, Durban, 30 October 1995.
17. Professor Klaus Nürnberger, interview, Pietermaritzburg, 25 October 1995.
18. Professor Johan Heyns, obituary by John Carlin, *The Independent*, 8 November, 1994, p. 14.
19. Professor Johan Heyns to John Carlin, *The Independent*, 1 February 1990.
20. John Carlin, *The Independent*, 8 November 1994, p. 14.
21. Nelson Mandela, during a speech in Durban, reported in *The Independent*, 7 November 1994, p. 10.
22. Serfontein, *Apartheid, Change and the NG Kerk*, pp. 162–3.
23. Mary Lean, *For a Change*, May 1989, p. 7.
24. Professor Nico Smith to Mary Lean, ibid.

25. Professor Nico Smith, interview, Pretoria, 17 October 1995.

26. Ibid.

27. *Koinonia*, Southern African Newsletter, October–December 1987, Vol 2, No 1, p. 4.

28. Professor Nico Smith, interview, 17 October 1995.

29. Tutu, *Desmond Tutu, Hope and Suffering*, p. 132.

30. Sir Laurens van der Post, 'Memories of a childhood on the veldt', BBC London, Radio 4, 4 December 1995.

31. Colin Legum, 'The Role of Mediators as Facilitators: Profile and Comment on Hendrik Wilhelm van der Merwe', in Andrew du Pisam and Koos van Wyk (eds), *Transitional Process, A South African Case Study*, May 1995, p. 2.

32. Ibid., p. 4.

33. Lionel Murcott, from *Tuis, A Poem Cycle for Breyten Breytenbach*, Barefoot Press, 1994, translated from the Afrikaans by the poet.

34. Breyten Breytenbach, *The True Confessions of An Albino Terrorist*, Taurus, 1984, p. 328.

35. Breyten Breytenbach, 'Dreams of Home', Paris, 18 February 1990, in *Leadership*, Vol 9, March 1990, p. 90.

36. Hugh Lewin, *Bandiet: Seven Years in a South African Prison*, Heinemann Educational Books, 1981, pp. 212–3.

37. Mary Benson, *A Far Cry, The Making of a South African*, Penguin, 1990, p. 183.

38. Quoted in *A Far Cry*, p. 171.

39. Carl Niehaus, from a lecture at the University of Pretoria in 1993, quoted in Carl Niehaus, *Fighting for Hope* (English edition), Human and Rousseau, Cape Town, 1994, p. 72.

40. Ibid., p. 54.

41. Ibid., p. 136.

42. Sir Laurens van der Post (in conversation with Jean Marc Pottiez), *A Walk with a White Bushman*, Penguin 1986, p. 298.

43. W.A. de Klerk, *F.W. de Klerk, The Man in His Time*, Jonathan Ball, Johannesburg, 1991, p. 124.

44. Ibid., p. 30.

45. *The Independent*, 16 March 1989.

46. Mandela, *Long Walk to Freedom*, p. 543.

47. F.W. de Klerk addressing the Los Angeles World Affairs Council, reported in *SA Times*, 3 November 1994, p. 4.

48. De Klerk, *F.W. de Klerk, The Man in His Time*, p. 30.
49. Churches Concern for Southern Africa Analysis, No 19, October 1990.
50. Quoted in *The Independent*, 23 February 1991, p. 10.
51. Pik Botha, interviewed by Donald Woods, BBC 2 'Assignment', 13 February 1991, reported in *The Independent*, 23 February 1991.
52. De Klerk, *F.W. de Klerk, The Man in His Time*, p. 61.
53. Desmond Tutu, foreword to Frost, *The Politics of Peace*, p. ix.
54. Quoted by Professor Kader Asmal, 25 May 1992, in a lecture on his installment as Human Rights Law Professor at University of the Western Cape, published by UWC, Series A, No 64, p. 18.
55. F.W. de Klerk to Mike Wooldridge, BBC Radio 4, 28 January 1991.
56. Allister Sparks, *Tomorrow Is Another Country*, Heinemann, 1995, p. 100.
57. See *South Africa 1990–1994, The Miracle of a Free Nation*, p. 51, published by the *Sunday Times*, printed by Don Wesley, Cape Town.
58. F.W. de Klerk, *SA Times*, 8 September 1993, p. 3.
59. F.W. de Klerk, speech on presentation of the Nobel Peace Prize, Oslo, 10 December 1993, p. 5 of text.
60. *The Independent*, 30 April 1993. p. 11.
61. Sparks, *Tomorrow Is Another Country*, pp. 92–3.
62. F.W. de Klerk, *Time* magazine, 3 January 1994, p. 37, interviewed by Jim Gaines, Joelle Attinger and Scott MacLeod.
63. Professor Sampie Terreblanche, quoted in *The Independent*, 23 February 1991.
64. Professor Colin Gardner, interview, Pietermaritzburg, 25 October 1995.
65. De Klerk, *F.W. de Klerk, The Man In His Time*, p. 139.
66. Nelson Mandela, *Time* magazine, 3 January 1994, pp. 37–8, interviewed by Jim Gaines, Koelle Attinger and Scott MacLeod.
67. Renier Schoeman, reported in *The Independent*, 23 February 1991, p. 10.
68. Marike de Klerk, *SA Times*, 25 May 1994.
69. *SA Times*, 24 November 1993, p. 4.
70. Fergal Keane, *The Bondage of Fear, A Journey Through The Last White Empire*, Viking, 1994, p. 223.
71. Ibid., pp. 215–6.
72. F.W. de Klerk, quoted in *SA Times*, 4 May 1994, p. 4.

73. 'South Africa Joins Sorry Collection', *SA Times*, 12 January 1994, p. 6.
74. F.W. de Klerk to Mike Wooldridge, BBC Radio 4, 28 January 1991.
75. Luthuli, *Let My People Go*, p. 176.
76. Dr Wilhelm Verwoerd, to a church group in a working-class coloured suburb on the Cape Flats, in *Leadership 1993*, Vol 12, No 5, p. 32.
77. Ibid., p. 34.
78. Ibid., p. 35.
79. Ibid., p. 36.
80. Ibid., p. 38.
81. Dr Wilhelm Verwoerd, 'Re-viewing Verwoerd's Vision: Reflections on the thought and actions of apartheid's architect,' private mss.
82. Dr Wilhelm Verwoerd, quoted in Sparks, *Tomorrow Is Another Country*, pp. 240–1.
83. Ibid.
84. Dr Wilhelm Verwoerd, interview, Stellenbosch, 21 November 1995.
85. RSR Mss 1/3 letters collection, D. Louw to I. Louw (secret), 16 September 1990, in Bill Nasson, *Abraham Esau's War, A Black South African's War in the Cape 1899–1902*, Cambridge University Press, 1991, p. 125.
86. Ibid., p. 130, quoting CA, AG 2020, Anglo-Boer War files, papers relating to the occupation of Calvinia led by the enemy, R.M. Calvinia, to SLD, 29 January 1902, *Graaff-Reinet Advertiser*, 6 February 1901; *Midland News*, 19 January 1901.
87. Ibid., p. 125.
88. Dr Alfred Biddle, ibid., p. 136.
89. Pierre Jeanne Gerber, interview, Johannesburg, 2 December 1995.
90. Ibid.
91. Rt Rev. Trevor Huddleston, *Christian*, No 4, 1994.

Chapter 4

1. Probler, *A Decisive Clash?* p. 175.
2. Oliver Tambo, Statement to the Ninth Extraordinary Session of the Foreign Ministers of the OAU, Dar Es Salaam, May 1975, in Tambo, *Oliver Tambo Speaks*, p. 98.
3. James Matthews, *Cry Rage*, SPROCAS Publications, Johannesburg, 1972, p. 1.

4. Oswald Mtshali, *Sounds of a Cowhide Drum*, Renoster Books, 1972, p. 24.

5. Mandela, *Long Walk to Freedom*, pp. 260–1.

6. *SA Times*, 30 November 1994. p. 5.

7. Zeki Ergas, *The Catharsis and the Healing*, Janus, 1994, p. 133.

8. Davenport, *South Africa, A Modern History*, p. 336.

9. Ibid., p. 356.

10. Edgar Bernstein, *My Judaism, My Jews*, Exclusive Books, 1964 (1965 reprint edition) p. 123, quoting the 1960 census.

11. Helen Suzman, *In No Uncertain Terms*, Sinclair Stevenson, 1993, p. 93.

12. Quoted by W.A. de Klerk in *South African Outlook*, December 1977, p. 150, in reflections on the published proceedings of the national conference of English-speaking South Africans, held in Grahamstown, July 1974.

13. Rev. Michael Crommelin, interview, Bloemfontein, 20 November 1995.

14. Canon Gonville ffrench-Beytagh, *Encountering Darkness*, Collins, 1973, p. 162.

15. David Welsh, *The Roots of Segregation*, Cape Town, Oxford University Press, 1971, quoted in Paul B. Rich, *Hope and Despair, English-Speaking Intellectuals and South African Politics 1896–1976*, British Academic Press, 1993, p. 10.

16. Guy Butler, from 'A Prayer for all my countrymen' in *Selected Poems*, Ad Donker, Johannesburg, n.d.

17. Trevor Huddleston, *Naught for Your Comfort*, Collins/Fontana, 1956, p. 44.

18. Shriddath Ramphal, 80th birthday celebrations for Trevor Huddleston, Central Hall, Westminster, 14 June 1993.

19. Huddleston, *Naught for Your Comfort*, p. 183.

20. Alan Paton, *Cry the Beloved Country*, The Reprint Society, 1948, p. 252.

21. Alan Paton, quoted in *New York Herald Tribune*, 20 October 1949, in Peter Alexander, *Alan Paton*, Oxford University Press, 1994, p. 249.

22. Alan Paton, *Journey Continued, an autobiography*, Oxford University Press, 1988, p. 47.

23. Luthuli, *Let My People Go*, p. 139.

24. Paton, *Journey Continued*, p. 234.

25. Ibid., p. 235.

26. Ibid., pp. 235–6.
27. Alexander, *Alan Paton*, p. 334.
28. Leslie Rubin to Peter Alexander, 27 November 1992, in *Alan Paton*.
29. 'First Things to Do: Repent', *Johannesburg Star*, 22 June 1970, in *Alan Paton*, p. 399.
30. *Toronto Globe and Mail*, 3 July 1976, ibid., p. 399.
31. Steve Biko, *I Write What I Like*, edited with a personal memoir by Aelred Stubbs, C.R., Bowerdean Press, 1978, p. 23.
32. Ibid., p. 66.
33. C.R.D. Halsi in Barney Pityana, Mamphele Ramphele, Malusi Mpumlwana and Lindy Wilson (eds), *Bounds of Possibility, The Legacy of Steve Biko and Black Consciousness*, David Philip/Zed Books, 1991, p. 105.
34. Aelred Stubbs, C.R., sermon at Mass, Priory Chapel of the Society of the Precious Blood, Masite, Lesotho, 25 September 1977, reproduced in *South African Outlook*, September 1977, p. 132.
35. Ibid., p. 131.
36. Ibid., p. 132.
37. Mamphele Ramphele, extract from her autobiography, *Mail and Guardian*, 3–9 November 1995, p. 27.
38. *South African Outlook*, November 1977, p. 169.
39. Biko, *I Write What I Like*, p. 215.
40. *Sunday Star*, 20 October 1991, p. 4.
41. Ibid., p. 3.
42. Ibid., p. 4.
43. Ibid., p. 3.
44. Farouk Asvat, *The Death of Steve in A Celebration of Flames*, Ad Donker, Johannesburg, 1987.
45. Pityana et al, *The Bounds of Possibility*, p. 11.
46. Ibid., p. 10.
47. Ibid., p. 256.
48. Mangosuthu G. Buthelezi, 14 March 1976, printed in supplement to *Pro Veritate*, March 1976, p. 2.
49. Ibid., p. 3.
50. Ibid., p. 4.
51. 'Biographies of Prominent Fort Harians – Mangosuthu Gatcha Buthelezi' by Professor Jacques Rousseau, *South African Outlook*, October 1978, p. 158.

52. Observation at meeting of Durban World Conference of Religions for Peace, 22 October 1995.
53. *South African Outlook*, September 1979, p. 135.
54. Ibid., p. 176.
55. M.T.W. Arnheim, *South Africa after Vorster*, Howard Timmins, 1979, p. 180.
56. In the first two years after its launch Inkatha had gone from 30,000 to 250,000 members according to a memorandum from Chief Buthelezi to Mrs Margaret Thatcher during a visit to Britain in August 1985, quoted in Mzala, *Gatcha Buthelezi, Chief with a Double Agenda*, Zed Books, 1988, p. 122.
57. Ibid., p. 193.
58. Chief Buthelezi, Address to National Council of Churches, September 1979, in *South African Outlook*, September 1975, p. 138.
59. From the political report of the National Executive Committee to the second National Consultative Conference, Lusaka, 16–23 June 1985, in Tambo, *Oliver Tambo Speaks*, pp. 146–7.
60. Mzala, *Chief with a Double Agenda*, p. 131.
61. Mangosuthu G. Buthelezi, *South Africa, My Vision of the Future*, Weidenfeld and Nicolson, 1990, p. 105.
62. Bishop Stanley Mogoba, interview, Durban, 27 October 1995.
63. R.W. Johnson, 'Spear of the Nation', *The Independent on Sunday*, 14 October 1990, p. 6.
64. Ibid., p. 3.
65. Jeff Guy, *The Destruction of the Zulu Kingdom, The Civil War in Zululand 1879–1884*, University of Natal Press, 1994, p. 246.
66. John Aitchison, in Klaus Nürnberger (ed), *A Democratic Vision for South Africa, Political Realism and Christian Responsibility*, Encounter Publications, Pietermaritzburg, 1991, p. 368.
67. Davenport, *South Africa, A Modern History*, p. 428.
68. Ibid., p. 429.
69. Canon Xundu Mcebisi, interview, Port Elizabeth, 7 November 1995.
70. Mzala, *Chief with a Double Agenda*, p. 179.
71. Chief Buthelezi, quoted in Phillip van Niekerk, *Work in Progress*, May 1989, p. 7, in *Chief with a Double Agenda*, p. 178.
72. *Chief with a Double Agenda*, p. 182.

73. Craig McEwan, interview, Cape Town, 15 November 1995. Craig McEwan is researching violence in South Africa under Professor Andre du Toit at the University of Cape Town.
74. Mzala, *Chief with a Double Agenda*, p. 233.
75. *The Independent*, 9 October 1987.
76. Mzala, *Chief with a Double Agenda*, p. 233.
77. Dr Sibusiso Bhengu, *The Guardian*, UK, 19 August 1986, in *Chief with a Double Agenda*, p. 163.
78. During a symposium at the University of Durban-Westville on 'Possible Alternatives for Peaceful Co-existence in South Africa', ibid., p. 231.
79. Willie Hofmeyr, MP for Claremont, symposium convened by the Islamic Unity Convention, City Hall, Cape Town, 12 November 1995.
80. Faren Kassim, MP, ibid.
81. Buthelezi, *South Africa, My Vision of the Future*, p. 73.
82. *The Sowetan*, 18 December 1992.
83. *Business Day; The Citizen; The Sowetan; The Star;* 7 April 1993.
84. Quoted by John Kane-Berman, *Political Violence in South Africa*, South African Institute of Race Relations, 1993, pp. 80–1.
85. Ibid., p. 83, quoting *Sunday Times*, 6 September 1992.
86. Cosmos Desmond, Memo to Peter Kerchhoff, PACSA, Pietermaritz-burg, September 1995.
87. Craig McEwan, interview, Cape Town, 15 November 1995.
88. Buthelezi, *South Africa, My Vision of the Future*, p. 6.
89. Ibid., p. 109.
90. The Rt Rev. Rubin Phillip, interview, Durban 3 November 1995.
91. Paton, *Journey Continued*, p. 15.
92. Ibid., p. 14. Alan Paton obtained this story from the Rev. A.G. Clarke's unpublished thesis 'For God or Caesar?' A *doek* is a cloth worn as a head covering.
93. Fatimer Meer, *Higher than Hope*, Hamish Hamilton, 1988.
94. Davenport, *South Africa, A Modern History*, p. 382.
95. Mrs I. Gandhi, interview, Durban, 30 October 1995.
96. Rt Rev. Rubin Phillip, interview, 3 November 1995.
97. *Daily News*, Durban, 18 October 1995, p. 12.
98. Fatimer Meer, interview, Durban, 3 October 1995.
99. Ibid.

100. Divali Message, *Daily News*, Durban, 18 October 1995, p. 12.

101. Davenport, *South Africa, A Modern History*, p. 382.

102. *SA Times*, 5 July 1995.

103. Rev. Simon Adams, interview, Stellenbosch, 20 November 1995.

104. *SA Times*, 8 March 1995.

105. *SA Times*, 31 May 1995.

106. Rev. Simon Adams, interview, Stellenbosch, 20 November 1995.

107. Professor Adam Small, interview, Cape Town, 21 November 1995.

108. Adam Small, 'There's Somethin' ', in *A Penguin Book of South African Verse*, edited with an introduction by Jack Cope and Uys Krige, Penguin, 1968, p. 241.

109. Dennis Brutus, 'A Letter to Basil, 11 November 1965', in *A Simple Lust*, Heinemann, 1973, p. 74.

110. Johann Magerman, 'All I want to do is to forgive you', BBC Radio, 13 April 1995.

111. 'Last Supper in Hortsley Street', *People to People Street* series, Channel 4 TV, 16 June 1985, in Frost, *The Politics of Peace*, p. 176.

Chapter 5

1. Serfontein, *Apartheid, Change and the NG Kerk*, p. 60.

2. Luthuli, *Let My People Go*, p. 154.

3. Address to World Consultation of the World Council of Churches, Holland, 16–21 June 1980, in Tambo, *Oliver Tambo Speaks*, p. 186.

4. Serfontein, *Apartheid, Change and the NG Kerk*, p. 61.

5. Ibid. Dr Piet Meiring was at the time a minister of the NGK congregation at Lynnwood. He made his remarks in his column in Beeld, 13 October 1981.

6. Ibid., p. 138.

7. Dr Jacques Kriel, *Die Vaderland*, 9 October 1978, cited ibid., p. 150.

8. Ibid., p. 182.

9. 'Racism and South Africa', statement adopted by the General Council of the World Alliance of Reformed Churches, 22 August 1982, reproduced in *South African Outlook*, December 1982, pp. 192–3.

10. 123 NGK Clergy Open Letter, *Star*, 10 June 1982.

11. Professor David Bosch, paper read on 11 September 1985 and reproduced in Klaus Nürnberger and John Tooke (eds), *The Cost of*

    Reconciliation in South Africa (NIR Reader No 1), MPO Cape Town, 1988, pp. 109–10.

12. Ibid.
13. *Church and Society 1990, A Testimony of the Dutch Reformed Church,* approved by the General Synod of the DRC, October 1990, published 1991 by the General Synodical Committee Commission with Pro Christo, p. 38.
14. Ibid., p. 39.
15. Professor Piet Meiring, ecumenical officer of the NGK, in *DRC News,* Vol 19 No 1, April 1995, p. 2.
16. Professor Piet Meiring, interview, Pretoria, 17 October 1995.
17. Colin James, obituary of the Most Rev. Robert Selby Taylor, Archbishop of Cape Town 1964–74, *The Independent,* 5 May 1995, p. 16.
18. *Ecunews,* 30/76, 17 September 1976, quoted in John de Gruchy, *The Church Struggle in South Africa,* SPCK, 1979, p. 4.
19. Archbishop Tutu, 'The Secular State and Religion', Archbishop Stephen Naidoo Memorial Lecture, 8 July 1992, Archbishop Tutu's archives, Cape Town, 1995.
20. See Ruth Lundie, *Victor,* Brevitas, Howick, KwaZulu-Natal, n.d.
21. *Pro Veritate,* August 1977, p. 11. Phakamile Mabije had been detained at his home on 27 June 1977 after alleged involvement in a stoning incident and had been due to appear in Kimberley Magistrates Court on a charge under the Riotous Assemblies Act the day after his death.
22. Aelred Stubbs, C.R., 'The Story of Nyamebko Barney Pityana', *South African Outlook,* October 1979, pp. 150–2.
23. Rev. Dr Barney Pityana, interview, Pretoria, 17 October 1995.
24. Denis E. Hurley, (ed) Nic Rhoodie, *The Church and Race Relations, South Africa Dialogue,* McGraw-Hill Book Company, Johannesburg, 1972, p. 469.
25. Bishop Peter Storey, lecture, Soweto, 11 October 1995.
26. Rev. Otto Ntshayana, interview, 24 November 1995.
27. J.L. McFall, *Trust Betrayed, The Murder of Sister Mary Aidan,* Nassional Boekhandel, 1963, p. 152.
28. Ibid., p. 150.
29. Ibid., p. 153.
30. *South African Outlook,* April 1977, pp. 50–2.
31. Pastoral Letter of the Southern Africa Catholic Bishops' Conference,

1 May 1986, in Nürnberger and Tooke (eds), *The Cost of Reconciliation in South Africa*, p. 56.

32. Letter to friends and supporters from Father Smangaliso Mkhatshwa, Secretary-General, Southern Africa Catholic Bishops' Conference, August 1987.

33. *SA Times*, 4 April 1994, p. 4.

34. Nürnberger and Tooke (eds), *The Cost of Reconciliation in South Africa*, p. 11.

35. Albert Nolan, *Challenge*, February–March 1995, p. 7.

36. Ibid.

37. Ibid., p. 30.

38. Ibid., p. 5.

39. Ibid., p. 4.

40. See Michael Sparks, 'A Consideration of the Kairos Document Ten Years On', *Johannesburg Star*, 24 July 1995.

41. Quoted to the Rev. Brian Brown, Africa Secretary of the Overseas Division of the Methodist Church, in 'The Church and Violence in Southern Africa', Churches Concern for Southern Africa occasional paper, No 1, 1993, p. 7.

42. *Journal of Theology for Southern Africa*, June 1988, No 63, special issue on Church and State, p. 70.

43. Ibid., pp. 80–1.

44. Nelson Mandela, statement to press at Pietermaritzburg Airport, 14 March 1993, in Philip, *Nelson Mandela Speaks*.

45. See Bernard Spong with Cedric Mayson, *Come Celebrate, 25 years of the South African Council of Churches*, SACC, 1993, p. 25.

46. Archbishop Denis Hurley, interview, Durban 30 October 1995.

47. John de Gruchy, *Cry Justice*, Collins, 1986, p. 201.

48. F.W. de Klerk to W.A. de Klerk, in *F.W. de Klerk, The Man In His Time*, p. 181.

49. Michael Cassidy (ed), *See I Will Heal Their Land*, papers from the South African Congress on Mission and Evangelism, Durban 1973, Africa Enterprise, 1974.

50. Michael Cassidy in Nürnberger and Tooke (eds), *The Cost of Reconciliation*, p. 76.

51. Rev. Dr Frank Chikane, foreword to Dr Louw Albert and Rev. Dr Frank Chikane (eds), *The Road to Rustenberg*, Struik Christian Books, 1991, p. 10.

52. Professor Willie Jonker, interview, Stellenbosch, 22 November 1995.
53. Albert and Chikane, *The Road to Rustenberg*, p. 92.
54. Ibid., p. 99.
55. Ibid., pp. 100–2.
56. Ibid.
57. Ibid., p. 79.
58. Ibid., p. 86.
59. Ibid., pp. 203–4.
60. Ibid., pp. 226–7.
61. Ibid., p. 20. See also Tutu, *The Rainbow People of God*, p. 214.
62. Ibid., p. 277.
63. Ibid., p. 278.
64. Ibid., p. 279.
65. Ibid., p. 280.
66. Ibid., p. 284.
67. Ibid., p. 285.
68. *From Cottesloe to Cape Town, Challenges to the Churches in a post-apartheid society*, WCC/PCR, 1991, No 30, p. 94.
69. SAPA., reported in *SA Times* 12 July 1995, p. 4.
70. Professor Piet Meiring, interview, Pretoria, 17 October 1995.
71. 'The Church in a Future South Africa' (from SACC meeting at Hammanskraal July 1975), in B. Johanson (ed), *The Church in South Africa Today and Tomorrow*, SACC, 1975, pp. 54–5.
72. Albert and Chikane, *The Road to Rustenberg*, p. 253.
73. Mrs Goba, interview, Durban, 27 October 1995.
74. Bishop Stanley Mogoba, SABC TV interview, Durban, 30 October 1995.
75. Stanley Mogoba, 'A Sign of Hope', in *South African Outlook*, February 1982, pp. 24 and 32.
76. Val Pauquet, interview, Johannesburg, 5 December 1995.
77. John Hall, in *In the Name of Peace*, published by *The Sowetan* in collaboration with the National Peace Secretariat, January 1995, p. 5.
78. Bishop Peter Storey, 'The National Peace Accord, The Secret of South Africa's Election "Miracle"', p. 1.
79. Ibid.
80. Bishop Stanley Mogoba to Lulama Luti, 'Moving the church in from the sidelines', in *Accent on Peace*, December 1993, p. 34.
81. Storey, 'The National Peace Accord', p. 2.

82. Ibid.
83. Bishop Peter Storey, in *In the Name of Peace*, p. 9.
84. Val Pauquet, interview, Johannesburg, 5 December 1995.
85. Rev. Dr Liz Carmichael, in *In the Name of Peace*, p. 8.
86. Karen McGregor, in *In the Name of Peace*, p. 10.
87. Bishop Stanley Mogoba, in Villa-Vicencio (ed), *The Spirit of Hope*, p. 188.
88. Archbishop Denis Hurley, in *In the Name of Peace*, p. 32.
89. Bruce Walker, in *In the Name of Peace*, p. 33.
90. Karen McGregor, in *In the Name of Peace*, p. 31.
91. Ibid., p. 33.
92. Ibid., p. 13.
93. Bishop Stanley Mogoba, *Accent on Peace*, December 1993, p. 37.
94. Bishop Stanley Mogoba, SABC TV interview, 30 October 1995.
95. Professor Pippin Oosthuizen, PACSA Newsletter, No 64, September 1995, p. 8.
96. Professor Pippin Oosthuizen, interview, Durban, 30 October 1995.
97. Rev. Buti Tlhagale, OMI, *Bringing the African Culture into the Churches* (private manuscript), pp. 6–7.
98. This and the following paragraph is a distillation of remarks made from the floor of a consultation on the problems of KwaZulu-Natal held at and convened by Africa Enterprise, 4 October 1995, Cascades, Pietermaritzburg.
99. Ibid.
100. Rev. Athol Jennings, interview, Durban, 31 October 1995.
101. See Michael Cassidy, *A Witness for Ever*, Hodder and Stoughton, 1995, p. 61 onwards.

Chapter 6

1. Nadine Gordimer, 'What being a South African means to me', *South African Outlook*, June 1977, p. 89.
2. Lord Shawcross, BBC Radio 4, 1 January 1996.
3. Reported in *SA Times*, 15 September 1993.
4. Promotion of National Unity and Reconciliation Bill B30B-95, p. 50.
5. *Cape Times*, 3 November 1995, p. 8.
6. *SA Times*, 3 August 1994, p. 2.
7. Ibid., 2 November 1994.

8. Professor Kader Asmal, 25 May 1992, inaugural lecture on installation as Professor of Human Rights Law at University of the Western Cape, Series A No 64, p. 9.

9. Professor Andre du Toit, (ed) Alex Boraine, Janet Lavy, *The Healing of the Nation?* Justice in Transition 1995, p. 98.

10. *SA Times*, 26 July 1995, p. 3.

11. Indemnity Act 1990 (Act No 35 1990). Indemnity Amendment Act 1992 (Act No 124, 1992). Further Indemnity Act 1992 (Act No 151, 1992).

12. *Mail and Guardian*, 3–9 November 1995, p. 11.

13. Dullah Omar, *SA Times*, 31 May 1995.

14. See Heribert Adam and Kogila Moodley, *The Negotiated Revolution (Society and Politics in post-apartheid South Africa)*, Jonathan Ball, Johannesburg, 1993, p. 155.

15. *The Independent*, 19 June 1995, p. 15.

16. Paula McBride, in *The World Paper*, April 1995, p. 4.

17. *SA Times*, 5 July 1995, p. 1.

18. Dullah Omar, Truth and Reconciliation Commission published by Justice in Transition on behalf of the Ministry of Justice 1995, p. 3.

19. Promotion of National Unity and Reconciliation Bill B 30B-95, p. 52.

20. Professor Hendrik van der Merwe, *The Argus*, 13 November 1995, p. 1.

21. Archbishop Tutu, interview with Panel, Cape Town, 13 November 1995.

22. Tony Leon, *Business Day*, 30 November 1995, p. 2.

23. *SA Times*, 27 April 1994, p. 4.

24. Phillip van Niekerk, *The Observer*, 24 December 1995, p. 13.

25. *Business Day*, 6 February 1996, p. 2.

26. *The Star and SA Times International*, 21 February 1996, p. 6.

27. *Sunday Times*, 11 February 1996.

28. *The Star and SA Times*, 8 May 1996, p. 9.

29. Ibid., 17 April 1996, p. 1.

30. Ibid., 8 May 1996, p. 9.

31. Rev. Buti Tlhagale, 'The Changing South Africa: The New Challenge', *Praxis* (Journal for Christian Business Management), Vol 3, No 2, June 1995, pp. 8–9.

32. Rev. Buti Tlhagale, interview, Pretoria, 12 October 1995.

33. *Justice and Peace News*, March 1995, p. 6.

34. Rabbi Ivan Lerner, *The Star and SA Times*, 24 January 1996, p. 8.

35. Bishop Peter Storey, *The Star and SA Times*, 31 January 1996, p. 9.

36. *SouthScan*, Vol 12, no 6, 14 February 1997, p. 44

37. Robert Brand, *The Star*, 6 March 1996.

38. Dr Charles Villa-Vicencio, *Sunday Times*, 22 October 1995.

39. Dr Wolfram Kistner, *Being Church in South Africa Today*, SACC, 1995, p. 107.

40. Fatimer Meer, interview, Durban 30 October 1995.

41. Rev. Robert Vithi, interview, Pretoria, 13 October 1995.

42. See Frost, *The Politics of Peace*, pp. 160–1.

43. Professor John de Gruchy, interview, Cape Town, 10 November 1995.

44. Du Toit, *The Healing of the Nation?*, p. 114.

45. Professor Hermann Giliomee is Professor of Political Studies at the University of Cape Town.

46. Rev. Vuyami Nyobole, interview, Grahamstown, 7 November 1995.

47. Ian Mackesie, interview, Durban, 30 October 1995.

48. Tshenvwani Simon Farisani, *Diary from a South African Prison*, Fortress Press, 1989, pp. 49–50.

49. Bishop Peter Storey, lecture to Methodist ministers in training, Soweto, 11 October 1995.

50. Tish White, interview, Johannesburg, 19 October 1995.

51. Victor Mabuso, interview, Durban, 29 October 1995.

52. Rev. Rob Robertson, 'The Erasmus Event', notes for Brian Frost, Cape Town, 22 November 1995.

53. See Spong with Mayson, *Come Celebrate*, pp. 96–7.

54. Rev. Dr Frank Chikane, *Challenge*, June–July 1995, p. 9.

55. Paul Erasmus, 'Confessions of an apartheid killer', *The Tiddler* (*The Observer* 'Little Bit Extra'), no 6, 1994.

56. *SouthScan*, vol 12, 14 February 1994, p. 44.

57. Mrs Naziopoh Plaatje, interview, Grahamstown, 8 November 1995.

58. Tokyo Sexwale, *Being Church in a New Land*, SACC 1995, pp. 14–15.

59. Walter Wink, *Engaging the Powers*, Fortress Press, 1991, p. 276.

60. Joe Seremane, interview, Pretoria, 13 October 1995.

61. Villa-Vicencio (ed), *The Spirit of Hope*, p. 126. See also *Work in Progress*, No 82, June 1992, and *Monitor*, December 1990.

62. Ibid.

63. May Hartley, *Sunday Times*, 29 August 1993, in *The Miracle of a Free Nation, South Africa 1990–1994*, published by the *Sunday Times*, Don Nelson, Cape Town, n.d., p. 110.

64. Nelson Mandela, *SA Times*, 8 September 1993, p. 5. Nelson Mandela was addressing a Johannesburg Forum discussing a strategy for peace and cooperation to end violence in South Africa's mini-bus taxi industry.
65. Ibid. In 1992 President F.W. de Klerk had ordered a probe into military intelligence activities after the Goldstone Commission investigating political violence had revealed evidence of an Army 'dirty tricks' campaign against the ANC.
66. Priscilla Kayne, *The World Paper*, April 1995, p. 2.
67. Winnie Mandela, reported in *SA Times*, 17 August 1994, p. 8.
68. Adam and Moodley, *The Negotiated Revolution*, pp. 95–6.
69. Ibid., p. 131, quoting Chris Hani, 'ANC units running wild', *Sunday Times*, 2 August 1992, p. 11.
70. Ken Owen, *Sunday Times*, 12 November 1995.
71. *The Star and SA Times*, 14 May 1997, p. 1.
72. *Time* magazine, 'Is Forgetting Possible?', 22 May 1995.
73. Derrick McBride, interview, Durban, 30 October 1995.
74. *Saturday Star*, 25 November 1995, section 2.
75. *Diamond Fields Advertiser*, 27 November 1995, p. 9.
76. *The Independent*, 21 February 1995, p. 11. 'Mr de Klerk said yesterday that the 1982 bombing of the London office of the ANC was "wrong and should not have been done".' He had never been a part of any decision by an apartheid government to commit a crime. 'I distance myself from such atrocities and from assassinations,' he told a news conference. The former South African spymaster Craig Williamson had claimed that agents of the former white government blew up the ANC's London HQ in 1982.
77. *SouthScan*, vol 12, no 6, 14 February 1997, p. 44.
78. Hope Papo, *The Star*, 6 December 1995, p. 13.
79. Ibid.
80. *Saturday Star*, 25 November 1995.
81. *The Star and SA Times*, 15 May 1996, p. 6.
82. Ibid., 14 May 1994, pp. 1 and 3. The ANC submission was handed in on 10 May 1997.
83. Ibid., 23 April 1997, p. 1.
84. *SA Times*, 30 August 1995, p. 3. To 700 members of the South African Students Congress, University of Cape Town.

85. Professor Hendrik van der Merwe, interview, Cape Town, 16 November 1995.
86. *The Star and SA Times*, 14 May 1997, p. 3.
87. Ibid., 1 May 1996, p. 10.
88. Dirk Coetzee, in Bernstein, *The Exile Experiences of South Africans*, p. 213.
89. Ibid.
90. Roger Finnigan, Network First, 'Confronting the Hitmen', ITV Yorkshire, 2 May 1995.
91. Bernstein, *The Exile Experiences of South Africans*, p. 213.
92. *The Star and SA Times*, 3 April 1996, p. 3.
93. Albie Sachs, *The Soft Vengeance of A Freedom Fighter*, Grafton, 1990, p. 199.
94. Ibid., pp. 198–9.
95. Ibid., p. 77.
96. *The Independent*, 31 May 1994.
97. Ibid.
98. *SA Times*, 10 April 1996, p. 4.
99. *SouthScan*, Vol 12, no 5, 7 February 1997, p. 35.
100. Tom Cohen, Associated Press, *The Independent*, 21 February 1995, p. 11.
101. *The Star and SA Times*, 14 September 1996, p. 6.
102. Ibid., 14 May 1997, p. 6.
103. *Mail and Guardian*, 5–11 January 1996, p. 4.
104. *The Star and SA Times*, 14 May 1997, p. 3.
105. P.W. Botha, *The Argus*, 22 November 1995, p. 29.
106. *The Star and SA Times*, 18 December 1996, p. 3.
107. Ibid., p. 28.
108. *The Star and SA Times*, 12 June 1996, p. 6.
109. Ibid., 14 May 1997, p. 3.
110. Chris Steyn, 'Spectrum', *The Star*, 11 November 1995, p. 15.
111. *Argus*, 31 October 1995.
112. *The Star and SA Times*, 7 May 1997, p. 1.
113. Ibid., 26 March 1997, p. 3.
114. Ibid., 21 May 1997, p. 4.
115. Ibid., 23 October 1996, p. 1.
116. Ibid., 21 May 1997, p. 3.

117. Quoted in editorial section of *The Star and SA Times*, 21 May 1997, p. 8.

118. Ibid., 14 May 1997, p. 1.

119. Ibid., 12 July 1997, p. 5.

120. Ibid., 2 July 1997, p. 5.

121. *The Guardian*, 11 December 1996.

122. *Star and SA Times*, 25 June 1997, p. 1.

123. Statement adopted by National Executive Committee of the SACC, *Regional Mail*, September–October 1992, p. 2. *Regional Mail* is a newsletter produced by the SACC.

124. Kistner, *Being Church in South Africa Today*, p. 49.

125. Professor Piet Meiring, interview, Pretoria, 17 October 1995.

126. Press Statement, Pretoria, 19 May 1995, translated by Mark Collier.

127. *The Star and SA Times*, 9 July 1997, p. 3.

128. Ibid., 11 June 1997, p. 9.

129. APS News and Features Bulletin, no 6, 9 June 1997.

130. John de Gruchy, *Christianity and Democracy*, Cambridge University Press, 1995, p. 216.

131. Ibid., p. 217.

132. Professor Denise Ackermann, Newsletter of A Religious Response to the Truth and Reconciliation Commission, Vol 1, No 5, November 1995, p. 2.

133. Nellis du Preez, letter to author, March 1996.

134. Bishop Stanley Mogoba, interview, Durban, 27 October 1995.

135. Dirkie J. Smit, 'The Truth and Reconciliation Commission – Tentative Religious and Theological Perspectives', *Journal of Theology for South Africa*, March 1995, p. 15. From a talk given originally in Afrikaans at a conference arranged by *Die Suid-Afrikan*.

136. Introduction to a Religious Consultation to the Truth and Reconciliation Commission, World Conference of Religions for Peace, South Africa, 1994.

137. *The Star and SA Times*, 26 June 1996, p. 8.

138. Father Michael Lapsley, *My Journey of Reconciliation, From Freedom Fighter to Healer*, p. 4., 28 April 1995.

139. Father Michael Lapsley, reported by Megan Walker in PACSA Newsletter no 62, Easter 1995, p. 4.

140. Paul van Zyl, interview, Johannesburg, 12 October 1995.

141. 'Ordinary People', Mail and Guardian TV, September 1994.

142. Paul van Zyl, interview, 12 October 1995.
143. Paul Williams, interview, Cape Town, 22 January 1995.
144. Frank Retief, *Tragedy to Triumph, A Christian response to trial and suffering*, Word Publishing, Nelson Word, Milton Keynes, UK, and Struik Christian Books, Cape Town, 1994, p. 86.
145. Ibid., p. 87.
146. Ibid., p. 144.
147. Ibid., p. 150.
148. *The Star and SA Times*, 19 July 1997, p. 2.
149. Ibid., 30 October 1996, p. 1.
150. Interview, Port Elizabeth, 7 November 1995.
151. *The Star and SA Times*, 10 December 1997, p. 1.
152. Ibid., 18 February 1998, p. 6.
153. *The Guardian*, 8 January 1998, p. 15.
154. *The Independent*, 8 January 1998, p. 13.
155. *The Star and SA Times*, 10 December 1997, p. 3.
156. Ibid., 17 December 1997, p. 3.
157. Ibid., 14 January 1998, p. 1.
158. *The Independent*, 17 December 1997, p. 7.
159. *The Star and SA Times*, 19 November 1997, p. 1.
160. Ibid., 22 October 1997, p. 4.
161. Ibid., 29 October p. 7. Archbishop Tutu was addressing the Cape Town Press Club.

Chapter 7

1. De Gruchy, *Christianity and Democracy*, pp. 217–8.
2. Joe Seremane, interview, Pretoria, 13 October 1995.
3. Land Claims under the Restitution of Land Rights Act (1994), Commission on Restoration of Land Rights.
4. Joe Seremane, interview, 13 October 1995.
5. Emma Mashinini, interview, Pretoria, 16 October 1995.
6. Reported in *SA Times*, 23 January 1994, p. 2.
7. R.W. Johnson, *The Times*, 22 January 1996, p. 9.
8. *The Natal Witness*, 25 September 1995, p. 9.
9. *The Sowetan*, 2 October 1995.
10. *Democracy in Action*, Vol 9, No 6, 15 October 1995, p. 16.
11. *The Economist*, 24 June 1995, pp. 37–8.

12. *The Regional Mail*, March–April 1993, No 10, p. 3.
13. James Barber and John Barratt, *South Africa's Foreign Policy*, Southern Books 1990, in association with South African Institute of International Affairs, p. 10.
14. William Mervyn Gumede, 'Unemployment resists feeble assaults', *The Star and SA Times*, 19 June 1996, p. 7.
15. Ibid., 14 February 1996, p. 4.
16. *Weekly Mail and Guardian*, 8–14 April 1994, p. 20.
17. Poverty Profile, IDASA, (ed) Conrad Barberton, Vol 1, No 1, October 1995, p. 1.
18. *The Times* magazine, 9 December 1995, p. 12.
19. Hugh Poper, *The Independent*, 16 March 1995.
20. SACOB Director General in *SA Times*, 24 August 1994, p. 9.
21. *The Reconstruction and Development Programme*, ANC, 1994, p. 6.
22. Ibid., p. 28.
23. Ibid., p. 31.
24. Ibid., p. 28.
25. Rev. Demetris Palos, interview, Johannesburg, 9 October 1995.
26. *The Mercury*, 20 October 1995, p. 8.
27. *Bloemnuus*, 1 November 1995, p. 3.
28. *Weekend Argus*, 25/26 November 1995, p. 27.
29. Walter Sisulu, *Saturday Star*, 2 December 1995, p. 5.
30. Quoted in *The Star and SA Times*, 1 May 1996.
31. *Sunday Times Business Times*, 23 July 1995, p. 8.
32. *After Apartheid: Regional Co-operation in Policy Focus 1994*, No 4, SA Overseas Development Council, Washington DC, p. 9.
33. Kim L. Robinson, Fulbright Scholar and Visiting Researcher at the Centre for Applied Legal Studies, University of Witswatersrand, *Saturday Star*, 2 December 1995, p. 11.
34. Robert Brand, 'New Big Step in Human Rights in South Africa', *The Star and SA Times*, 27 November 1996, p. 5.
35. John Jackson, *Justice in South Africa*, Secker and Warburg. 1980, p. 64.
36. Louis du Plooy, interview, Cape Town, 22 January 1995.
37. Rev. Dr Barney Pityana, interview, Pretoria, 17 October 1995.
38. *Cape Times*, 1 November 1995, p. 5.
40. *Accent on Peace*, December 1993, pp. 70 and 73.

41. Centre for the Study of Violence and Reconciliation Annual Report 1994, p. 21.
42. *Guardian*, 8 May 1995, quoting Reuters.
43. *SA Times*, 12 January 1994, p. 2.
44. Laurie Nathan, interview, Cape Town, 23 November 1995.
45. *The Independent*, Section 2, 20 July 1995, p. 5.
46. *SA Times*, 3 May 1995, p. 3.
47. *The Independent*, Section 2, 20 July 1995, p. 5.
48. *The Times*, 10 May 1996, p. 17.
49. *Daily Telegraph*, 10 April 1996, p. 12.
50. David Beresford, *The Guardian*, 10 May 1996, p. 14.
51. *Daily Telegraph*, 10 May 1996, p. 12.
52. R.W. Johnson, *The Times*, 10 May 1996, p. 11.
53. Editorial, *The Independent*, 13 February 1995, p. 14.
54. Loek Gromans, World Conference of Religions for Peace Committee meeting, 22 October, 1995.
55. General Constand Viljoen, Sunday Profile, *Sunday Times*, 13 November 1995.
56. Parliamentary Whip, IDASA Parliamentary and Monitory Service, 1 September 1995, p. 5.
57. Ibid.
58. Speaker Frene Ginwala, welcome to President Joachim Chissano, 1 March 1995.
59. *The Argus*, 2 March 1995, p. 31.
60. Harvey Tyson, *Straddling the World in South Africa's New World*, A Leadership Publication 1991, p. 14.
61. Barney Desai, information secretary PAC, ibid., p. 16.
62. Zilka Efrat, 'SA companies rush in where western rivals fear to trade', *Sunday Times Business Times*, 23 July 1995, p. 4.
63. Teboho Loate, interview, Bloemfontein, 30 November 1995.
64. ANC Reconstruction and Development Programme 1994, p. 69.
65. Quoted in H. Giliomee and L. Schlemner, *From Apartheid to Nation-Building*, Oxford University Press, 1989, p. 18.
66. Father Albert Nolan, interview, Johannesburg, 9 October 1995.
67. Adam and Moodley, *The Negotiated Revolution*, p. 74.
68. Joe Seremane, *Leadership*, January 1986, p. 96.
69. Neville Alexander, *Work in Progress*, November 1993, pp. 14–15.
70. Ibid.

71. Professor Johan Degenar, *Nations and Nationalism*, IDASA, 1991, p. 5.
72. Ibid., p. 12.
73. Ibid., p. 14.
74. Rev. Dr Charles Villa-Vicencio, interview, Cape Town, 16 November 1995.
75. Tokyo Sexwale, *Church and State* in *Being Church in a New Land*, SACC 1993, p. 11.
76. Ibid., p. 14.
77. Bishop Peter Storey, lecture to Methodist theological students, Soweto, 11 October 1995.
78. *From Cottesloe to Cape Town, Challenges for the Churches in a post-apartheid society*, WCC/PCR 1991, No 30, p. 116.
79. Dr Emilio Castro, address, ibid., p. 15.
80. Canon Xundu Mcebesi, interview, Port Elizabeth, 7 November 1995.
81. Dr Manas Buthelezi, in Spong with Mayson, *Come Celebrate*, p. 47.
82. Rev. Dale White, interview, Johannesburg, 6 December 1995.
83. Dr Frank Chikane in Villa-Vicencio (ed), *The Spirit of Hope*, p. 70.
84. Bishop Peter Storey, ibid.
85. Canon Mcebisi, ibid.
86. Luthuli, *Let My People Go*, pp. 37–8.
87. Villa-Vicencio (ed), *The Spirit of Hope*, p. 70.
88. Professor W. Jonker, interview, Stellenbosch, 22 November 1989.
89. W.A. Visser t'Hooft, citing Bieler 1961 (Le Pensée Economique et Sociale de Calvin, Geneva) p. 297 and Calvin's Commentary on Habbakuk 2:6, Bieler p. 305, in Wilson, *Freedom for My People*, p. 209.
90. David du Plessis in Cassidy (ed), *I Will Heal Their Land*, p. 295.
91. Rt Hon John Major, MP, Speech to South African Parliament National Assembly and Senate, 20 September 1994.
92. *Cape Times*, 21 March 1995, p. 1.
93. Ibid., p. 5.
94. Queen Elizabeth II, reported in *Argus*, southern edition, 20 March 1995, p. 1.
95. 20 March 1995, quoted in a letter to Mr J.A. Marais, Leader of the HNP, from A.J. Noble of the Political Section of the British High Commission, Cape Town, 1 September 1995.

96. *Argus*, 21 March 1995, p. 1.
97. *Weekend Argus*, 18–19 March 1995, p. 20.
98. Ibid., p. 9.
99. Kaiser Nyatsumba, 'Forgiveness but...' *The Argus*, 22 March 1995, p. 24.
100. Smuts, *Jan Christian Smuts*, pp. 83–4.
101. *The Guardian*, 10 June 1996, p. 8.
102. *The Star and SA Times*, 27 March 1996, p. 1.
103. The previous three paragraphs are based on an interview with the Rev. Dan Le Cordeur in Mpophomeni on 26 October 1995.
104. Sheena Duncan, interview, Johannesburg, 9 October 1995.
105. See Sparks, *Tomorrow Is Another Country*, pp. 233–5.
106. Rian Malan, *My Traitor's Heart*, Vintage, 1991, p. 318.
107. Ibid., p. 413.
108. Ibid., pp. 424–5.
109. In Heidi Holland, *Born in Soweto, Inside the Heart of South Africa*, Penguin, 1994, p. 139.
110. Sylvia Collier, interview, Cape Town, 18 November 1995.
111. Rev. Dr Donald Cragg, interview, Johannesburg, 6 October 1995.
112. Gilbert Zephanie Tony Ngwenge, interview, Kimberley, 28 November 1995.
113. Aelred Stubbs, C.R., eulogy preached at Requiem Mass celebrated for Mangaliso Sobukwe, Priory Chapel of the Society of the Precious Blood, Masite, Lesotho, 1 March 1978, in *South African Outlook*, August 1978, p. 118.
114. Ibid.
115. Rev. J. Fourie, interview, Durban, 20 October 1995.
116. Joe Seremane, interview, Durban, 20 October 1995.
117. Dr Alex Boraine, quoted in Benjamin Pogrund, *How Can a Man Die Better? Sobukwe and Apartheid*, Peter Halbraum, 1990, p. 364.
118. Rev. Arthur East, interview, Kimberley, 28 November 1995.
119. See Don Mattera, *Azanian Love Song*, Justified Press (a division of William Waterman, Rivonia), 1994, p. 79.
120. Archbishop Denis Hurley, interview, Durban, 31 October 1995.
121. *The Independent*, 12 July 1996, p. 9.
122. *Guardian*, 12 July 1996, p. 8.
123. *The Independent*, 9 July 1996, p. 9.
124. *Guardian*, 12 July 1996, p. 8.

Epilogue

1. 24 April 1963. In Jomo Kenyatta, *Suffering without Bitterness*, East Africa Publishing House, 1968, p. 201.
2. Elspeth Huxley, *Out in the Midday Sun*, Chatto and Windus, 1985, p. 202, quoting from a speech she heard made by Jomo Kenyatta in May 1963.
3. Robert Mugabe, address to the United Nations, 26 August 1980, Ministry of Tourism and Information, Zimbabwe.
4. See Frost, *The Politics of Peace*, p. 161.
5. W.A. de Klerk, in *F.W. de Klerk, The Man in His Time*, p. 154.
6. Professor Adam Small, interview Cape Town, 23 November 1995.
7. Ronnie Kasrils, in Bernstein, *The Exile Experiences of South Africans*, p. 181.
8. Estelle Hudson, interview, Durban, 31 October 1995.
9. Nelson Mandela, *The Independent*, 15 January 1996.
10. Ebrahim Rasool, in Villa-Vicencio (ed), *The Spirit of Hope*, p. 240.
11. *The Star and SA Times*, 9 July 1997, p. 3.

List of abbreviations

ANC	African National Congress
APLA	Azanian People's Liberation Army
ARM	African Resistance Movement
AWB	Afrikaner Weerstandsbeweging (Afrikaner Resistance Movement)
AZAPO	Azanian People's Organization
BCM	Black Consciousness Movement
COSATU	Congress of South African Trade Unions
DRC	Dutch Reformed Church
GEAR	Growth, Employment and Redistribution Programme
GNU	Government of National Unity
HNP	Herstige Nationale Party
IDAMASA	Interdenominational African Ministers' Federation
IDASA	Institute for a Democratic Alternative in South Africa
IFP	Inkatha Freedom Party
MK	Umkhonto we Sizwe (Spear of the Nation)
NGK	Nederduitse Gereformeerde Kerk
NHK	Nederduitsch Hervormde Kerk
NIR	National Initiative for Reconciliation
NP	National Party
NUSAS	National Union of South African Students
PAC	Pan-Africanist Congress
PACSA	Pietermaritzburg Council for Social Action
RDP	Reconstruction and Development Programme
SACC	South African Council of Churches
SADF	South African Defence Force
SAIC	South African Indian Congress
SANDF	South African National Defence Force
SAP	South African Police
SASO	South African Student Organization
SPROCAS	Study Project on Christianity in an Apartheid Society

TRC	Truth and Reconciliation Commission
UCCSA	United Congregational Church of Southern Africa
UDF	United Democratic Front
UWUSA	United Workers Union of South Africa

Index